U0594607

主　编：黄兴亚　孙永林　周　青

副主编：段忠玉　冯寒英　黄　莺

刘丹丹　展淑卿　赵少钦

编　委（按首字母顺序排列）：

把　明　白　璐　段忠玉

冯寒英　黄兴亚　黄　莺

姜　丹　焦　娇　刘丹丹

卢佳梅　马　静　潘玲华

沈　月　孙　雯　孙永林

王　艳　吴　非　展淑卿

赵少钦　周　青　周叶函

左媛媛

走近

Approaching Chinese Culture

主　编：黄兴亚　孙永林　周　青

副主编：段忠玉　冯寒英　黄　莺

刘丹丹　展淑卿　赵少钦

云南大学出版社

Yunnan University Press

图书在版编目（CIP）数据

走近中国文化：汉、英 / 黄兴亚等主编. 一昆明：云南大学出版社，2015
ISBN 978-7-5482-2299-6

Ⅰ.①走… Ⅱ.①黄… Ⅲ.中华文化—研究生—教材—汉、英 Ⅳ.①K203

中国版本图书馆CIP数据核字（2015）第087105号

责任编辑：熊晓霞
装帧设计：刘　雨

Approaching Chinese Culture

主　编：黄兴亚　孙永林　周　青
副主编：段忠玉　冯寒英　黄　莺
刘丹丹　展淑卿　赵少钦

出版发行：云南大学出版社
印　装：昆明市五华区教育委员会印刷厂
开　本：787mm×1092mm　1/16
印　张：19.75
字　数：323千
版　次：2015年6月第1版
印　次：2015年6月第1次印刷
书　号：ISBN 978-7-5482-2299-6
定　价：38.00元

社　址：昆明市翠湖北路2号云南大学英华园内
邮　编：650091
电　话：（0871）65033244　65031071
网　址：http://www.ynup.com
E-mail：market@ynup.com

前　言
Preface

中国文化，也叫中华文化或华夏文明，是中国 56 个民族文化的总称，是中华文明在演化过程中形成的一种反映民族特质和风貌的民族文化，是民族历史上各种思想文化、观念形态的汇聚，是各种民族文明、风俗和精神的总称，是人类文明的一个重要组成部分。中国文化源远流长，影响甚广，在中国 5 000 年文明里，虽然经历了社会制度变迁和朝代的更替，中国文化始终保持了完整的面貌和独特的风采，要走进中国文明，就要走近中国文化。

进入 21 世纪，在世界经济全球化的进程中，世界各国间跨文化交流越来越频繁。一方面，大量的中国人走出国门去学习和工作；另一方面，来自世界各地的人，也纷纷涌入中国学习或工作。对一个来到中国学习或工作的外国人而言，由于风俗习惯、思维方式存在差异和对历史文化背景知识缺乏了解，往往会不可避免地有交往障碍和冲突，要克服这些交往的障碍和冲突，就要走近中国文化。对一个走出国门到国外学习和工作的中国人而言，学习中国传统文化可以增加对历史的了解、对文化的了解，丰富自己的知识面，培养民族自豪感和增加民族凝聚力，同时，也有助于把具有鲜明民族特色的，历史悠久、博大精深的中国文化传播到世界各地。

本书是云南中医学院汉语国际教育专业硕士学科学位点教材建设的一部分，用中文和英文两种文字简要介绍了中国文化，由于篇幅所限，不能也不可能把中国文化一并囊括，只能择其重点进行介绍。本书的英语部分由中文翻译而成，所以内容大致相同，旨在让世界上讲英语的外国朋友了解地道、传统的中国文化，也能为那些想把中国传统文化介绍给外国朋友的中国人提供一定的参考。同时，也为那些想了解中国文化的学习者提供一个学习的机

会。本书可以作为本科生、研究生、留学生及广大学习者了解中国传统文化、拓展人文知识和增强文化素养的教科书。

本书的主编由云南中医学院的黄兴亚、周青、孙永林担任。黄兴亚负责全书中文部分的编写，同时，负责全书的统稿、审稿和英文部分校译和修改工作。周青和孙永林负责本书的策划、编写人员的协调和本书的审批和出版的相关事宜。孙永林还负责了全书英语部分的审定和把关工作。第一章“五十六个民族简介”的英语翻译由潘玲华负责，第二章“龙文化”的英语翻译由黄兴亚负责，第三章“中国古代四大发明”的英语翻译由赵少钦负责，第四章“中国的宗教文化”的英语翻译由孙雯负责，第五章“中国礼仪文化”的英语翻译由冯寒英完成，第六章“中国传统婚俗文化”由沈月负责，第七章“中国人的忌讳文化”的英语翻译由展淑卿负责，第八章“中国汉族传统服饰文化”的英语翻译由周叶函负责，第九章“中国八大菜系”的英语翻译由赵少钦负责，第十章“中国茶文化”的英语翻译由黄莺负责，第十一章“酒文化”的英语翻译由展淑卿负责，第十二章“中国传统节日文化”的英语翻译由马静负责，第十三章“中医文化”的英语翻译由焦娇负责，第十四章“中国建筑”的英语翻译由冯寒英负责，第十五章“中国园林艺术文化”的英语翻译由把明完成，第十六章“中国的风物特产”的英语翻译由刘丹丹完成。另外，段忠玉、白璐、王艳、吴非、左媛媛、卢佳梅为本书的出版提供了无私的帮助，在此，一并表示衷心的感谢。

本书在编写过程中，力求做到内容丰富、论述全面，因此参阅了相关的各种文献，浏览了相关的网页，借鉴了诸多学者和专家的研究成果，在此，表示衷心的感谢。由于编者水平有限，时间仓促，书中难免有疏漏之处，恳请广大读者批评指正。

黄兴亚

2014/12/22

目　录
Contents

第一章　中国五十六个民族简介

中国自古以来就是一个统一的多民族国家。新中国成立后，通过识别并经中央政府确认的民族共有56个。由于汉族以外的55个民族相对于汉族的人口较少，习惯上被称为“少数民族”。

中国各民族分布的特点是大杂居、小聚居，相互交错居住。汉族地区有少数民族聚居，少数民族地区有汉族居住。这种分布格局是由于在长期历史发展过程中各民族间相互交往、流动而形成的。

一、汉　族

汉族占中国人口的92%，是中国56个民族中人口最多的民族，也是世界上人口最多的民族，遍布全中国。汉族是中国古代华夏族同其他一些民族同化、融合形成的。汉代开始称汉族。汉族使用的语言是汉语。现代汉语以北方方言为基础，北京语音为标准音。汉族使用的文字叫汉字。汉族受儒、道、佛学思想影响，崇尚仁义忠孝。重要节日有春节、端午节、重阳节等。

二、蒙古族

蒙古族主要分布在内蒙古、吉林、辽宁、黑龙江、新疆、甘肃、青海、宁夏等省区，善畜牧、骑射，住蒙古包。蒙古族使用的文字叫蒙古文。每年夏秋之际的那达慕大会是蒙古族传统节日。

三、回　族

回族主要聚居在宁夏回族自治区（占全国回族总人口的17.7%），其余

大多数散布全国各地。汉语为回族的共同语言。回族服饰与汉族基本相同，所不同者主要体现在头饰上，回族男子多戴白色或黑色、棕色的无檐小圆帽；妇女多戴盖头。回族人信仰伊斯兰教。开斋节和古尔邦节是回族的两个盛大节日。

四、藏　族

藏族是中华民族的重要一员，主要聚居在西藏自治区（占全国藏族总人口的 45.9%），其余分散在四川、青海、甘肃、云南等省部分地区。藏族多从事农牧业，使用藏文，多信仰喇嘛教。藏历新年是藏族传统节日。藏族喜穿藏袍、长靴，饮酥油茶，主食糌粑。

五、维吾尔族

维吾尔族主要聚居在新疆维吾尔自治区，其余分布在湖南常德等地。维吾尔族有自己的语言和文字，信仰伊斯兰教。维吾尔族有经营农牧业和手工业的悠久传统，擅长植棉和瓜果园艺业。维吾尔族是一个能歌善舞的民族。花帽是维吾尔族服饰的组成部分，也是维吾尔族美的标志之一，男女老幼皆喜戴四楞小花帽。民族节日有古尔邦（库尔班）节、肉孜节等。

六、苗　族

苗族主要分布在贵州省（占苗族总人口的 49.8%），其中主要聚居在黔南布依族苗族自治州、黔西南布依族苗族自治州和黔东南苗族侗族自治州，其余分布在湖南、云南、广西、海南等省区。苗族有自己的语言，现今大部分人通用汉文。苗族的手工艺品主要有刺绣、蜡染、剪纸和首饰制品，可谓绚丽多彩。苗族的飞歌、芦笙舞享有盛名。苗族节日多，主要有十月苗年和纪念民族英雄亚努的“四月八”。

七、壮　族

壮族是中国少数民族中人口最多的民族，主要分布在广西壮族自治区及云南、广东等省。壮族有本民族的语言文字。壮族的铜鼓、岩壁画和壮锦很有名。壮族民间喜欢对唱山歌。中元节是壮族地区仅次于春节的大节日。

八、布依族

布依族主要分布在黔南布依族苗族自治州、黔西南布依族苗族自治州和安顺地区，其余分布在云南、广西等省区。布依族有自己的语言文字，现多通用汉语、汉文。布依族生产方式以农业为主，种植水稻的历史较为悠久。布依族妇女擅纺织、蜡染。布依族擅歌舞，山歌内容形式多样，常以歌代言。民族节日六月六是仅次于春节的盛会，相传为纪念布依族起义领袖的节日。

九、朝鲜族

朝鲜族主要分布在吉林省，最大的聚居区是延边朝鲜族自治州，其余分布在黑龙江、辽宁等省。朝鲜族有自己的语言文字。朝鲜族擅长在寒冷的北方种植水稻。朝鲜族喜好本民族歌舞及摔跤、荡秋千、压跳板等体育活动。朝鲜族喜着素白色服装。特色食品是冷面和泡菜。

十、满　族

满族主要分布在辽宁省（占满族总人口的 50.4%），其余分布在河北、黑龙江、吉林、内蒙古等省区。满族有自己的语言和文字，现普遍习用汉文、汉语。满族民族体育活动有跳马、滑冰等。

十一、侗　族

侗族主要分布在贵州省，集中分布在黔东南苗族侗族自治州、铜仁市的玉屏侗族自治县，其他分布在湖南、广西等省区。侗族有自己的语言，现在大部分通用汉文。侗族主要从事农业生产，以种植水稻为主，特产糯谷，以香禾糯最享盛名。侗族妇女擅长织侗锦。侗族擅长唱歌。侗族节日有春节、祭牛节、吃新节等。

十二、瑶　族

瑶族主要分布在中国的广西、湖南、云南、广东、贵州和江西等省区。瑶族有自己的语言。瑶族多从事农林业活动，狩猎业也占有一定地位，还精于染织和刺绣。瑶族爱唱歌，节日几乎月月有。

十三、白　族

白族主要聚居在云南省西部以洱海为中心的大理白族自治州，少部分散居住在四川、贵州、湖南等地。白族有自己的语言，无文字，大多数白族通晓汉语。白族擅长农业，并创造了灿烂的白族文化，如大理三塔、剑川石窟、鸡足山佛教建筑群等。三月街又称“观音市”，是白族的盛大节日和街期，另一个盛大节日是七月火把节。白族的民族音乐、戏曲独具特色。

十四、土家族

土家族主要聚居在湖南湘西土家族苗族自治州、湖北恩施土家族苗族自治州。土家族有自己的语言，绝大部分人通用汉语、汉文。土家人织造技艺较高，与摆手舞一同被称为“土家艺术之花”。土家族大端午、六月六等节日都要祭土王。土家族几乎是人人会编、会唱山歌。

十五、哈尼族

哈尼族有99.5%聚居于云南红河和澜沧江的中间地带。哈尼族有自己的语言，无文字。哈尼族人擅长种梯田，有的梯田高达数百级。常用自己染织的青布制衣，男子以黑或白布裹头，妇女系绣花腰带。哈尼历法以农历十月为岁首，过“十月节”即是过新年。哈尼人能歌善舞。

十六、哈萨克族

哈萨克族主要分布在新疆维吾尔自治区（占该民族总人口的99.8%），主要聚居区在伊犁哈萨克自治州，其余分布在甘肃。哈萨克族有自己的语言和文字，大都信仰伊斯兰教。哈萨克族大部分从事畜牧业。民族体育叼羊、摔跤、骑射、姑娘追等，大都为马上功夫。

十七、傣　族

傣族主要分布在云南省，主要聚居在西双版纳傣族自治州和德宏傣族景颇族自治州，其余分布在四川、广东等省。傣族有自己的语言和文字。傣族有“旱傣”“水傣”“花腰傣”之分，不同的装饰代表着其支系的服饰文化。

傣族擅长种水稻和热带作物。傣族多信仰南传上座部佛教。妇女传统着装为短衣、筒裙。傣家民居竹楼颇具特色。清明前后的傣历年泼水节是傣族传统节日。傣族能歌善舞，创造了丰富多彩的文化艺术。

十八、黎　族

黎族主要分布在海南省（占黎族总人口的92.0%），主要聚居区在海南岛中部、西南部各黎族自治县，其余分布在湖南等省。黎族有自己的语言，无文字，许多黎族群众兼说汉语，通用汉文。黎族的生产方式以农业为主，是最早的纺织先民。黎族妇女精于以木棉纺织黎锦。黎族人能歌善舞，黎族民歌曲调优美。

十九、傈僳族

傈僳族主要分布在云南省（占该民族总人口的96.9%），主要聚居区在滇西北怒江傈僳族自治州，其余分布在四川。傈僳族有自己的语言和文字。住房为竹木结构，中置火塘。傈僳族擅歌舞，每年十月“收获节”是傈僳族最重要的节日，是日，人们狂饮高歌，通宵达旦。

二十、佤　族

佤族分布在云南省，主要聚居在云南省西南部的西盟、沧源、孟连、耿马等县。佤族有自己的语言和文字。佤族生产方式以农业为主。佤族同胞能歌善舞，常见的舞蹈是“圆圈舞”，跳舞时不分男女老少，舞者手拉手，边唱边跳，气氛十分热烈。

二十一、彝　族

彝族主要分布在云南省，其余分布在四川、贵州等省。彝族有自己的语言文字。最大的彝族聚居区是云南红河哈尼族彝族自治州、楚雄彝族自治州和四川凉山彝族自治州。包头是彝族的典型服饰。夏历六月二十四日的火把节为其最隆重的传统节日。

二十二、畲　族

畲族主要居住在福建、浙江两省的广大山区，其余分布在江西、广东和安徽省境内。畲族有自己的民族语言，大部人讲当地方言。没有本民族文字，通用汉语文字。畲族以种植稻和茶为生。擅长刺绣、编织。山歌被称为畲族文化明珠。畲族民族节日三月三祀祖。

二十三、高山族

高山族主要居住在中国台湾省，其余散居福建、浙江等沿海地区。高山族有自己的语言，没有通用的民族文字，散居于大陆的高山族通用汉语文字。高山族以稻作农耕经济为生，以渔猎生产为辅。高山族擅长雕塑、制陶、编织等工艺。高山族擅长歌舞，其独特的舞乐形式叫“杵杵乐”，妇女手持长杵绕石臼舂米，伴以悦耳歌声。

二十四、拉祜族

拉祜族主要分布在云南省（占拉祜族总人口的99.4%），主要聚居在澜沧江流域的普洱市、临沧市以及西双版纳傣族自治州、红河哈尼族彝族自治州。拉祜族有自己的语言和文字，大多数人通汉语和傣语。擅长狩猎，农业以茶、药、剑麻等的种植为主。传统的芦笙舞、口头文学“陀普科”（谜语）为群众所喜闻乐见。

二十五、水　族

水族分布在贵州省（占水族总人口的93.0%），主要聚居在三都水族自治县。通用汉文字，有自己的语言，古时有水书，仿汉字反写，又称“反书”，仅限于宗教活动使用。水族从事农业，以种植水稻为主。传统佳酿为九阡酒。水族喜爱铜鼓舞、芦笙舞、大歌、酒歌等歌舞。妇女喜戴银饰项圈手镯。水族历法以农历九月为岁首，农历十一月的端节是水族最大节日。

二十六、东乡族

东乡族主要聚居在甘肃省临夏回族自治州的东乡族自治县，其余分布在新疆、宁夏等省区。东乡族有自己的语言，无文字，通用汉语、汉文。东乡族主要信仰伊斯兰教。生产方式以农业为主，兼营畜牧业。东乡族几乎人人都爱编唱“花儿”，其曲调高亢悠扬。

二十七、基诺族

基诺族主要分布在云南省（占基诺族总人口的99.0%），主要聚居在云南省西双版纳傣族自治州景洪市的基诺山基诺族乡，其余分布在四川、湖南等省。基诺族有自己的语言，无文字，过去多靠刻竹木记事。基诺族主要从事农业，擅长种普洱茶。典型的民族服饰是砍刀布和尖顶帽。基诺族人喜歌舞。三月间的新年是基诺族的重要节日。

二十八、景颇族

景颇族主要分布在云南（占该民族总人口的99.4%），主要聚居区在德宏傣族景颇族自治州。景颇族有自己的语言，无文字，曾以刻木结绳记事。景颇族能歌善舞，有的舞蹈是千人以上的集体舞，伴以鼓乐。男女均着黑色对襟短上衣，妇女围艳丽的围裙，喜戴银饰物。

二十九、珞巴族

96.8%的珞巴族集中在西藏自治区东南部地区，其余散布在四川、贵州、辽宁等省。珞巴族有自己的语言，没有本民族文字，少数人通晓藏语、藏文。长期保留着刻木结绳记数、记事的原始方法。主要从事农业，兼狩猎，擅长射箭，竹编工艺精巧。妇女戴银、铜制耳环、手镯。主要食物大米饭，也食糌粑。信仰喇嘛教。

三十、纳西族

纳西族是云南特有的少数民族，主要聚居在丽江市古城区、玉龙纳西族自治县、宁蒗、永胜、维西、香格里拉、德钦等县（市），其余分布在四川省的盐源、盐边、木里等县。纳西族有自己的语言，有自己的象形文字，明末清初，接受了汉族文化，汉文便逐渐为纳西族民众普遍使用。

三十一、门巴族

门巴族主要分布在西藏自治区，主要聚居在西藏墨脱县和错那县。门巴族有自己的语言，无本民族文字，通用藏语、藏文。普遍信仰藏传佛教。

三十二、土 族

土族主要分布在青海省，主要聚居区在互助土族自治县，其余分布在甘肃、云南、贵州等省。土族有自己的语言，无文字，通汉语，用汉文。多信仰喇嘛教。土族擅长歌舞、体育，一年多次的“花儿会”是他们对唱“花儿”的盛大节日。

三十三、赫哲族

赫哲族主要分布在黑龙江省的饶河、抚远两县，聚居在街津口、四排、八岔3个民族乡。赫哲族有自己的语言，无文字，大多数人通用汉语、汉文。有丰富的口头文学传说故事，普遍喜好音乐、即兴编词歌唱。

三十四、阿昌族

阿昌族主要分布在云南省，有自己的语言，无文字，兼通汉语，使用汉文。主要从事农业，擅长种植水稻，打制铁器技艺高。阿昌族民间口头文学十分丰富，对歌和象脚鼓舞、猴舞广为流行。

三十五、布朗族

布朗族主要分布在云南省，主要聚居在勐海县布朗山区。布朗族主要从事农业，擅长种普洱茶。普遍信仰南传上座部佛教。布朗人喜跳刀舞，青年人喜跳集体舞“圆圈舞”。口头文学主要有抒情叙事诗。

三十六、保安族

保安族主要分布在甘肃省，主要聚居区在积石山保安族东乡族撒拉族自治县，其余分布在青海、新疆等省区。通汉语，用汉文。主要从事农业，冶铁、制作保安腰刀有名。习俗受伊斯兰教影响较深。擅长吹奏丝竹乐，喜唱“花儿”和宴席曲，舞姿刚健。

三十七、达斡尔族

达斡尔族主要分布在内蒙古自治区，主要聚居区在莫力达瓦达斡尔族自

治旗，其余分布在黑龙江、新疆等省区。清代多用满文，现多普遍使用汉文。达斡尔族主要从事农业，妇女擅长织绣，制作狍皮坎肩。达斡尔族人喜好歌舞。

三十八、德昂族

德昂族主要分布在云南省，主要聚居地在德宏的芒市、临沧的镇康。通用傣文、汉文字。信仰南传上座部佛教。主要从事农业，擅长种茶。传统手工艺为银器制作。德昂族的住宅多竹楼。民族乐器有铓锣、象脚鼓等。

三十九、独龙族

独龙族主要分布在云南省，主要聚居区在贡山独龙族怒族自治县。有自己的语言，无本民族文字。主要从事农业。独龙族人过去有文面的习俗，相信万物有灵。腊月过年，喜跳牛锅庄舞。

四十、俄罗斯族

俄罗斯族主要分布在新疆维吾尔自治区，主要居住在伊犁、阿勒泰等地。俄罗斯族有自己的语言，使用俄文。主要从事商业、服务业和园艺、养畜、养蜂业等。生活习俗、服饰等基本上与独联体俄罗斯民族相同。

四十一、鄂伦春族

鄂伦春族主要分布在黑龙江省（占51.9%）和内蒙古的鄂伦春自治旗（占44.5%）。一般通用汉语、汉文。鄂伦春人男女都擅骑射，妇女擅刺绣、制作皮制品和桦皮器皿。男女老少都擅歌舞，编唱民歌、仿动物起舞。

四十二、鄂温克族

鄂温克族主要分布在内蒙古自治区，主要聚居区在呼伦贝尔盟的鄂温克族自治旗，其余分布在黑龙江和北京等省市。牧区通用蒙古语和蒙古文，农区通用汉语和汉文。宗教信仰以萨满教为主。鄂温克人口头文学丰富，民歌悠扬，舞蹈豪放。

四十三、京　族

京族主要分布在广西壮族自治区（占 86.9%），主要聚居北部湾内京族三岛上，其余散布在贵州、广东等省。京族有自己的语言和文字，但很早以来就通用汉语、汉文。主要从事渔业，积累了丰富的经验。京族青年男女喜对歌，舞蹈有跳天灯，民族乐器独弦琴音色悠扬。

四十四、柯尔克孜族

柯尔克孜族主要分布在新疆维吾尔自治区（占 97.9%），主要聚居区在克孜勒苏柯尔克孜自治州，其余分布在黑龙江省。有自己的语言，无文字。现在居南疆者通用维吾尔语、文字，居北疆者通用哈萨克语、文字。大都信仰伊斯兰教，部分信仰喇嘛教。主要从事畜牧业，部分从事农业。柯尔克孜族擅长歌舞。柯尔克孜族历法年初的诺劳孜节相当于汉族的春节。

四十五、毛南族

毛南族主要分布在广西壮族自治区（占 98.2%），主要聚居区在桂北环江毛南族自治县。通用汉、壮语和汉文字。主要从事农业，有饲养菜牛（食用牛）的丰富经验。擅长雕刻、编织。喜好歌唱。祭祀神灵、祖先的五月庙节是毛南族特有节日。

四十六、仫佬族

仫佬族主要分布在广西壮族自治区北部山区，90% 聚居于罗城仫佬族自治县。有自己的语言，无本民族文字，多数人通汉语和壮语，通用汉文。民族节日以庆丰收、保平安的“依饭”最隆重。

四十七、怒　族

怒族主要分布在云南省怒江傈僳族自治州的泸水、福贡、贡山、兰坪县。怒族有自己的语言，无文字，大都使用汉文。主要从事农业，也从事狩猎、采集业。怒族人喜歌舞，以此表达喜怒哀乐。服饰特点：妇女耳戴垂肩大铜环，成年男子腰佩砍刀，肩背弓弩。

四十八、普米族

普米族主要聚居区在云南省兰坪白族普米族自治县。通用汉文。多信仰喇嘛教。普米族能歌善舞，婚丧喜庆都举行对歌。普米族大过年即过春节，届时要举行赛马、摔跤等活动。

四十九、羌　族

羌族主要聚居区在四川省西北部阿坝藏族羌族自治州。羌族是中国最古老的民族之一。通用汉文字。主要从事农牧业，擅长打井和石砌建筑技术。传统工艺有挑花刺绣、编织等。羌族人民能歌善舞，伴奏乐器中的竹笛，称羌笛，是中国著名的古乐器之一。

五十、撒拉族

撒拉族主要聚居在青海省循化撒拉族自治县，其余分布在青海、甘肃、新疆等省区。撒拉族有自己的语言，无文字，通汉文。撒拉族普遍信仰伊斯兰教，其生活习俗大体与回族相似。口头文学丰富多彩，撒拉族山歌“花儿”受藏族影响，普遍带有颤音，婉转动听。

五十一、塔吉克族

塔吉克族主要分布在新疆维吾尔自治区西南部的塔什库尔干塔吉克自治县，其余分布在莎车、泽普、叶城和皮山等县。有自己的语言，普遍使用维吾尔文。

五十二、塔塔尔族

塔塔尔族分布在新疆维吾尔自治区。现一般通用维吾尔文或哈萨克文，多信仰伊斯兰教。居住北疆城镇的塔塔尔族多经商，一部分人从事手工业或畜牧业。民族音乐、舞蹈节奏鲜明活泼。还有赛马、摔跤、拔河等民族体育活动。

五十三、乌孜别克族

乌孜别克族散居在新疆维吾尔自治区 85% 以上的市、县、城镇，部分分

布在农牧区。有自己的语言，现通用维吾尔文和哈萨克文。多信仰伊斯兰教。居住城镇的多经商，尤其以丝绸业为主，居住乡村的从事农牧业。妇女擅长刺绣。乌孜别克族头戴各式瓜帽，喜喝奶茶。乌孜别克族舞蹈轻盈，音乐悠扬。

五十四、锡伯族

锡伯族主要分布在新疆维吾尔自治区伊犁哈萨克族自治州的察布查尔锡伯族自治县和辽宁、吉林等省，其余主要分散居住在北方各省及全国各地。有本民族语言和文字。锡伯族原是游牧民族，后发展农业，兼营畜牧业。民间文学神话传说丰富，锡伯族能歌善舞。爱好摔跤、骑射等民族体育活动。节日与汉族、满族大致相同，农历四月十八日是锡伯族人从东北迁往新疆的纪念日，每年都举行庆祝活动。

五十五、仡佬族

仡佬族主要分布在贵州省，以北部的道真仡佬族苗族自治县、务川仡佬族苗族自治县分布较集中。通用汉语，普遍使用汉文。主要从事农业。多民间故事、诗歌、谚语。音乐、舞蹈优美朴素，“八仙”乐曲富有民族特色。

五十六、裕固族

裕固族主要聚居区在甘肃省肃南裕固族自治县，其余分布在新疆、青海等省区。通用汉语、汉文。主要信仰萨满教和喇嘛教。裕固族主要从事畜牧业。擅长织绣、造型艺术。多民间传说故事。民歌曲调优美、内容丰富。

Chapter 1 Brief Introduction of Chinese 56 Ethnic Groups

Since ancient times, China is a unified multi-ethnic country. After the establishment of People's Republic of China, there are altogether 56 ethnic groups that have been recognized and identified by China's Central Government. As the majority of the population is the Han ethnic group, the other 55 of which are generally called the ethnic minorities.

China's ethnic groups live together over vast areas while some live in individual concentrated communities in small areas. In some cases, minority peoples can be found living in concentrated communities in areas inhabited mainly by the Han people, while in other cases the situation is just the other way round. This distribution pattern has taken shape throughout China's long history of development as ethnic groups migrated and mingled.

1. Han Nationality

The Han people, accounting for 92.0% of China's population, are not only China's largest ethnic group among 56 ethnic groups, but also one of the most populous nationalities in the world, who spread all over the country. Han nationality is China's ancient Huaxia nationality that is assimilated and fused with other nationalities. It has been called Hans from Han Dynasty. The language, which Han Chinese speak, is Chinese language. Modern Chinese language originates from the dialect spoken in northern China and is based on the Beijing accent. The written language used by Han nationality is called Chinese Character. Influenced by

Confucianism, Taoism, Buddhism and upholds humaneness, the Han people advocate loyalty, benevolence, filialness and justice. The main festivals for Han people are Spring Festival, Dragon Boat Festival, Double Ninth Festival, and so on.

2. Mongolian Nationality

Mongolian nationality mainly live in Inner Mongolia, Jilin, Liaoning, Heilongjiang, Xinjiang, Gansu, Qinghai, Ningxia, and other provinces and regions. Mongolian nationality is not only excelling in cattle breeding, but also good at riding and shooting. The house, in which they live, is called yurt. The written language of the Mongolian is called Mongolian script. The Nadamu Fair, which is held in Fall and Spring, is a traditional festival for Mongolian nationality.

3. Hui Nationality

The Hui nationality, mainly resides in Ningxia Hui Autonomous Region, which account for 17.7% of Hui People, the rest of whom scatter across the country. The language, which Hui people speak and use, is Chinese language and Chinese Character. The style of clothing for Hui nationality is very similar to Han people. The difference mainly is reflected on the headdress. The men love wearing bonnet and the women like wearing headscarf. Hui people mainly follow Islam. Eid (also called Rozah) and Corbon are two main folk festivals for Hui nationality.

4. Tibetan Nationality

Tibetan nationality is one of the vital members of the Chinese ethnic peoples. Most Tibetan people settle in Tibet Autonomous Region, which account for 45.9% of all the Tibetans. And the rest scatter in Sichuan, Qinghai, Gansu, Yunnan and other provinces. Tibetan people are mainly engaged in agriculture and animal husbandry. The language, which they use, is Tibetan language. Most Tibetan people follow Lamaism. Tibetan New Year is Tibetan people's traditional festival. Tibetan people like dressing robes and boots in customary clothing. They like drinking Tibetan buttered tea. *Zanba*, which is roasted highland barley flour, has long been a staple in Tibet.

5. Uighur Nationality

Uighur people mainly settle in Xinjiang Uygur Autonomous Region, the rest of whom distribute in other such places as Changde in the north of Hunan Province. The Uighur people have their own language and characters. The religious belief, which they follow, is Islam. Uighur people have a long tradition of running agriculture and husbandry and handicrafts. They are skillful in cotton planting and fruits gardening. Uighur people are all good at singing and dancing. Hats floret, which is an integral part of the Uighur ethnic costumes, is one of the hallmarks of the Uygur beauty. Men and women of all ages are fond of wearing a hats floret. Traditional festivals are Corban Festival, the Rozah Festival, and so on.

6. Miao Nationality

The Miao people primarily settle in Guizhou Province, accounting for 49.8%. Most Miao people inhabit in Qiannan Buyi and Miao Autonomous Prefecture, Qianxi'nan Buyi and Miao Autonomous Prefecture and Qiandongnan Miao and Dong Autonomous Prefecture and a small number of Miao people live in Hunan, Yunnan, Guangxi, Hainan and other provinces. Handicrafts of the Miao nationality are mainly embroidery, batik, paper-cut and ornaments, which are colorful. The *Lusheng* (a reed-pipe wind instrument) is their favorite musical instrument. Hmong song, which is a traditional music of the Miao people, and Lusheng Dance of Miao nationality enjoy a high reputation. There are a large number of festivals in Miao people's life, such as Miao Year and "April 8" to perpetuate the memory of the national hero.

7. Zhuang Nationality

Zhuang people, one of the largest populations of Chinese minority groups, mainly live in Guangxi Zhuang Autonomous Region, and Yunnan, Guangdong and other provinces. Zhuang people have their own language and characters. Bronze drum, rock paintings and Zhuang brocade are all very famous. Zhuang people enjoy singing

antiphonal folk songs. The Hungry Ghost Festivals is a second important vital festival, which is second only to Spring Festival in Zhuang regions.

8. Buyi Nationality

Buyi people primarily scatter in Qiannan Buyi and Miao Autonomous Prefecture, Qianxi'nan Buyi and Miao Autonomous Prefecture and Anshun City, the rest in Yunnan, Guangxi and other provinces. Buyi people have their own language and characters, but now Chinese is commonly in use. Buyi people, who are dominated by agriculture, have a long history of growing rice. Buyi women are good at textile and batik. Buyi people are experts in singing and dancing. The contents of folk songs are in variety. Buyi people always sing songs to express their feelings. Double Sixth Festival is a great pageant only next to Spring Festival and it is a day in memory of the uprising Buyi leaders.

9. Korean Nationality

Korean people mainly live in Jilin Province, the rest of whom scatter in Heilongjiang Province, Liaoning Province, and so on. The largest area inhabited by the Korean people is Yanbian Autonomous Prefecture. Korean people have their own language and characters. Korean people have a way with growing rice in the cold North. They are fond of singing folk songs, dancing and sports activities such as wrestling, swinging, springboard, preferring wearing plain white clothing. Specialty is cold noodles and pickles.

10. Man Nationality

Man people mainly live in Liaoning Province, accounting for 50.4% of all Man people. The rests scatter in the Hebei, Heilongjiang, Jilin Provinces, and Inner Mongolia Autonomous Region. Man people has its own language and characters but Man people learn and adopt the Chinese language of dominant Han generally conventional Chinese Mandarin. Sports of the Man people are the vaulting horse, skating, and so on.

11. Dong Nationality

Dong people, who mainly live in Guizhou Province, are clustered together in Qiandongnan Miao and Dong Autonomous Prefecture, Yuping Dong Autonomous County, others scattering in Hu'nan and Guangxi Provinces. Dong people have their own language, and now most of them use Chinese language. Dong people are mainly engaged in agriculture, especially growing rice. The specialty is glutinous rice. The Kam Sweet Rice is probably the most famous. Dong women are good at brocading and singing. The special festivals of Dong people are the Spring Festival, Offering Cattle Festival and Eating Newly Riped Grains Festival.

12. Yao Nationality

Yao people mainly live in China's Guangxi, Hu'nan, Yunnan, Guangdong, Guizhou, Jiangxi Provinces, and so on. Yao people have their own language. Yao people are primarily engaged in agroforestry, hunting also occupying a certain position. Yao women are also skillful in textile and embroidery. Yao people enjoy singing and they celebrate festivals nearly every month.

13. Bai Nationality

Bai people mainly inhabit in the Erhai Lake, centered Dali Bai Autonomous Prefecture in west Yunnan, only a few scattering in Sichuan, Guizhou, Hunan and other places. Bai people have their own language, yet without characters, and a majority of them know Chinese. Bais are expert in agriculture, and create the brilliant Bai culture, such as the Three Pagodas, Jianchuan Grottoes, Jizu Mountain Buddhism Buildings, etc. The Third Month Fair, also known as Guanyin Market, is Bai Minority's grand festival and market-day. There is another grand festival in July, which is called the Torch Festival. Folk music and opera of Bai people show their unique characteristics.

14. Tujia Nationality

Tujia people mainly live in Xiangxi Tujia and Miao Autonomous Prefecture in

Hu'nan Province and Enshi Tujia and Miao Autonomous Prefecture in Hubei Province. The Tujia people have their own language, yet most people speak Mandarin Chinese and write with Chinese Character. Tujia people are skilled at weaving craft, and its weaving craft and Hand-waving Dance are known as the art of Tujia flower. They will offer sacrifice to the chieftain of the Tujia nationality in Dragon Boat Festival, Double Sixth Festival, and so on. Nearly every Tujia people enjoy singing and making up folk songs.

15. Ha'ni Nationality

99.5% of Ha'ni people inhabit in central zone between the Honghe River and the Lancangjiang River in Yunnan Province. Ha'ni Minority Ethnic Group have its own language, yet without characters. Ha'ni people are clever at planting in terraced fields, some as high as hundreds of levels. They commonly make their garments with dying and weaving green cloth. Men wrap their heads with a piece of black or white cloth, while woman wear embroidered belts. Ha'ni calendar begins with the lunar October; therefore, October Festival is Ha'ni's New Year. Ha'ni people are good at singing and dancing.

16. Kazak Nationality

Kazak People mainly live in Xinjiang Uygur Autonomous Region, accounted for 99.8% of the whole Kazaks, most of whom live in the Yili Kazak Autonomous Prefecture. The rest scatter in Gansu Province. They have their own language and characters. Most of them follow Islam. Kazaks people are mostly engaged in animal husbandry. National sports include lamb tussling, wrestling, horseback archery, the girls' chase, mostly belonging to the kung fu on the horse.

17. Dai Nationality

The Dai people, mainly living in Yunnan Province, live in Xishuangbanna Dai Autonomous Prefecture and Dehong Dai and Jingpo Autonomous Prefecture. The rest scatter in Sichuan, Guangdong and other provinces. The Dai nationality has its own

language and character. The Dai nationality is classified as "Handai", "Shuidai" and "Huayaodai". Different clothing decoration represents dress culture of their branches. They are skilled at planting rice and tropical crops. Most of them believe in Hinayana. Women traditionally dress jacket and tight skirt. Dai's bamboo house is really characteristic. The Dai calendar year's Water-splashing Festival is a traditional festival usually held before the Tomb-sweeping Day. Dai people, skilled at sing and dancing, have created rich and colorful culture and art.

18. Li Nationality

Li people mainly live in Hainan Province, accounting for 92.0% of whole Li nationality. They mostly live in Li Autonomous Counties in the central and southwest of the Hainan Island, the rest of whom inhabit in Hunan Province. Li people have their own language and characters. Many of Li people speak Chinese. Li people, dominated by agriculture, are the earliest minority group that can spin. Li women are good at brocading by cotton. Li people are skilled at dancing and their folk songs are melodious.

19. Lisu Nationality

Lisu people mainly live in Yunnan Province, accounting for 96.9% of whole Lisu Nationality. They mostly live in Nujiang Lisu Autonomous Prefecture in northwest Yunnan. The rest scatter in Sichuan Province. Lisu people have their own language and characters. Their houses are built with bamboo and wood with a fireplace. Lisu people are skilled at singing and dancing. They will sing and drink to their hearts' content when celebrating Harvest Festival in October every year.

20. Wa Nationality

Wa people mainly live in Yunnan Province, most of whom mainly live in the Ximeng, Cangyuan, Menglian, Gengma Counties of southwest Yunnan Province, etc. Wa people have their own language and characters. Wa nationality's economy is dominated by agriculture. They are both good singers and dancers. Their national

dance is circling dance. Men, women and children, hand in hand, sing and dance happily and the atmosphere is quite lively.

21. Yi Nationality

Yi people mainly live in Yunnan Province, the rest of whom scatter in Sichuan, Guizhou and other provinces. Yi people have their own language and characters. Honghe Ha'ni and Yi Autonomous Prefecture and Chuxiong Yi Autonomous Prefecture in Yunnan Province, and Liangshan Yi Autonomous Prefecture in Sichuan Province are the largest settlement for Yi people. Headcloth is the typical dress of Yi nationality. The Torch Festival, usually celebrated in June 24th of lunar calendar is the most boisterous traditional festival of Yi nationality.

22. She Nationality

She people mainly live in the mountainous area of Fujian and Zhejiang Provinces. The rest distribute in Jiangxi, Guangdong and Anhui Provinces. She people have their own national language and most of them speak the local dialects. They don't have Character and commonly use Chinese language and character. She people enrich their family by planting tea. They are good at embroidery, weaving and such kind of folk craft. Folk song is known as the pearl of She minority culture. Double Third Day Festival of She people is usually concerned with ancestors worship.

23. Gaoshan Nationality

Gaoshan people mainly live in China's Taiwan Province, and the rest scatter in Fujian, Zhejiang and other coastal areas. Gaoshan people have their own language but have no Character. Gaoshan people scatter in the mainland speaking Chinese language and using Chinese characters. Gaoshan people are agrarian economy-oriented and be supplemented by fishing and hunting production. Gaoshan people are good at sculpture, pottery, weaving, etc. Gaoshan people are fond of singing and dancing. There is a unique form of dance music called "pestle Chule". Women thrash rice with long stone pestle, accompanied by melodious songs.

24. Lahu Nationality

Lahu people mainly distribute in Yunnan Province, accounting for 99. 4% of the whole Lahu Nationality. Lahu people mainly live in Pu'er and Lincang Cities, which are in Lancang River drainage area, Xishuangbanna Dai Autonomous Prefecture and Honghe Ha'ni and Yi Autonomous Prefecture. Lahu people have their own language and characters. Most people can speak both Chinese language and Dai language. They are good at hunting. The agriculture is mainly on planting tea, medicine, sisal, and so on. The traditional Lusheng dance and *Tuopuke* of oral literature (quizzes) are very popular among the masses.

25. Shui Nationality

Shui people mainly live in Guizhou, accounting for 93. 0% of the whole Shui group. Shui people inhabit in Sandu Shui Autonomous County. They speak and write in Chinese language and Character. Sui people have their own language. In ancient time, Shui people have their own characters, called Shui Characters, which imitate reversed Chinese Character, which also known as reversed character but they are just used in religious activities. Shui people engage in growing rice. Jiuqian wine is their traditional vintage wine. Shui people like such entertainment activities as Bronze Drum dance, Lusheng Dance, songs, and toasting songs. Women are fond of wearing a silver necklace and bracelet. Shui people's calendar begins with the lunar calendar in September. Duan Festival, which celebrated in 11th month lunar calendar, is their biggest festival.

26. Dongxiang Nationality

Dongxiang people mainly live in Dongxiang Autonomous County of Linxia Hui Autonomous Prefecture. The rest scatter in Xinjiang, Ningxia and other autonomous regions. Dongxiang people have their own language but no characters. They generally use Chinese language and Character. They believe in Islam. Dongxiang people's economy is dominated by agriculture and animal husbandry. Almost every Dongxiang

people love singing *Hua'er*, a folk song, the tune of which is sonorous and melodious.

27. Ji'nuo Nationality

Ji'nuo people mainly live in Yunnan Province, accounting for 99.0% of the whole Ji'nuo people. They mainly live in Ji'nuoshan Ji'nuo County of Jinghong City of Xishuangbanna Dai Autonomous Prefecture in Yunnan Province, the rest of whom scatter in Sichuan, Hunan and other provinces. Ji'nuo people have their own language, without characters. They keep records by carving bamboo. Ji'nuo people mainly engage in agriculture, especially planting Pu'er tea. Typical national costumes are a machete and peaked cap. Ji'nuo people like singing and dancing. Their new year celebrated in March is a grand festival.

28. Jingpo Nationality

Jingpo people mainly scatter in Yunnan Province, accounting for 99.4% of the whole Jinpo population. They live together in Dehong Dai and Jingpo Autonomous Prefecture. Jingpo people have their own language but no characters. They ever kept a record of events by carving wood and knotting ropes. Jingpo people are skilled in dancing and singing. More than one thousand people perform the group dance, accompanied by the drum music. Both men and women wear black Duijin jacket (a traditional Chinese costume) and women like wearing gorgeous apron and silver ornaments.

29. Lhoba Nationality

96.8% Lhoba people live in the southeastern Tibet Autonomous Region, the rest of whom scatter in Sichuan, Guizhou, Liaoning and other provinces. Lhoba people have their own language but no characters. A few people have a good command of Tibetan language. They have been keeping a record of events by carving wood and knotting ropes for a long time. They are predominantly engaged in agriculture, but sometimes are engaged in hunting. They are good at archery. Moreover, their bamboo craft is exquisite. Women wear earrings and bracelets which are made of silver and copper. Their principle food is rice, sometimes tsampa. They follow Lamaism.

30. Naxi Nationality

Naxi nationality is one of the unique minority groups of Yunnan Province. They mainly inhabit in Lijiang City, Yulong Naxi Autonomous County, Ninglang, Yongsheng, Weixi, Shangrila, and Deqin. The rest scatter in Yanyuan, Yanbian and Muli Counies of Sichuan Province. Naxi people have their own language and hieroglyphs. They accepted the Han people's culture during the late Ming and early Qing Dynasty, then Chinese language and Character are gradually and widely used among the people of Naxi nationality.

31. Monba Nationality

Monba people mainly settle in Tibet Autonomous Region, living in Motuo and Cuona Counties. Monba people have their own language but no character. Tibetan language and Tibetan character are in common use. The common belief of Monba people is Tibetan Buddhism.

32. Tu Nationality

Tu people mainly live in Qinghai Province. They mainly live in Huzhu Tu Autonomous County. The rest scatter in Gansu, Yunnan, Guizhou and other provinces. Tu people have their own language, but no characters. Chinese language and Chinese Character are used universally among Tu people. They follow Lamaism. Tu people are good at singing, dancing and sports. *Hua'erhui* Assembly, which is held several times a year, is their grand festival, in which the young men and women sing in antiphonal style.

33. Hezhe Nationality

Hezhe people mainly live in Raohe and Fuyuan County of Heilongjiang Province and inhabit in Jiejinkou, Sipai, and Bacha of ethnic towns. Hezhe nationality has its own language, but no characters. Chinese language and Chinese Character are in

common use. They have rich legends of oral literature and are fond of music and impromptu singing.

34. Achang Nationality

Achang people mainly live in Yunnan Province. They have their own language but no characters. They also can speak Chinese language and use it. They are mainly occupied with rice cropping. They are quite experienced in forging iron. Achang nationality is very rich in folk oral literature, songs, the elephant-foot drum dance, and monkey dance are popular.

35. Bulang Nationality

Bulang people mainly live in Yunnan Province, who mainly settle in Bulang mountainous areas in Menghai County. They are mainly occupied by agriculture and good at planting Pu'er tea. They believe in Hinayana. Bulang people are fond of sword performance. Young people like circling dances. Oral literature is mainly lyric epics.

36. Bao'an Nationality

Bao'an people mainly live in Gansu Province. The rest scatter in Qinghai, Xinjiang and other provinces and regions. They mainly live in Bao'an, Dongxiang and Salar Autonomous County of Jishishan . Chinese language and Character are in common use. They are mainly engaged in agriculture and famous for smelting iron and forging Bao'an broadsword. Islam has a profound influence on the Bao'an customs. They are skilled in playing music. They enjoy singing *Hua'er* and feast songs. Their dancing movements and postures are vigorous.

37. Daur Nationality

Daur nationality mainly lives in Inner Mongolia Autonomous Region. The rest scatter in Heilongjiang, Xinjiang and other provinces and regions. They are living in Morin Dawa Daur Autonomous Banner. Man language is adopted during Qing Dynasty but nowadays Chinese language is in common use. Daur people are largely engaged in agriculture. Women are good at weaving and embroideries, who are skilled in roe deer leather waistcoat. They are fond of songs and dances.

38. De'ang Nationality

De'ang people mainly live in Yunnan Province. Their ethnic enclave is in Luxi County in Dehong Prefecture and Zhenkang County in Lincang City. Dai and Chinese language are both commonly in use. They believe in Hinayana. They are dominated by agriculture and good at planting tea. Traditional craft is the production of silverware. De'ang people typically live in bamboo building. Ethnic musical instruments have Mangluo gong, elephant-foot drum, etc.

39. Dulong Nationality

Dulong people mainly live in Yunnan Province. They inhabit in Gongshan Dulong and Nu Autonomous County. They have their own language but no characters. They are mainly engaged in agriculture. Dulong people used to have a habit of cheeks tattoos. They believe that all things have spirit. National festival is the lunar New Year's Day. They are fond of dancing Niuguozhuang dance.

40. Russian Nationality

Ethnic Russians mainly live in Xinjiang Uygur Autonomous Region. They settle in such places as Yili, Altai, and so on. The Russians Nationality has its own language and use Russian character. They are mainly engaged in the business, services and gardening, stock raising, beekeeping, etc. Life customs, clothing are basically the same as Russian people in the Commonwealth of Independent States.

41. Oroqen Nationality

Oroqen people mainly live in Heilongjiang Province, accounting for 51.9% of the whole population and Oroqin Autonomous Banner of the Inner Mongolia Autonomous Region accounting for 44.5% of the whole. Chinese language and Character are commonly in use. The Oroqen people are good at riding and

shooting. The women are skilled in embroidery and making leather products and birchbark wares. Men and women all enjoy singing and dancing. They like making up, singing folk songs and imitating animals to dance.

42. Evenki Nationality

Ewenki people mainly live in Inner Mongolia Autonomous Region. They mainly live in Evenki Autonomous Banner, the rest of whom scatter in the Heilongjiang Province, Beijing City, and so on. In pastoral areas Mongolian language and Mongolian characters are generally used, while in the agricultural area Mandarin Chinese and characters are commonly used. They mainly follow Shamanism Religion. Ewenki people are rich in oral literature. Their folk songs are melodious. The style of the dance is bold.

43. Jing Nationality

Jing people mainly live in Guangxi Zhuang Autonomous Region, accounting for 86.9% of the whole Jing people. They settle in three islands of the Northern Bay. The rest scatter in Guizhou and Guangdong Provinces. Jing people have their own language and characters, but generally they have been using Chinese language and Character from early times. They are dominated by fishing and have profound experience in it. Young men and women are keen on singing to each other and dancing. The typical folk dance of Jing people is *Tiaotiandeng*. Their ethnic musical instrument is called *Duxianqin*, a single-string instrument, which has a melodious sound.

44. Kirzig Nationality

Kirzig people mainly live in Xinjiang Uygur Autonomous Region, settling in Kirzig Autonomous Prefecture. The rest scatter in Heilongjiang Province. They have their own language but no characters. Kirzig people who live in northern Xinjiang use Kazakh language and character. Most Kirzig people follow Islam and Lamaism. They mainly are engaged in animal husbandry and some agriculture. Kirzigs enjoy singing and dancing. Nuolaozi Day at the beginning of the year in Kirgiz calendar is equivalent the Spring Festival of Han Chinese.

45. Maonan Nationality

Maonan people mainly live in Guangxi Zhuang Autonomous Region, accounted for 98.2% of the whole Maonan people. They settle in Huanjiang Maonan Autonomous County in northen Guangxi Zhuang Autonomous Region. Chinese language and Zhuang language are in common use. They are mainly engaged in agriculture and are experienced in breeding beef cattle. They are good at carving and weaving and fond of singing. Temple Day in May to sacrifice gods and ancestors is a special festival for Maonan people.

46. Mulao Nationality

Mulao people mainly live in the northern mountainous areas in Guangxi Zhuang Autonomous Region. 90% of whole Mulao people live in Luocheng Mulao Autonomous County. They have their own language but no characters. Most of Mulao people know Chinese language and Zhuang language. Chinese Character are in common use. The ethnic festival, Yifan Festival, to celebrate harvest and pray for security and peace is the grandest one.

47. Nu Nationality

Nu people mainly live in Lushui, Fugong, Gongshan and Lanping of Nujiang Lisu Autonomous Prefecture. They have their own language but no characters. They are dominated by agriculture, hunting and gathering. Nu people are fond of singing and dancing to express happiness and sadness. Women wear big copper rings. Adult men always carry a chopper with a crossbow in the shoulder.

48. Pumi Nationality

Pumi people mainly live in Lanping Bai and Pumi Autonomous County in Yunnan Province. Chinese language is in common use. They follow Lamaism. Pumi

people enjoy singing and dancing. Singing in antiphonal style will be held in weddings and funerals. Pumi people's Spring Festival is their grandest festival, in which horse racing, wrestling and other activities will be held.

49. Qiang Nationality

The Qiang people mainly live in Aba Tibetan and Qiang Autonomous Prefecture of Sichuan Province. Qiang nationality is one of the oldest nationalities in China. Chinese language and Character are in common use. They engage in agriculture and animal husbandry. They are good at well sinking and stone building technology. Cross-stitch embroidery and knitting are their traditional arts. Qiang people are keen on singing and dancing. *Qiangdi*, an accompaniment musical instrument, is one of the famous ancient musical instruments in China.

50. Sala Nationality

Sala people mainly live in Xunhua Sala Autonomous County in Qinghai Province. The rest scatter in Qinghai, Gansu, Xinjiang, and other provinces and regions. Sala people have their own language but no characters. They follow Islam. Their living customs are similar to Hui people. Their oral literature is very profound. Influenced by Tibetan, folk song, *Hua'er*, is normally with tremolo and sounds beautiful.

51. Tajik Nationality

Tajik people mainly live in Taxkorgan Tajik Autonomous County in the southeast of Xinjiang Uygur Autonomous Region. The rest scatter in Shache, Zepu, Yecheng, Pishan and other counties. They have their own language and use Uygur characters.

52. Tatar Nationality

Tatar people mainly live in in Xinjiang Uygur Autonomous Region. Uygur characters and Kazakh characters are commonly in use. They follow Islam. Tatar people living in the border towns are mainly engaged in business, part of who are engaged in manufacturing or animal husbandry. Folk dance music rhythm is bright and lively. National sports activities such as horse racing, wrestling, and tug of war are their favorite ones.

53. Uzbek Nationality

Uzbeks scatter in more than 85% towns, counties, prefectures in Xinjiang Uygur Autonomous Region, some of whom live in pastoral areas. They have their own language. Uygur character and Kazakh character are in common use. They follow Islam. Uzbeks, who live in cities and towns, are mainly engaged in business, silk, etc. , others, living in rural areas, run agriculture, animal husbandry. Women are good at embroidery. Uzbek people like wearing all kinds of hats, and drinking milky tea. Ethnic Uzbeks dance lightly with melodious music.

54. Xibo Nationality

Xibo people mainly live in Chabucha'er Xibo Autonomous County in Yili Prefecture of Xinjiang Uygur Autonomous Region, Liaoning and Jilin Provinces, the rest of whom scatter in northern provinces and other regions all over the country. They have their own language and characters. Xibo people are originally hordes. They are gradually engaged in agriculture and animal husbandry. Xibo people have rich folk literature and legends. Xibo people are good at singing and dancing as well as some sports activity such as wrestling and horseback archery. Their festivals are almost the same with Han people and Man people. The April 18th in the lunar calendar is the Memorial Day on which Xibo people move to Xinjiang from the northeast. They hold celebrations every year.

55. Gelao Nationality

Gelao people mainly live in Guizhou Province especially in Daozhen County and Wuchuan Gelao and Miao Autonomous County of northern Guizhou. Chinese language and Character are commonly in use. They are mainly engaged in agriculture. Gelao people have many folk tales, poems and proverbs. Their songs and dances are simple

but beautiful. The music, the Eight Immortals, is full of their unique characteristics.

56. Yugu Nationality

Yugu People mainly live in Yugu Autonomous County in the south of Gansu Province, the rest of whom settle in Xinjiang, Qinghai and other provinces and regions. Chinese language and Character are commonly in use. They follow Shamanism and Buddhism. Yugu people are mainly engaged in animal husbandry and are good at silk embroideries and plastic art. There are many folk legends. Folk songs are melodious and rich in content.

第二章　龙文化

中国是龙文化的发源地，龙文化源远流长，在中华民族文化发展史上占有重要的地位。龙文化是中国传统文化的标志。在历史长河中，龙是中华民族的象征，作为中华民族共同的崇拜物、神、艺术形象，沟通了中华大地上不同民族、不同信仰的人们之间的关系，增进了各民族的相互理解和团结，对促进民族融合、文化统一起到了积极作用。

一、龙的起源

中国龙只是一种传说中的虚构动物。中国龙看起来是一种由许多动物组合起来的动物，通常认为是由九种动物组合而成："角似鹿，头似驼，眼如兔，项似蛇，腹如蜃，鳞如鱼，爪似鹰，掌似虎，耳如牛"。

中国龙起源于原始图腾文化，但本质却超越了图腾文化。一些学者认为，龙起源于中国古代不同的原始部落，具体来说，是以蛇为图腾的华夏族东征西讨，逐渐兼并了崇奉鹿、骆驼、兔、鳄、鱼、鹰、牛等图腾的部落。为了加强团结，这就需要一个综合性的崇拜物作为共同的图腾。于是以自己的蛇图腾为本体，吸收被征服或加盟部落图腾崇奉物中的某一突出特征，综合而成似蛇非蛇、似鱼非鱼、似兽非兽的新的图腾，由此升华成了自然界不曾有过的"龙"。因此，中国龙是诸多氏族部落崇拜的图腾经过美化的综合体，是构成中华民族凝聚力的共同图腾之偶像。

二、龙的演变

春秋以前的龙，可以称为"古代龙"。古代龙多匍匐爬状，结构形态粗

陋，蛇身兽头，保持着爬行动物的特点。其形状极为丰富，也异常怪异，带着一身粗野与狂放、暴力与恐怖，展示着神秘的威力。这不仅反映着上古时代各地文化未经系统化之前的形态，同时也反映着部落兼并战争的文化特点。

战国到唐代的龙，可称之为“中世龙”。这是龙的形态变化最大的一个时期。中世龙开始蜕去了爬行动物的特点，从匍匐走向飞腾。龙的体态多呈S形，显得刚健有力。中世龙不管形状和姿态怎么样变化除圆形造型外，其头大多奋力高举或引颈欲鸣，有引身向上飞动的趋势。这方面与古代龙和现代龙大不相同。

宋代以后，龙的形态基本定型，可称之为“现代龙”。其主要特点是蜿蜒多变，通体华美，虽然仍然保持着不可一世的威严，但却失去了中世龙头的威猛。其头角由短变长，呈叉状，展示的是一种威仪的气度。上腭由卷变直，口由深变浅，原始龙带血的巨口，变成了满足生存需求的觅食工具。身躯延长，须发长飘，身体的各个部分表现得极为协调，优美的姿态更富有神韵。此时，“角似鹿，头似驼，眼如兔，项似蛇，腹如蜃，鳞如鱼，爪似鹰，掌似虎，耳如牛”的形象基本确定下来，而广为后世效仿并保留至今。

自从封建帝王杜撰出君权神授一说，龙的形象就成了其最好的替身，所以古代的皇帝认为自己是“真龙天子”，也即真龙和上天的儿子。于是，皇帝的衣服成了“龙袍”，皇帝的椅子被叫作“龙椅”，皇帝出行用的车马叫“龙辇”，皇帝的子女叫“龙种”，皇帝生气了叫“龙颜大怒”。

三、龙的分类

传说天龙守卫天庭，拉神车。神龙是掌管天气的雷神，长着人身龙头，有鼓一样的肚子。伏藏龙是地下世界金银珠宝的守卫，主管火山。地龙掌管五湖四海，决江开渎。应龙是修炼了千年，长出了双翼的龙，相传应龙是上古时期黄帝的神龙，它曾奉黄帝之令讨伐过九黎族部落酋长蚩尤，并杀了蚩尤而成为功臣。蛟龙是无角的龙，是水中霸主，擅于兴风作浪。蟠龙是湖中之龙，蛰伏在地而未升天。黄龙是无角之龙，往往用来象征帝王。飞龙是生有双翼，能腾云驾雾之龙。青龙是“四灵”之一，主管东方。

四、龙生九子的传说

老大囚牛（Qiúniú），喜音乐，蹲立于琴头。

老二睚眦（Yázì），嗜杀喜斗，刻镂于刀环、剑柄吞口。

老三狴犴（Bì'àn），形似虎，有威力，生平好讼，常见于古代牢门之上，震慑囚犯，民间有虎头牢的说法，是辨明是非，伸张正义的神兽。

老四狻猊（Suānní），形如狮，喜烟好坐，倚立于香炉足上，随之吞烟吐雾。

老五饕餮（Tāotiè），嘴馋身懒，好吃好喝，其形象常见于古代烹饪鼎器上，夏商青铜器便可见饕餮纹，为有首无身的狰狞猛兽，是品尝美味、鉴赏佳肴的"美食家"。

老六椒图（Jiāotú），形似螺蚌，性情温顺，常见于大门上，衔环守夜，阻拦小人，是求学、求子、升职的保护神。

老七赑屃（Bìxì），龟形有齿，力大好负重，常背负石碑于宫殿中，是长寿、吉祥、走鸿运的保护神。

老八螭吻（Chīwěn），又名鸱（Chī）尾或鸱吻，好张望，常站立于建筑物屋脊，作张口吞脊状，是宅院守护、驱邪纳福、安居乐业的神兽。

老九貔貅（Píxiū），又叫辟邪，生性凶猛，专吞金银，肚大无肛，只进不出，即能招财，又能守护财富、掌握财运，是招财进宝的保护神。

五、龙的体现

中国是龙的故乡，中华民族是龙的传人，中华民族历来信龙、尊龙、祭龙，并把美好的理想和愿望寄予龙，相信龙会给人们带来好运，赐予幸福。龙是神灵和权威的象征，龙的观念、龙的形象已经渗透到社会的各个方面。

在中华民族的历史长河中，作为中国独特文化现象之一的龙，出现在政治、经济、文化、艺术、建筑等各个领域。从秦砖汉瓦到木雕石刻，从古寺塔林到钟鼎华表，从皇室宫殿到民间生活用品，从绘画剪纸到民间传说，到处都体现着中国龙文化。从节日风俗到娱乐风俗以及各种喜庆活动，象征吉祥的龙灯往往就会出现在人们面前。龙的图像在许多工艺品、建筑物及其他器物上也大量出现，各种字体的"龙"字书法作品也在许多场合展现出来。龙象征吉祥，代表理想，代表力量。

在一些重大庆典中，往往也有龙的形象出现，如舞龙、赛龙舟等等。龙在中国政治、文学、艺术、习俗及宗教信仰中都有着极其重要的作用。

Chapter 2 Chinese Dragon Culture

China is the birthplace of Chinese dragon culture. Dragon culture has a long history in China, which occupies an important position in the development of the cultural history of Chinese ethnic peoples. Chinese dragon culture is a sign of Chinese traditional culture. In the long China's history, the dragon is a symbol for the Chinese ethnic peoples. As a common worship or a god, which is an artistic image for Chinese ethnic peoples, Chinese dragon links up the relationship of different ethnic peoples with different beliefs in China and enhances the mutual understanding and the unity of all the nationalities, which plays a positive role in the ethnic fusion and cultural unity.

1. The Origin of the Dragon

Chinese dragon is a legendary animal in the fictions. The dragon looks like a combination of many animals, which is often described visually as a composite of parts from nine animals, the horns of a deer, the head of a camel, the eyes of a rabbit, the neck of a snake, the abdomen of a large cockle, the scales of a fish, the claws of an eagle, the paws of a tiger, and the ears of an ox.

Chinese dragon originates from primitive culture of totems, but the essence is beyond the totem culture. Some scholars believe that Chinese dragon originates from totems of different tribes in ancient China. Specifically speaking, ancient Huaxia Tribe, who takes the snake as their totem, gradually conquers other tribes, who take the deer, camel, rabbit, cockle; fish, eagle, tiger, and ox as their respective

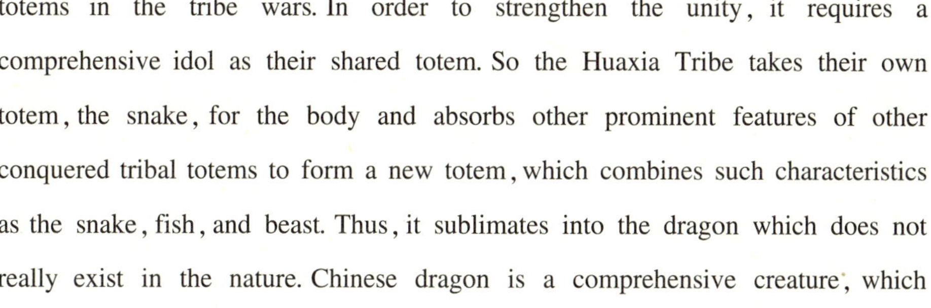

totems in the tribe wars. In order to strengthen the unity, it requires a comprehensive idol as their shared totem. So the Huaxia Tribe takes their own totem, the snake, for the body and absorbs other prominent features of other conquered tribal totems to form a new totem, which combines such characteristics as the snake, fish, and beast. Thus, it sublimates into the dragon which does not really exist in the nature. Chinese dragon is a comprehensive creature, which combines the totems, which many other tribes worship. Chinese dragon becomes a shared totem of Chinese ethnic peoples, which constructs the Chinese national cohesion.

2. The Evolution of Chinese Dragon

The dragons before the Spring and Autumn Period can be called the "Ancient Dragon", many of which have an image of crawling, which is humble in structure and morphology, with a snake's body and animals' head, and share some reptilian characteristics. The shape of the dragon then is extremely rich, but rather extremely weird. The dragon takes on an image of roughness, wildness, violence and terror, showing a mysterious power, which not only reflects the cultural system in the ancient times, but also embodies the cultural characteristics of tribal conquest and annexation war.

The dragons from the Warring States Period to Tang Dynasty can be called the "Medieval Dragon". In this period the dragon undergoes the biggest changes in the morphology. The Medieval Dragon begins to remove the reptilian characteristics, from creeping towards flying. The dragon's body takes on the shape of "S", which is vigorous. No matter what changes the Medieval Dragon undergoes in the dragon posture or in the dragon shapes, besides its circular shape, the dragon's head is mostly struggling to uphold to make a roar or have a tendency of flying, which is quite different from the Ancient Dragon and the Modern Dragon.

After Song Dynasty, the dragon form its basic shape, which can be called "Modern Dragon", the main characteristic of which is winding, changeable and gorgeous. The Modern Dragon, though it still maintains a mighty majesty of a

dragon, loses the fierce of a Medieval Dragon. Their horns become longer than that of Medieval Dragon, which take on a forked shape, showing a laudable tolerant spirit. The palate becomes straight from a rolled shape. The mouth becomes deeper than it is before. The blooded giant mouth of an Ancient Dragon turns to be the foraging tools to meet the needs of survival. The dragon's body is lengthened with long elegant beard and hair. Each part of the dragon's body is quite coordinated with a beautiful posture and a romantic charm. At this time, the image of the dragon, which has the horns of a deer, the head of a camel, the eyes of a rabbit, the neck of a snake, the abdomen of a large cockle, the scales of a fish, the claws of an eagle, the paws of a tiger, and the ears of an ox, is basically established, which is emulated and followed by later generations.

Since the Chinese feudal emperors fabricate the divine right of emperors, the image of the dragon has become the best substitute of the feudal emperors. The feudal emperors become "the real dragon and the sons of the heaven", which are sent by God to rule the world. Thus, the emperor's clothes are called "dragon robes". The chair, which the feudal emperors sit, is called "dragon chair". The closed carriage, which the feudal emperors take for travel, is called the "dragon chariot". The emperor's children are called "dragon tatsutane". The feudal emperors' anger is called "dragon fury".

3. The Dragon's Classification

According to the old legend, Tianlong Dragon, the dragon in the heaven, guards the heaven and pulls the carts in the heaven. Shenlong Dragon, the Thor, is in charge of the weather. It has a human body and a dragon's head with a drum-like belly. Fuzanglong Dragon, who guards the gold, silver and jewelry in the underground world, is in charge of volcano. Dilong Dragon, an earth dragon, which is in charge of rivers and lakes, takes the responsibility of opening the rivers. Yinglong Dragon is the dragon, who sprouts two wings after thousand of self-cultivating. It is said that Yinglong Dragon is a dragon of Huangdi, who is the alliance leader of ancient Huaxia Tribal. Yinglong Dragon follows Huangdi's order

to crusade against Chiyou, who is the alliance leader of Jiuli ethnic tribal in ancient times. Yinglong Dragon killed Chiyou and became a hero. Jiaolong Dragon, a flood dragon, who is a hornless dragon, is the overlord in the water, who is capable of invoking storms and floods. Panlong Dragon is the lake dragon, who is dormant in the ground without ascending to the heaven. Huanglong Dragon, a yellow dragon, is a hornless dragon, which is often used to symbolize the feudal emperors. Feilong Dragon, a flying dragon, which has two wings, can fly in the sky. Qinglong Dragon, a blue dragon, which is one of "four spirit" in Chinese culture, is in charge of the East.

4. The Legend of the Nine Sons of Dragons

The first son of the dragon, who is called Qiuniu, loves music and becomes a decoration for music instrument, such as two-stringed bowed violin(*Huqin*).

The second son of the dragon, who is called Yazi, loves fighting. Yazi is often carved in many different knife rings and handles of swords.

The third son of the dragon, who is called Bi'an, shapes like a tiger. Bi'an, who is powerful, loves adventure. Therefore, it often appears on the ancient prison door to deter prisoners. There is an allegation of tiger prison, which is circulated among the people in the past. It is said that Bi'an, the third son of the dragon, is a mythical animal, who can distinguish between the right and wrong and have the justice to be done.

The fourth son of the dragon, who is called Suanni, shapes like a lion and likes smoke and sitting. Suanni usually rests on the feet of an incense burner swallowing and spitting the smoke.

The fifth son of the dragon, who is called Taotie, is greedy and lazy. Taotie likes delicious food and drink. Therefore, Tiaotie is often found in ancient cooking tripods and other devices. The design of Taotie, which is a ferocious beast with a head but without body, can be found in the bronze vessels of Xia and Shang Dynasties. It is a gastrologist who is capable of tasting and appreciating the delicious delicacies.

The sixth son of the dragon, who is called Jiaotu, shapes like a snail mussel and has a gentle temperament. Jiaotu, who is the guardian of going to school, praying for children and promotion, often appears on the door with a ring in mouth, guarding for the safety and keeping out of the villains.

The seventh son of the dragon, who is called Bixi, shapes like a turtle with teeth and possesses tremendous strength and likes bearing a heavy burden. Bixi, who is usually found to bear a heavy stone tablet in the palaces, is the guardian of long-live, luck and good fortune.

The eighth son, who is called Chiwen or Chiwei, likes looking up and down. Chiwen, who is usually found to stand on the roof of a building with a posture of opening the mouth to swallow the ridge, is the mythical animal for guarding houses, expelling evils, invoking blessings and enjoying a good and prosperous life.

The ninth son, who is called Pixiu or Bixie, is violent by nature, specially swallowing gold and silver. Pixiu, who is a monster with a huge belly but without an anus, always takes but never gives. Therefore, Pixiu is the guardian of making money and bringing in wealth and treasure.

5. The Embodiment of the Dragon

China is the hometown of the Chinese dragon. The Chinese ethnic peoples are descendants of the Chinese dragon. The Chinese ethnic peoples always believe in the dragons, worship dragons, and offer sacrifices to dragons. They often place their beautiful ideals and wishes on the dragon and believe that the dragon will bring them good luck and give them happiness. The dragon is a symbol of divine and authority. The concept and the image of the dragon have penetrated into every aspects of Chinese society.

In Chinese history, the dragon, as one of China's unique cultural phenomena, appears in such various fields as politics, economy, culture, art and architecture. Chinese dragon culture is embodied everywhere, from the bricks in Qin Dynasty or the tiles in Han Dynasty to wood carvings or stone carvings, from

ancient temples or the forest of towers to vessels or bells or ornamental columns, from the royal palace to folk living articles, from paintings or paper-cuts to folk legends. From the festivals or customs to the entertainment customs or festive activities, the dragon, which is the symbol of auspiciousness, often appears in front of people. The dragon's image also appears in many arts, crafts, buildings and other utensils. Various forms of Chinese character, "龙", which means the dragon, also appear in many occasions as calligraphy works. The dragon is a symbol of auspiciousness, which represents the ideal and strength.

The image of the dragon can be seen as well in such grand celebrations as dragon performance, dragon boat race, and so on. The dragon plays a very important role in Chinese politics, literature, art, customs and religious belief.

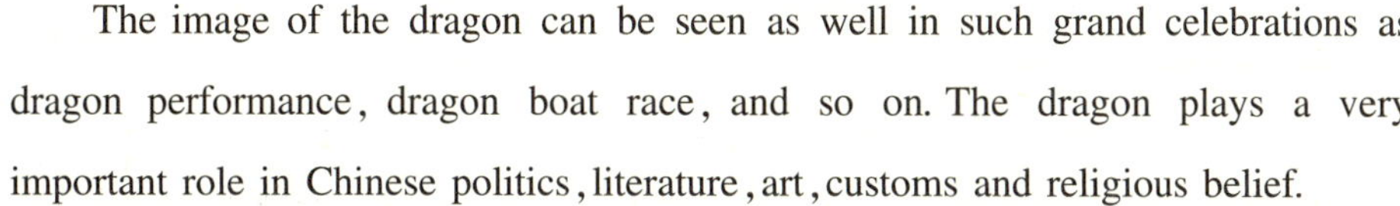

第三章　中国古代四大发明

四大发明是指中国古代对世界发展具有革命性意义的四种发明——指南针、造纸术、火药、印刷术。四大发明对中国古代的政治、经济、文化的发展产生了巨大的推动作用，对世界的发展也产生了非常大的影响。

一、指南针

指南针是利用磁铁在地球磁场中的南北指极性而制成的一种指向仪器，有多种形体。

主要组成部分是一根装在轴上可以自由转动的磁针。磁针在地磁场作用下能保持在磁子午线的切线方向上。磁针的北极指向地理的南极，利用这一性能可以辨别方向。指南针常用于航海、大地测量、旅行及军事等方面。

指南针的发明是中国劳动人民在长期的实践中对物体磁性认识的结果。由于生产劳动，人们接触了磁铁矿，开始了对磁性质的了解。人们首先发现了磁石引铁的性质，后来又发现了磁石的指向性，经过多方的实验和研究，终于发明了可以用于辨别方向的指南针。

早在战国时期，中国先民已用天然磁石制成指示方向的司南之勺。

三国魏时，马钧利用磁铁和差速齿轮制造了能指示方向的机械装置——指南车。

宋代科学家沈括在其《梦溪笔谈》中记载了制作指向用的磁针的方法。

水浮法——将磁针上穿几根灯心草浮在水面，就可以指示方向。

碗唇旋定法——将磁针搁在碗口边缘，磁针可以旋转，指示方向。

指甲旋定法——把磁针搁在手指甲上面，由于指甲面光滑，磁针可以旋

转自如，指示方向。

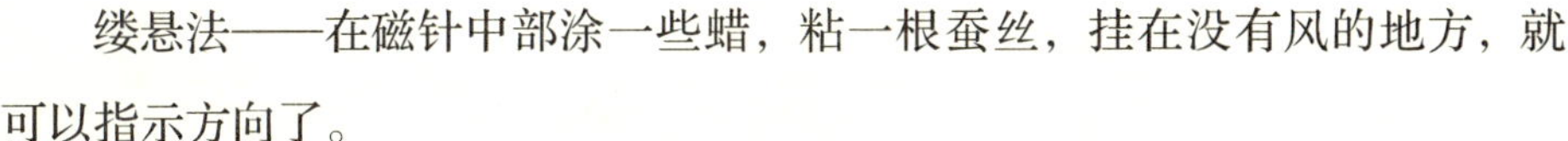

缕悬法——在磁针中部涂一些蜡，粘一根蚕丝，挂在没有风的地方，就可以指示方向了。

沈括还对四种方法做了比较，他指出，水浮法的最大缺点是水面容易晃动从而影响测量结果。碗唇旋定法和指甲旋定法，由于摩擦力小，转动很灵活，但容易掉落。沈括比较推崇的是缕悬法，他认为这是比较理想而又切实可行的方法。事实上沈括指出的四种方法已经归纳了迄今为止指南针装置的两大体系——水针和旱针。

后来，确定方向除了要有指南针之外，还需要有方位盘相配合。最初使用指南针时，可能没有固定的方位盘，随着测方位的需要，出现了磁针和方位盘一体的罗盘。方位盘是24向，盘式为圆形。这样一来，只要看一看磁针在方位盘上的位置，就能断定出方位来。

至晚在北宋后期，指南针已用于航海；南宋时，已使用针盘导航。

指南针的发明，对于海上交通的发展和经济文化的交流，起到了极大的作用。

二、造纸术

造纸技术的发明，是中华民族对世界文明做出的贡献之一。在纸尚未发明之前，古埃及人曾用纸莎草，古印度人用贝树叶，古巴比伦人用泥砖，古罗马人用蜡版，欧洲人则用中亚细亚人制作的小山羊皮等当作记事材料。

在中国，商代用甲骨，西周用青铜器，春秋时则用竹简、木牍、缣帛等作为记事材料；此外，还曾将抽丝织绸和制取丝棉时残絮的薄片用于书写。

上述材料甲骨、竹简和木牍都很笨重，战国时思想家惠施外出讲学，带的书简就装了五车，所以有“学富五车”的典故。缣是细绢，帛是丝织品的总称，在缣帛上写字时，便于书写，不但比简牍写得多，而且还可以在上面作画，但缣帛昂贵且来源较少，只能供少数王公贵族使用，不能适应社会文化发展的需要。

东汉元兴元年（105 年），蔡伦在前人造纸术的基础上，改革和推广了造纸技术。他用树皮、麻头及敝布 、渔网等为原料，经搓、捣、抄、烘等工艺制成了适合书写的植物纤维纸，人称“蔡侯纸”。这种纸的出现使纸成为普遍

使用的书写材料。蔡侯纸是现代纸的起源。值得注意的是，蔡伦只是改进造纸术，而不是纸的发明人。

纸的发明及应用，对社会历史的记载与保存，对文化思想的交流与传播，发挥了重要作用。

造纸术在7世纪经朝鲜传到日本，8世纪中叶传到阿拉伯，到12世纪，欧洲才仿效中国的方法开始设厂造纸。

三、火　药

火药是中国古代四大发明之一。因为是用硝石、硫黄和木炭这三种物质混合制成的，而当时人们都把这三种东西作为治病的药物，所以取名“火药”，意思是“着火的药”。

早在商周时期，人们在冶金实践中已经广泛使用木炭，之后制作火药的原料硫黄、硝石又为人们所熟知，为火药的发明准备了条件。

自秦汉以后，炼丹家用硫黄、硝石等物炼丹，从偶然发生爆炸的现象中得到启示，逐渐发现硫黄、木炭和硝石按照一定的比例混合后，混合物有燃烧和爆炸能力，再经过多次实践，找到了火药的配方。火药在中国唐代初年就已经发明了。

唐武德四年（621年），一个叫李畋的人将火药装入竹筒制成“爆竹”，用于驱除瘴气，也用于婚丧喜庆，开创了火药应用的先河。

唐朝末年，火药开始应用到军事上。公元904年，唐朝人郑潘制成“发机飞火”，进攻豫章，这是火药用于军事的开始。人们利用抛射石头的抛石机，把火药包点着以后，抛射出去，烧伤敌人，这是最原始的火炮。

后来人们将球状火药包扎在箭杆头附近，点着引线以后，用弓箭将火药射出去烧伤敌人。

还有把火药、毒药，再加上一些沥青、桐油等，捣在一起做成毒球，点着以后，用弓箭射出，杀伤敌人，这就是后来的“万人敌”。

到了宋朝，人们将火药装填在竹筒里，火药背后扎有细小的“定向棒”，点燃火管上的火硝，引起筒里的火药迅速燃烧，产生向前的推力，使之飞向敌阵爆炸，这是世界上第一种火药火箭。

以后又发明了火铳和枪，这些都是用竹管制成的原始管形火器，是近代

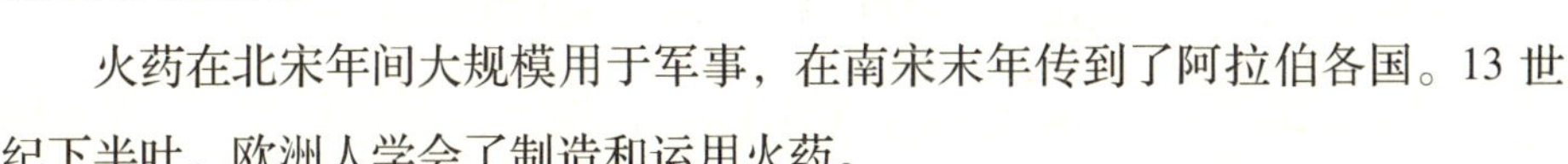

枪炮的老祖宗。

火药在北宋年间大规模用于军事，在南宋末年传到了阿拉伯各国。13 世纪下半叶，欧洲人学会了制造和运用火药。

四、印刷术

印刷术是中国古代四大发明之一。活字印刷术被公认为世界最伟大的发明之一。在印刷术发明前人们用手抄书，既费时，又费力，还容易出错。

到了隋唐，人们从印章和拓片中受到启发，把字雕刻在木板上，使它成为反的凸字。然后刷上墨，铺上纸，书页一张一张地就印成了。但是，每印一种新书，木板就得从头雕起，速度很慢，如果刻版出了差错，又要重新刻起，劳作之辛苦，可想而知。

北宋刻字工人毕昇在公元 1004 年至 1048 年间，用质细且带有黏性的胶泥，做成一个个四方形的长柱体，在上面刻上反写的单字，一个字一个印，放在土窑里用火烧硬，形成活字。然后按文章内容，将字依顺序排好，放在一个个铁框上做成印版，再在火上加热压平，就可以印刷了。印刷结束后把活字取下，下次还可再用。这种印刷方法虽然原始简单，却与现代铅字排印原理相同，使印刷技术进入了一个新时代。

活字印刷术问世不久，便传到世界各国，对促进人类文化交流和文明进步做出了巨大的贡献。

Chapter 3 The Four Great Inventions of Ancient China

The four great inventions refers to four inventions in ancient China, which made revolutionary significance to the development of the world, namely compass, papermaking, gunpowder and printing. They promoted the development of ancient China's politics, economy and culture and imposed great influence on the development of the world.

1. Compass

Compass, which is made according to the characteristics of magnet's north and south polarity in earth magnetic field, is a kind of directional instrument, which has various forms.

The main component of the compass is a magnetic needle fixed on an axis that can rotate freely. The magnetic needle remains on the tangent line of magnetic meridian under the function of magnetic field. People adopt the function of the north pole of the magnetic needle, which points to the south, to recognize direction, which is widely applied to navigation, geodetic survey, travel and military at that time.

The invention of the compass is the result of Chinese people's recognition on magnetism in the process of their long-term social practice. People get to know magnetite and start to understand the magnetic properties due to productive work. First, they have discovered the properties of magnet can appeal iron, and then find the directive property of magnet. After a series of experiments and researches,

the compass is invented finally.

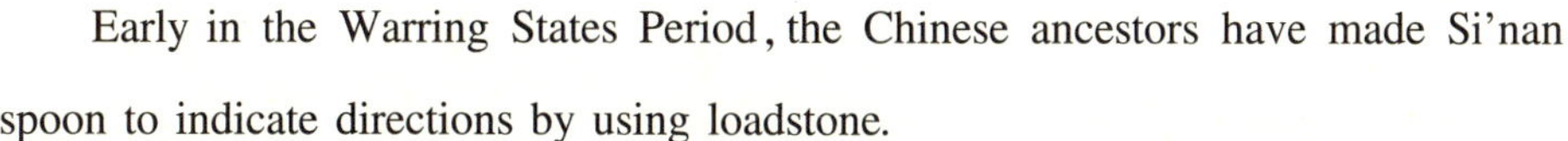

Early in the Warring States Period, the Chinese ancestors have made Si'nan spoon to indicate directions by using loadstone.

During the period of the Three Kingdoms of Wei, Ma Jun makes a mechanism device called south-pointing chariot by adopting magnet and differential gear for indicating directions.

Shen Kuo, a scientist in Song Dynasty records the methods for making magnetic needle used for recognizing directions in his *Dream Pool Essays.*

Floating Method the magnetic needle can indicate directions by putting some rushes on it and floating on the surface of water.

The Method of Fixing on the Edge of a Bowl fixing the magnetic needle on the edge of a bowl, it can rotate freely to indicate directions.

The Method of Fixing on the Fingernail fixing the magnetic needle on the smooth fingernail, it can rotate freely on the smooth fingernail and indicate directions.

Wisping and Hanging Method applying some wax on the magnetic needle and sticking a silk on it, and then hanging it in a place without wind, it can indicate directions.

Shen Kuo has compared the four methods and mentions that the biggest shortcoming of floating is the swaying of the water surface, which may influence the measuring result. Though the methods of fixing on the edge of a bowl and fixing on the fingernail can rotate easily due to small friction force, it drops out often. Shen Kuo has a high regard for wisping and hanging. He thinks it is an ideal and operable method. In fact, the four methods for making magnetic needle mentioned by Shen Kuo have concluded the two main systems of compass devices, water needle and dry needle.

Except the needles for indicating directions, an azimuthal plate also needed to cooperate with the needle. Initially, there is no fixed azimuth plate in a compass. With the demand for measuring the azimuth, a compass with needles and an azimuthal plate turns up. There are 24 directions in an azimuthal plate with a round

disc. Therefore, we can easily find the azimuth by taking a look at the location of the magnetic needle on the azimuthal plate.

In the later stage of Northern Song Dynasty, compass has been applied to navigation. In Southern Song Dynasty, needle dial compass has been used for navigation.

The invention of compass has made great contribution to the development of marine traffic and the exchange of economy and culture.

2. Papermaking

The invention of papermaking is one of the contributions that Chinese people have made to the world civilization. The ancient Egyptians use papyrus; ancient Indians take pattra leaves; ancient Chaldaics apply bricks; ancient Romans adopt wax plate; Europeans select the nerbris made by the Asia Minor people as a tool to keep a record of events before the real paper is invented.

In China, people in Shang Dynasty use oracle bone, in Western Zhou Dynasty apply bronze ware and in the Spring and Autumn Period adopt bamboo slip, inscribe wooden tablet and silk fabrics as their recording materials. In addition, the sheets and slices of silk weaving and making silk floss are used for writing at that time.

The materials mentioned above are heavy and hard to carry. Hui Shi, an ideologist in the Warring States Period brings five carriages of bamboo books to give lectures in other states at that time. Therefore, the literary quotation of "Xue fu wu che", which means a person is learned and what he learns can fill up five carriages, comes into being at that time. *Jian* is the general name of thin silk and *Bo* is the general name of silk fabrics. It is easy to write on *Jian* and *Bo*. We can write more words on *Jian* and *Bo* than write on bamboo scripts, and we can even draw on *Jian* and *Bo*. However, *Jian* and *Bo* are expensive and hard to find, which can only offer the nobles in the palace to use it and it cannot meet the demand of social and cultural development.

In Eastern Han Dynasty (105 A. D.), Cai Lun, an eunuch, reforms and spreads the papermaking skill based on the ancient people's papermaking experience. He

takes bark, fibre, rag and fishing net as raw material to make plant fibre paper for writing by dampen, smash, forming and pressing, and baking. The paper made by Cai Lun at that time is called Caihou Paper, and from then on, paper becomes a widespread writing material. Caihou Paper is the origin of modern paper. It should be noted that Cai Lun is not the inventor of paper, and he just improves the papermaking skill.

The invention and application of paper plays an important role in recording and preserving social history, exchanging and spreading cultural thoughts.

Papermaking spreads to Japan via North Korea in 7th century. It is transmitted to Arab in the middle of 8th century. And till 12th century, European countries imitate the papermaking factories of China to make paper.

3. Gunpowder

Gunpowder is one of the four great inventions of ancient China. Gunpowder is made by the mixture of saltpeter, sulfur and charcoal, which are used for treating diseases at that time, so gunpowder is called *Huoyao*, which means flaming medicine.

Early in Shang and Zhou Dynasties, charcoal is widely used in metallurgy practice. Later people get familiar with saltpeter and sulfur, which lay a foundation for the invention of gunpowder.

Since Qin and Han Dynasties, alchemists apply saltpeter and sulfur to get alchemy. They get inspiration from the explosive happened accidentally and find that the mixture of saltpeter, sulfur and charcoal according to certain rate have the ability of burning and explosive. They find the formula for making gunpowder after several times' practice. Gunpowder has been invented in the early years of Tang Dynasty.

In Tang Dynasty (621 A. D.), Li Tian makes fireworks by filling in bamboo tube with gunpowder, which creats the pioneer of gunpowder usage.

During the late Tang Dynasty, gunpowder is applied to military. In 904 A. D., Zheng Pan invents *Fajifeihuo*, a flamethrower, to attack Yuzhang, which is the symbol of gunpowder used in military. People adopt the basilisk to cast gunpowder package after lighting it to burn enemy, which were the original cannon.

Later, people wrap the ball-like gunpowder package up near the arrow shaft, shooting it to burn enemy after its leading wire is lighted.

People smashed gunpowder, toxicant, pitch prill and tung oil together to make a poisonous ball, shooting it out after it is lighted to kill enemy, which was called *Wanrendi.*

In Song Dynasty, gunpowder is filled into a bamboo tube and there are some tiny bars on the gunpowder. When the nitre is lighted, the gunpowder in the bamboo tube will burn rapidly and it will fly to the enemy position by forward push power, which is the first gunpowder rocket in the world.

Then, roer and gun are invented, both of which are original tubular firearms made from the bamboo tube, which are the old ancestor of modern guns.

During Northern Song Dynasty, gunpowder is widely used in military and spreads to Arabic countries in late Southern Song Dynasty. In the second half of the 13th century, Europeans learn to make and use gunpowder.

4. Printing

Printing is one of the four great inventions of ancient China. Movable Type Printing is one of the greatest inventions acknowledged universally in the world. People copy the book by hand before the Movable Type Printing is invented, it takes time and great efforts to copy books by hand, and mistakes are hard to avoid.

During Sui and Tang Dynasties, inspired from seal and rubbings, people carve the characters on the board and make it to be reversed and embossed characters. Then, paste the ink and lay a piece of paper on the board. The book is printed by one sheet after another, but the board has to be carved from the beginning when printing each new book. If there are some mistakes on it, all the work has to restart from the beginning, therefore, you can imagine how hard the work is.

From 1004 – 1048 A. D. , Bi Sheng, a man who carves characters, in Northern Song Dynasty uses fine and sticky plaster to make a squared cylinder, on which he carves retrography characters on it, with one character on one squared cylinder, and then burn it hard in an earth kiln to make printing characters. Later, the characters

are ordered according to the contents and are put on a metal frame to make printing form, heated and pressed on a fire. When the printing form are made, the printing can be started. When the printing is finished, the printing characters can be brought down and can be reused. The printing method is primitive but simple, the theory of which is same to modern characters' typesetting and printing, which leads the printing technology into a new era.

Movable Type Printing spreads to various countries in the world after its invention, which made great contributions to the improvement of human beings' cultural exchange and the progress of civilization.

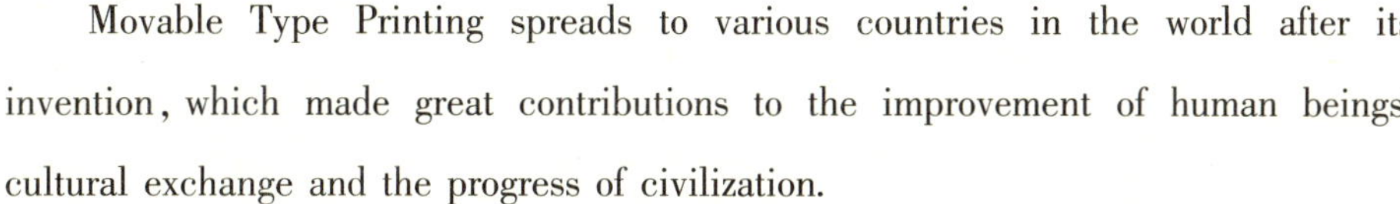

第四章　中国的宗教文化

今天，中国是一个多宗教并存，并且宗教信仰自由的国家。中国公民可以自由地选择和表达自己的信仰和表明宗教身份。在中国，宗教信徒信奉的主要有原始宗教、道教、佛教、伊斯兰教和基督教等。

一、原始宗教

宗教起源于原始社会，原始宗教的产生，以神灵观念为标志。根据考古发现和文献记载，中国在远古时期流行有自然崇拜、鬼魂崇拜、图腾崇拜、生殖崇拜等原始宗教形式。

自然崇拜包括对自然物和自然现象的崇拜。人们对自然物的崇拜，包括对天、地、日、月、星辰、雷、电、水、火、山、石等自然物的崇拜。远古时期，人们对自然现象（云、风、雨、电闪、雷鸣）无法解释，充满了敬畏之心。因此就产生了雷公、电母、风婆婆等诸位天神的传说。

鬼魂崇拜的产生是因为先民相信人死后灵魂不灭，死者的灵魂将继续生活在幽冥之界，因此就产生了鬼魂崇拜。

祖先崇拜即信仰祖先所代表的经验、智慧和权威，将随其灵魂而永存，成为一种超自然的力量而护佑氏族成员。随着祖先崇拜习俗的传承，民族始祖成为民族种姓的象征，他们经古史传说的神化，被奉为神人或圣人，夏族的禹、商族的契、周族的后稷都是原始民族的始祖。

图腾崇拜是自然崇拜和祖先崇拜经结合而产生的。“图腾”一词的意义是族徽标记，上古民族的祖先一般以动植物为图腾。

生殖崇拜是基于重视氏族或部落的人口繁衍而产生的对生殖力的崇拜。

二、道　教

道教是中国土生土长的宗教，是中国传统文化的重要组成部分。因其与民间风俗、习惯联系密切，是了解中国民间信仰和民间文化的重要途径。

道教创立于东汉后期，以蜀地（四川）张陵的“五斗米道”和豫州巨鹿郡（今河北省巨鹿县）张角创立的“太平道”为标志，奉老子为教主，以《道德经》为主要经典。

道教是以神仙信仰为核心，以长生为人生目的，在汉代黄老道家理论的基础上，综合了上古时代的神仙传说，吸收古代神仙家的方术，融合了阴阳五行学说和民间巫术和鬼神信仰而形成的一种宗教。

道教的标记为八卦太极图。“太极图”由两条黑白的“阴阳鱼”组成。白鱼表示阳，黑鱼表示阴。白鱼中有一黑眼睛，黑鱼之中有一白眼睛，表示阳中有阴、阴中有阳之理，说明了阴阳交感生万物的道理。阴阳分化则为两仪，两仪生四象，再由四象生八卦，八卦代表自然界的事物，说明阴阳运动衍生万物。大千世界，从宏观天体到微观粒子，无不是一分为二又合二为一的，并且都处在不断的运动变化之中。太极和八卦组合成了太极八卦图，成为道教的标记。

三、佛　教

佛教是外来宗教，中国佛教是指佛教在中国的发展的特殊形式或中国化的佛教。中国佛教经历了漫长的发展岁月，在封建社会各阶层中曾有广泛的影响，是中国传统文化的组成部分。

佛教在中国的传播与发展可以分为三个时期：西汉为传入期；三国和魏晋南北朝是发展时期，在此期间，汉人以对待中国的神仙方术的眼光对待佛教；隋唐时期是佛教在中国发展的鼎盛时期，形成了中国佛教的十大宗派；宋以后，佛教逐步衰微。各大宗派逐步趋向融合。

另外，佛教还先后传入中国的少数民族地区，其中藏传佛教俗称喇嘛教，是中国佛教的一支，主要传播于藏族、蒙古族等聚居的地区。

中国佛教教义在前期以“般若学”为主，主张用“空观”看世界，认为一切事物和现象都是空幻不实的；后期则以“涅槃学”为主，主要讲如何成

佛、成佛的理据以及成佛的阶段等。

佛教传入中国后对中国文化的影响极大，尤其是对雕塑、建筑和绘画等方面的影响。

佛教在中国的传播还产生了大量的佛教雕塑，佛教雕塑在中国雕塑史上产生了大量的艺术精品，从敦煌、云冈、龙门石窟到遍布各地的大小寺庙，佛像、菩萨像、天王像及罗汉像等琳琅满目，千姿百态。

佛教在中国的传播还产生了大量的佛教绘画，佛教绘画在中国绘画史上有着重要的地位，如敦煌莫高窟壁画场面宏大，色彩富丽，线条飘逸自如，人物栩栩如生，面部表情多呈安详之状，形神兼备，体现了高超的艺术造诣。

佛教在中国的传播还产生了大量的佛教建筑，在中国建筑史上有着重要的地位。佛教建筑包括佛寺建筑、佛塔和石窟。

中国著名的佛寺建筑精品有河南洛阳白马寺、浙江杭州灵隐寺、江苏镇江金山寺、湖北武汉归元寺、四川峨眉山伏虎寺、安徽九华山天台古寺、河南嵩山少林寺等。

中国的佛教名山有山西五台山、四川峨眉山、浙江普陀山、安徽九华山等。

中国著名的佛塔建筑精品山西五台山塔林、河南登封嵩山少林寺塔林、山东省济南市灵岩寺塔林、宁夏青铜峡塔林、云南景洪市飞龙山白塔林等。

四、基督教

基督教是外来宗教，基督教传入中国历经四个巅峰时期。第一个巅峰是在唐朝贞观九年（635 年），基督教的一个分支聂斯托利派传入中国，史称景教。会昌五年（845 年），唐武宗灭佛，基督教被殃及，流传了 210 年的景教在中原绝迹。

基督教传入中国的第二个巅峰是在 13 至 14 世纪。元代基督教再次传入中国。当时流传的主要有两个派：一派是景教；另一派是天主教的圣方济各派，这是天主教首次传入中国，时间是 1289 年，但流传不广，基督教在中国的传播随着元朝的灭亡又告中断。

第三个巅峰是明清之际，随着葡萄牙、西班牙、荷兰等国对中国的殖民入侵，基督教第三次传入中国。天主教的耶稣会是这一时期的主要流派。

第四个巅峰是鸦片战争后基督教新教大规模传入中国。1840 年鸦片战争后，中国沦为半殖民地半封建国家，传教士倚仗不平等条约，在中国的土地上到处设立教堂、修道院，兴办学校、孤儿院，用各种方法传播、发展基督教的各个派别。到新中国成立前夕，共有天主教徒 320 余万人，大小天主堂 15 000 座。

基督教在中国的传播，带来了许多富有特色和魅力的旅游资源，如具有历史意义的教堂，具有基督教特色的建筑、习俗等。

五、伊斯兰教

伊斯兰教是外来宗教，在唐永徽二年（651 年）传入中国。伊斯兰教传入中国主要有两条路，即陆路和海路。陆路是沿丝绸之路传入，从大食（今阿拉伯），经波斯（今伊朗），过天山南北，穿过河西走廊，进入中原。海路是沿着香料之路而传入，即从大食，经印度洋，到天竺（今印度），经马六甲海峡，到中国东南沿海广州和泉州等地。

伊斯兰教在中国的传播播种于唐代，萌芽于五代，发展于宋代，繁荣于元代，衰落于明清。

在中国，信仰伊斯兰教的少数民族主要集中在西北地区，如回族、维吾尔族、哈萨克族、柯尔克孜族、塔吉克族、乌孜别克族、塔塔尔族、东乡族、撒拉族、保安族等。

Chapter 4 Chinese Religions

At present, there are various religions in China. People have the freedom of religious belief. Citizens of China may freely choose and express their religious beliefs and make clear their religious affiliations. In China, people believe in primitive religion, Taoism, Buddhism, Islam, and Christianity.

1. Primitive Religion

Religion originates in primitive society. The origin of primitive religion is marked by the concepts of gods. According to archaeological research and documents, Chinese ancestors worshiped the nature, ghosts, totems, reproductivity, etc.

Chinese worship natural objects and natural phenomena. People worship the natural objects, including the Heaven, the Earth, the Sun, the Moon, stars, the thunder, the lightning, water, fire, mountains, stones, and so on. In ancient times, people can not explain natural phenomena (clouds, wind, rain, lightning, thunder), so people deal with nature with fear and respect. For this reason, there are a lot of legends of the gods, such as the legends about Leigong, who is the Thunder God, Dianmu, who is the Goddess of Lightening, Fengpopo, who is the Goddess of Wind, and so on.

Chinese ancestors worship ghosts because they believe that the soul will keep living in the Hell after death.

The Chinese worship their own ancestors because they believe the souls of

their ancestors, which represents experience, wisdom and authority, will live forever. That is a supernatural power, which can protect their clan members. Influenced by the practices of ancestor worship, the ethnic ancestors become the national symbol of the caste. Deified by ancient legends and ancient history, the ethnic ancestors are regarded as sons of god or saints. Yu, the ancestor of Xia people, Xie, the ancestor of Shang people, and Houji, the ancestor of Zhou people are regarded as the ancestors of the Chinese people.

The Chinese totems worship is influenced by both of the nature worship and ancestor worship. Totem is defined as the symbol of a clan. In most cases, plants and animals are used as totems by Chinese ancestors.

Reproductivity worship is based on the great importance of the population that determines the size and development of a clan or a tribe.

2. Taoism

Taoism is the only true native-born Chinese religion. It is an important part of Chinese traditional culture. It is an important way to understand the Chinese beliefs and culture, because it is closely related to Chinese custom.

Taoism is evolved into a religious faith in late Eastern Han Dynasty. The credit for turning Taoism into a religion is generally given to Zhang Ling from Shu Area (now Sichuan Province), who formally established his Celestial Masters Movement, and Zhang Jiao, from Julu County of Yuzhou Prefecture (now Julu County in Hebei Province), who established his Peace Movement. The founder of Taoism is believed by many people to be Laozi who lived in the late Spring and Antumn Period. The record of his beliefs is the *Tao Te Ching*.

The core of Taoism is the belief Immortals. The purpose of Taoism is seeking for longevity. Taoism is a religon, which is based on the theory of Daoism, created by Huangdi and Laozi in the Han Dynasty, colligating the legends of the Immortals from ancient times, absorbing the astrology of the Immortals, mixing together the theory of *Yin-Yang* and Five Elements, folk witchcraft and the faith of supernatural beings.

The symbol of Taoism is called Taiji Bagua map, which is made of the Eight Diagrams and Taiji Diagram, which is consisted of a "Black Fish", the Yin, and a "White Fish", the Yang. There is a white eye in the "Black Fish" and a black eye in the "White Fish", which indicates that there is Yin in Yang and vice versa. It illustrates the truth that the interaction between Yin and Yang generates everything in the world. The differentiation of Yin and Yang becomes the *Liangyi*, from which 4 images and from 4 images 8 trigrams emerge. The 8 trigrams represent everything in the world. It refers to a power which envelops, surrounds and flows through all things, living and non-living. The Tao regulates natural processes and nourishes balance in the Universe. It embodies the harmony of the opposites. The combination of the Taiji Diagram and Eight Diagrams makes up Taiji Bagua map, which is regarded as the symbol of Taoism.

3. Buddhism

Buddhism is a foreign religion. Chinese Buddhism is a special form of the development of Buddhism in China, or sinicized Buddhism. Chinese Buddhism has experienced long years of development. There is a widespread influence in the various strata in Chinese feudal society. It is one of important parts of Chinese traditional culture.

The spread and development of Buddhism in China can be divided into three periods. The Western Han Dynasty, which is an incoming period. The Three Kingdoms Period and the Nanbeichao Period, which can be regarded as a period of development, in which the Chinese treats the Buddhism as astrology of Immortals. During Sui and Tang Dynasties, it is a period of great prosperity of Buddhism in China. The ten sects of Buddhism in China come into being in this period. After Song Dynasty, Buddhism in China gradually declines. The various sects of Buddhism gradually fuse.

Buddhism has been introduced to the ethnic minority areas in China. The Tibetan Buddhism, which is known as Lamaism, is one of branches of Chinese Buddhism, mainly spread in areas inhabited Tibetan, Mongolian and other regions.

The doctrine of Chinese Buddhism is mainly about Prajna in the early stage, which advocates viewing the world with a "view of emptiness". In the later stage, Chinese Buddhism is mainly about Nirvana, which mainly talks about how to become a Buddha, the principles of becoming a Buddha and the Buddha and the different stages of becoming a Buddha.

The introduction of Buddhism to China imposes great influence on Chinese culture, especially the impact on sculpture, architecture, and painting.

The spread of Buddhism in China leaves a large number of Buddhist sculptures. A lot of Buddhist sculptures are fine arts in the history of Chinese sculpture. From Dunhuang, Yungang, Longmen Grottoes to the temples all over China, there are different kinds of Buddha, Bodhisattva, Heavenly King and Arhats dazzling with different sizes and postures.

The spread of Buddhism in China also leaves a large number of Buddhist paintings, which has an important position in the history of Chinese painting, for example, the Mogao Grottoes in Dunhuang murals spectacular, with rich and beautiful colors, elegant lines and freely lifelike characters, on which the vivid facial expression is mixed with a serene status, reflecting the superb artistic attainments.

The spread of Buddhism in China also leaves a large number of Buddhist architectures, which has an important position in the history of Chinese architecture. Buddhist buildings include Buddhist temples, pagodas, and grottoes.

The famous Buddhist temples in China include Baimasi Temple in Luoyang City of Henan Province, Lingyinsi Temple in Hangzhou City of Zhejiang Province, Jinshansi Temple in Zhenjiang City of Jiangsu Province, Guiyuansi Temple in Wuhan City of Hubei Province, Fuhusi Temple on Emeishan Mountain in Sichuan Province, Tiantaisi Temple on Jiuhuashan Mountain in Anhui Province and Shaolinsi on Songshan Mountain in He'nan Province.

The famous Buddhist mountains in China include Wutaishan Mountain in Shanxi Province, Emeishan Mountain in Sichuan Province, Putuoshan Mountain in Zhejiang Province, Jiuhuashan Mountain in Anhui Province, etc.

China's famous stupa architectures include the Pagoda Forest on Wutaishan

Mountain in Shanxi Province, the Pagoda Forest in Shaolinsi Temple on Songshan Mountain in Dengfeng City of He'nan Province, the Pagoda Forest in Lingyansi Temple in Ji'nan City in Shandong Province, the Pagoda Forest in Qingtongxia City in Ningxia Hui Autonomous Region, the Pagoda Forest on Feilongshan Mountain in Jinghong City of Yunnan Province, etc.

4. Christianity

Christianity is a foreign religion. The spread of Christianity in China has experienced four climax. The first climax is in the ninth year of Zhen'guan (635 A. D.) in Tang Dynasty, in which Nestorianism, a branch of Christianity, has been introduced to China, known as the *Jingjiao* (Nestorianism) in the history. In the 15th year of Huichang (845 A. D.), the Emperor Wuzong thoroughly does away with Buddhism in. Christianity is deadly influenced. As a result, Jingjiao, which has spread in China for 210 years, extincts in the Central Plains of China.

The second climax of the spread of Christianity in China is from the 13th to 14th Century. In Yuan Dynasties, Christianity is once again introduced into China. There are two religious sects of Christianity prevailing in China. One sect is Jingjiao (Nestorianism) and the other is the Catholic Franciscan factions, in which the Catholicism is introduced into China for the first time in 1289 A. D., but not widely spread. With the demise of Yuan Dynasty, the spread of Christianity in China breaks off.

The third climax of the spread of Christianity in China is in Ming and Qing Dynasties. With the colonial invasion of Portugal, Spain, Holland and other countries in China, Christianity is introduced into China for the third time. The Catholic Jesuit is the main school of this period.

The fourth climax of the spread of Christianity in China is after the Opium War, in which Protestant is introduced to China in a large scale. After the Opium War in 1840, China becomes a semi-colonial and semi-feudal country. Relying on unequal treaties missionaries use various ways to spread Christianity and develop different sects of Christianity, such as building churches, monasteries, schools, orphanages. To

the eve of China's liberation, there are more than 3,200,000 Catholics and 15,000 Catholic Churches in China.

Owing to the spread of Christianity in China, there are many distinctive and charming tourist resources, such as historic churches, architectures and customs with Christian characteristics.

5. Islam

Islam is a foreign religion, which is introduced to China in the second years of Yonghui, a Chinese era name in Tang Dynasty (651 A. D.). Islam is introduced into China by means of two roads, overland route and sea route. That Islam is introduced into China by the overland route is along the Silk Road, which begins from the Arab Empire (now Arabia), via Persia (now Iran), across the north and south of the Tianshan Mountains, through the Hexi Corridor, into the Central Plains of China. That Islam is introduced into China by the sea route is along the spice route, which begins from the Arab Empire, by the India Ocean, to Tianzhu (now India), through the Strait of Malacca, to such the cities in southeast coast of China as Guangzhou and Quanzhou, etc.

The spread of Islam in China are sown in Tang Dynasty, germinates in the Five Dynasties, develops in Song Dynasty, flourishes in Yuan Dynasty, and declines in Ming and Qing Dynasties.

The ethnic minorities, who believe in Islam, mainly live in the northwest regions of China, such as the Hui, Uighur, Kazak, Kirgiz, Tajik, Uzbek, Tatar, Dongxiang, Salar, Bao'an nationalities, etc.

Owing to the spread of Islam in China, there are many Islam styled architecture with unique features and glamour.

第五章　中国礼仪文化

中国在世界上享有“文明古国”“礼仪之邦”的盛誉。在绵延数千年的历史进程中，中国人的祖先创造了灿若云霞的中国文化。在博大精深的中国文化宝库中，礼仪从来就占有相当重要的地位。“礼”在社会中无时不在，出行有礼，坐卧有礼，宴饮有礼，婚丧有礼，寿诞有礼，祭祀有礼，征战有礼，等等。

礼仪，作为在人类历史发展中逐渐形成并积淀下来的一种文化，始终以某种精神的约束力支配着每人的行为，是适应时代发展，促进个人进步和成功的重要途径。可以说，人类文明从礼仪开始。

中国传统文化中“礼”的内容涉及广泛，包含了整个社会的等级制度、法律规定和道德规范，以及用来表现“礼”的内容的各种礼节规则和礼节仪式等。中国古代有“五礼”之说，祭祀之事为吉礼，冠婚之事为喜礼，宾客之事为宾礼，军旅之事为军礼，丧葬之事为凶礼。

一、行走之礼

在行走过程中，也有行走的礼节。古代常行趋礼，趋礼是指地位低的人在地位高的人面前走过时，一定要低头弯腰，以小步快走的方式对尊者表示礼敬，这就是“趋礼”。

在传统的行走礼仪中，还有“行不中道，立不中门”的原则，即走路不可走在路中间，应该靠边行走，站立不可站在门中间。这样既表示对尊者的礼敬，又可避让行人。

二、见面之礼

古代宾主相见的最常见的礼节是揖礼，也称拱手礼、抱拳礼。一般性的打招呼，行拱手礼。如果到别人家做客，在进门与落座时，主客相互客气行礼谦让，这时行的也是揖礼。除社交场合外，向人致谢、祝贺、道歉及托人办事等也常行揖礼。身份高的人对身份低的人回礼也常行揖礼。

社会对至尊者还有跪拜礼，即双膝着地，手、头依次触地叩拜，即所谓叩首。

现今跪拜礼只在偏远乡村的拜年活动中能够见到，一般不再施行。在当今社会人们相见，一般习用西方社会传入的握手礼。

三、入座之礼

在中国，社会礼仪秩序井然，何种身份坐何位置都有一定的规矩，如果坐错席位，不仅主人不高兴，而且还会被认为是失礼的。

坐席有主次尊卑之分，尊者上坐，卑者末坐。一般来说，室内座次以东向为尊，即贵客坐西席上，主人一般在东席上作陪。年长者可安排在南向的位置，即北席。陪酒的晚辈一般在北向的位置，即南席。

如果自己不能把握坐何种席次，最好的办法是听从主人安排。

入座之后，吃东西时人体尽量靠近桌子，不吃东西时，身体尽量靠后。如有贵客光临，应该立刻起身致意。

四、饮食之礼

饮食礼仪在中国占有极重要的地位。迎宾的宴饮称为“接风”“洗尘”，送客的宴席称为“饯行”。

宴饮之礼无论迎送都离不开酒品，“无酒不成礼仪”。宴席上饮酒有许多礼节，客人需待主人举杯劝饮之后，方可饮用。客人如果要表达对主人的盛情款待的谢意，也可在宴饮的中间举杯向主人敬酒。

在进食过程中，同样先有主人执筷劝食，客人方可动筷。

古代还有一系列进食规则，如“当食不叹”“共食不饱、共饭不泽手”“毋投骨于狗”等。

五、拜贺之礼

拜贺之礼是在节庆期间，晚辈或下级向尊长和上级的礼敬，同辈之间相互拜贺的礼仪，如古代元旦官员朝贺、民间新年拜年之礼。

在古代，拜贺之礼一般要行跪拜礼，行礼时，不仅要态度恭敬，口诵贺词，俯首叩拜，而且也得有贺礼一同奉上。

六、庆吊之礼

庆吊之礼是指人生大事中的一系列礼仪。人的一生要经历诞生、成年、婚嫁、寿庆、死亡等若干阶段，围绕着这些人生节点，形成了一系列人生礼仪。

（一）满月礼

子孙繁衍是家族大事，诞生礼自然隆重热闹。婴儿满月时，亲戚朋友纷纷上门恭贺，并馈赠营养食品与幼儿鞋帽、衣物。

（二）成年礼

小孩长大成人时要行成年礼，成年礼在中国社会称为冠笄之礼。男子 20 岁行加冠礼，重新取一个名号，表示该男子具有了结婚、承担社会事务的资格。女子 15 岁行绾发加笄礼，表示到了出嫁的年龄。

（三）婚　礼

婚嫁是人生的大事，中国人十分看重。婚礼的高潮在迎亲，新郎要到女家亲自迎娶新娘，新婚夫妇拜堂行执手礼。大婚之日，亲友纷纷前来恭贺，主人要大宴宾客。

（四）寿诞礼

寿诞礼，一般在四十岁以后开始举行。生日那天有庆生仪式，亲友送寿礼致贺。

(五) 丧　礼

最后一道人生仪礼是丧礼。中国人重视送亡，丧礼仪式很完备。丧礼是白喜事，亲戚朋友都来吊唁热闹，但为了表示哀悼心情，人们要奉上挽联、挽幛或礼品、礼金。

七、奉茶之礼

中国历来就有“客来敬茶”这一民俗。最基本的奉茶之礼，就是客人来访马上奉茶。奉茶前应先请教客人的喜好。俗话说：酒满茶半。奉茶时，茶不要太满，以八分满为宜。水温不宜太烫，以免客人不小心被烫伤。同时有两位以上的访客时，端出的茶色要均匀，并要配合茶盘端出，左手捧着茶盘底部，右手要扶着茶盘的边缘。主人给客人斟茶时，客人要用食指和中指轻叩桌面，以致谢意。

八、握手之礼

握手是现代在相见、离别、恭贺或致谢时相互表示情谊、致意的一种礼节，双方往往是先打招呼，后握手致意。

握手时，主人、长辈、上司、女士主动伸出手，客人、晚辈、下属、男士再相迎握手。

握手时，一定要用右手握手，要紧握对方的手，时间一般以 1 ~3 秒为宜。过紧地握手，或是只用手指部分漫不经心地接触对方的手都是不礼貌的。

多人同时握手时应顺序进行，切忌交叉握手。

在任何情况下拒绝对方主动要求握手的举动都是无礼的，但手上有水或不干净时，应谢绝握手，同时必须解释并致歉。

九、言谈举止之礼

在人际交往中，要多听少说，善于倾听别人讲话是一种高雅的素养。因为认真倾听别人讲话，表现了对说话者的尊重，人们也往往会把忠实的听众视作可以信赖的知己。

聆听别人讲话，必须做到耳到、眼到、心到，同时还要辅以其他的行为

和态度。

聆听别人讲话时，要注视说话者，保持目光接触，不要东张西望。单独听对方讲话时，身子要稍稍前倾；面部保持自然的微笑，表情随对方谈话内容有相应的变化，恰如其分地频频点头；不要中途打断对方，让他把话说完；适时而恰当地提出问题，配合对方的语气表述自己的意见；不离开对方所讲的话题，但可通过巧妙的应答，把对方讲话的内容引向所需的方向和层次。

十、待客之礼

在日常生活中，接待来访客人是一门艺术。讲究待客的礼节，热情、周到、礼貌待客就会赢得朋友的尊敬。如果不注意待客礼节，就会使客人不悦，甚至因此而失去朋友。

（一）准　备

预先知道客人来访，要提前做好接待准备工作。整理好房间，准备好茶杯、烟具、糖果等。主人要仪容整洁，自然大方。蓬头垢面，或穿着睡衣短裤会客是不礼貌的。

（二）迎　客

客人来到门前，应主动出门迎接，请客人进屋。如果客人是第一次来访，应该给家里其他人介绍一下，并互致问候。然后热情地给客人让座、上茶，给会吸烟的客人递烟。

（三）交　谈

与客人交谈时要心平气静，不要频繁看表，不要呵欠连天，以免对方误以为你在下逐客令。

（四）告　辞

客人告辞时，家里在场的人，都应该微笑起立，亲切道别，让客人感到这个家庭的每个成员都是热情好客的。

（五）还　礼

如果客人带来了礼品，主人应表示谢意，并在送客时适当还礼。

（六）送　客

送客时一般应送到大门口或街口。常客、老熟人或一般来访者，也可随意一些，送出门口或送到楼梯口，致意告别即可。把客人送出门后，注意回身关门不能过重，以免客人误以为主人对他不满而生疑虑。

十一、敬酒之礼

中国人的好客，在酒席上发挥得淋漓尽致。人与人的感情交流往往在敬酒时得到升华。中国人敬酒时，往往都想对方多喝点酒，以表示自己尽到了主人之谊，客人喝得越多，主人就越高兴，说明客人看得起自己，如果客人不喝酒，主人就会觉得有失面子。

敬酒分文敬、回敬、互敬、代饮、罚酒。

（一）文　敬

文敬是传统酒德的一种体现，也即有礼有节地劝客人饮酒。酒席开始，主人往往在讲上几句话后，便开始了第一次敬酒。这时，宾主都要起立，主人先将杯中的酒一饮而尽，并将空酒杯口朝下，说明自己已经喝完，以示对客人的尊重。客人一般也要喝完。在席间，主人往往还分别到各桌去敬酒。

（二）回　敬

回敬是客人向主人敬酒。

（三）互　敬

互敬是客人与客人之间的敬酒，为了使对方多饮酒，敬酒者会找出种种必须喝酒的理由，若被敬酒者无法找出反驳的理由，就得喝酒。在这种双方寻找论据的同时，人与人的感情交流得到升华。

（四）代　饮

“代饮”是不失风度，又不使宾主扫兴的躲避敬酒的方式。本人不会饮酒或饮酒太多，但是主人或客人又非得敬上以表达敬意，这时，就可请人代酒。代饮酒的人一般与他有特殊的关系。在婚礼上，男方和女方的伴郎和伴娘往往是代饮的首选人物，故酒量必须大。

（五）罚　酒

罚酒是中国人敬酒的一种独特方式。罚酒的理由也是五花八门的，最为常见的可能是对酒席迟到者的“罚酒三杯”。罚酒有时也不免带点开玩笑的性质。

Chapter 5 Chinese Traditional Etiquette

China enjoys a good reputation as "ancient civilization" and "a state of courtesy" in the world. In the historical course, which stretches for thousands of years, Chinese ancestors have created magnificent culture. In brilliant and gorgeous cultural treasure of China, the etiquette and rituals have always occupied a very important position. In the society, from travelling, daily behaviors, banquettes and weddings to funerals, birthdays, sacrifice and military activities, *Li*, the etiquette, is all-pervading.

Etiquette, as a culture evolved and accumulated gradually in the history of human development, always dominates everyone's behaviors spiritually, which is an important access to adapt to the new eras, personal development and personal success. In a manner speaking, human civilization begins with etiquette.

Li, the etiquette, in traditional Chinese culture covers a lot, including the hierarchical system, the law and ethics of the whole society, as well as the various rules and rituals which are used to express the etiquette. There were five kinds of etiquette in ancient China, in which sacrifice rites are named as *Jili*, crowning and marital rites are called *Xili*, rites of guest receptions are regarded as *Binli*, rites of military affairs are looked on as *Junli* and funeral and burial rites are regarded as Xiongli.

1. Walking Etiquette

During the walk, there are also walking manners. In ancient time, *Quli*,

which is also called bowing etiquette, is often used in walking. *Quli*, is a rite, which refers to a person who is in low position, when walking in front of another person, who is in higher position, should bow and run with short strides and quick steps, to pay his respect for seniority.

In the traditional walking etiquette, there is a principle that "neither walk in the middle of the road nor stand in the middle of the doors" to be followed. Simply speaking, when walking, you should walk along either side of the road instead of in the middle of the road. While standing, you should not stand in the middle of doors. In this way, not only can politeness be expressed to the seniority, but also can avoid hampering pedestrians.

2. Meeting Etiquette

In ancient China, the most common etiquette when meeting guests is *Yili*, which is also called Gongshou etiquette and fist-and-palm salute. Gongshou etiquette is commonly used for general greeting. If you pay a visit to someone, *Yili* will be used. When the guest entering the gate and taking a seat, the host and the guest both make a bow with hands folded in front to show politeness and modesty. Besides the above social occasions, it is also used to express acknowledgements, congratulations, apologies, or asking for help. Moreover, when a person, who is in higher position, returns a salute to a person who is in lower position, *Yili* is also commonly in use.

In traditional Chinese society, to express the supreme respect to the person, who is in higher position, Kowtow etiquette is commonly in use. People bow down upon their knees with the head and hands touching the ground and bowing in a servile manner. But now this etiquette can only be seen in remote villages in the Spring Festival. In modern society, handshaking from western society is a common etiquette when meeting friends or relatives.

3. Seating Etiquette

In China, the social etiquette is in good order. The seating position contains

certain rules. Different identities have different seating positions. Taking a seat improperly will not only upset the host, but also is considered impolite and rude.

The seats at table can be divided into seats of honor and the least prominent seats. The respected take the former ones, while the inferior take the latter ones. Generally speaking, seats to the east are the best, which is for the distinguished guests, with the host's company sitting in the east. The seniors can be arranged in northern seats facing the south, while the younger generation accompanying the guests sits in the southern seats.

If you do not make sure where to sit, you had better follow the arrangement of the host.

After taking a seat, your body is expected to be close to the table when you are eating, but far away from the table when you are not eating. If distinguished guests come to visit, you should immediately stand up in salutation.

4. Dinning Etiquette

Dinning etiquette occupy a very important position in China. Welcome dinner is called *Jiefeng*, or *Xichen*, which means giving a reception in honour of a guest from afar. Farewell feast is named *Jianxing.*

However, the wine is an inseparable part both in welcome and farewell feasts. "No feast can be done without wine." There are many drinking etiquette. Guests are to be advised to drink a toast by the host. Guests, who want to express their gratitude to the host's hospitality, also can drink a toast to the host in the middle of the feast.

During the dinner, guests cannot begin to eat until the host persuades them to eat with chopsticks. In ancient time, many rules for dinner were established, for example "no sighing when eating", "when dining with others, you should not eat too much and keep your hands clean", "do not throw the bones to dogs", and so on.

5. Celebrating Etiquette

Celebrating etiquette refers to the etiquette that during the festivals, the

younger generation or the inferior show reverence to the elderly or the superior, or the mutual greetings among their peers. For instance, in China, on New Year's Day, the officials must come and pay their respect for the emperor. New Year's calls were paid among the folks.

In ancient times, celebrating etiquette requires people to bow in worship on bended knees with respectful attitudes, to chant congratulatory words, and to give gifts.

6. Congratulation and Condolence Etiquette

Congratulation and condolence etiquette refers to a series of rituals of key events in human life, such as birth, adulthood, marriage, birthday celebration, and death, from which a series of life rituals are formed.

(1) The Etiquette of Celebrating the First Month of a Newborn Baby

Giving birth to an offspring is a big event for a family, so naturally the birth celebration is grand and lively. When the baby is a month old, relatives and friends will come to congratulate and send nutritious food as well as clothing and shoes for children.

(2) The Etiquette of Adult Ceremony

When the children grow up to be an adult, *Guanjili*, also known as Adult Ceremony, in Chinese society is to be held. The man in 20-year-old takes initiation rite, *Guanli*, and gains a new name to indicate that he has the qualifications to marry and undertake social affairs. The woman in 15-year-old binds her hair and takes initiation rite, *Jili*, to show she is ready for marriage.

(3) Marriage Etiquette

Marriage is a major event in life, which is highly valued in Chinese society. The climax of the wedding is *Yingqin*, which means that the bridegroom goes to the bride's home to escort her back to the wedding, and the newlyweds perform formal bows in the old custom, which is called *Zhishouli*. On the day of the wedding, relatives and friends come up to congratulate on the wedding and the host family banquets all guests.

(4) Birthday Etiquette

Birthday is celebrated after the age of forty in general. On the birthday, birthday ceremony is performed and relatives and friends send birthday gifts and congratulations.

(5) Funerals Etiquette

The last etiquette in one's life is funeral etiquette. Chinese people attach great importance to death etiquette, so funeral etiquette is well developed. Relatives and friends come to offer condolences and they also send elegiac couplet, elegiac scrolls, gifts, or money to express mourning.

7. Etiquette of Offering Tea

Offering tea to the guest is a traditional Chinese folk custom, which is called *Fengchali*. The most basic explanation of it is that when a guest comes to visit you, you should offer him/her a cup of tea immediately. You have to consult the preference of the guest before you serve the tea. There is an old saying "full wine but half tea", which indicates that the teacup should not be too full and 80% is appropriate. The water should not be too hot, so that the guest does not accidentally burn. At the same time, if there are more than two visitors, the cups of tea offered should be the same with tea trays. The host takes the bottom of tea tray with the left hand, and holds the edge of it with the right hand. When the host offers tea to the guest, he/she is expected to tap on the desktop with the index finger and middle finger to show his/her gratitude.

8. Etiquette of Handshaking

Handshaking is commonly used upon meeting, greeting, parting, offering

congratulations, or expressing gratitude. With the purpose of conveying mutual emotions, the two sides greet each other first and then shake hands together.

Guests, the junior, the inferior, and the male usually have to wait for the host, the elderly, the superior, and the female to offer their hands before shaking.

When shaking hands, you must use the right hand to hold firmly the hand of the other side for 1 to 3 seconds. Too tight or too weak handshakes like contacting the hands with your fingers are both impolite.

When many people shake hands together, you are expected to shake hands one by one and avoid cross handshakes.

Generally, it is considered to be rude to reject a handshake. If your hands are wet or dirty, you can decline but have to explain it and apologize for it.

9. Etiquette of Speech and Deportment

In interpersonal communication, being a good listener is elegant for the reason that being a serious listener shows the respect to the speaker and people also tend to put the listener as trusted confidant.

Listening to people, you must use your ears, eyes, and heart, together with other actions and attitudes.

When listening to others, you'd better have your eyes on the speaker, maintaining eye contact and do not look around. If you are the only listener, your body leans slightly forward, and your face maintains natural smile. The expressions are corresponding with the content of the conversation, and you need nod appropriately. Do not interrupt the speaker. Raise questions and present your own opinions properly. Do not leave the topic, but you can lead the content into the direction and level you desire through clever response.

10. Etiquette of Guest Receptions

In daily life, the reception of visitors is an art. Exquisite hospitality etiquette, warmness, thoughtfulness, and courteousness will help you win the respect from

friends. If you don't pay attention to the rites, you will make guests unpleased, even lose their friendship.

(1) Preparation

As soon as you know the visit, preparation for the reception work should be done in advance. Tidy up the room and prepare the tea set, cigarettes and candy. The host should be well-groomed with natural manners. Uncombed hair and dirty face or pajamas are not acceptable.

(2) Welcoming

When guests come near your house, you should go outside the door to welcome them and ask them to enter the house. If the guest visits your home for the first time, you should introduce him/her to the rest of the family and exchange greetings. Then you enthusiastically ask the guest to take a seat, offer tea, and give a cigarette when necessary.

(3) Conversations

When you are talking with the guest, keep calm and avoid checking your watch frequently and yawning. Otherwise, your guest considers you are showing him/her the door.

(4) Farewell

When a guest leaves, all the people at home should smile and stand up to give a warm farewell, which let the guest feel that all the members of the family are hospitable.

(5) Gift in Return

If the guest takes a gift when visiting, the host should express his/her gratitude and send a gift in return when the guest leaves.

(6) Seeing the Guest Out

When a guest finishes the visit, the host usually accompanies him/her to the door or the street, but for the frequent visitors, old acquaintances, or common visitors, it is more casual. Farewell at the door or the foot of the stairs are both OK. After showing the guest the door, you must close the door gently, otherwise the guest may misunderstand your feelings to him/her by a slamming door.

11. Toasting Etiquette

Chinese hospitality is presented thoroughly in the banquet, where emotions are exchanged and improved by drinking wines. The more the guest drinks, the happier the host will be. The host holds that if the guest drinks more, it indicates that he thinks highly of the host, while if the guest do not drink, the host will lose face.

Proposing a toast can be divided into *Wenjing*, *Huijing*, *Hujing*, *Daiyin*, and *Fajiu.*

(1) Wenjing

Wenjing meaning that the host politely persuades the guests to drink, is a reflection of the traditional Chinese wine morality. At the beginning of the banquet, the host often speaks a few words, and then he/she starts the first toast. At this time, all the people have to stand up, then the host will drink the first cup neatly and display the empty cup to the guest as a sign of respect to the guests. Guests generally finish off their wine. In the banquet, the host often separately goes to the various tables to propose a toast.

(2) Huijing

Huijing means that the guests propose a toast to the host in return.

(3) Hujing

Hujing means mutual toasting among the guests. In order to propose others to

drink more, the person who proposes a toast has to find all sorts of reasons to persuade others to drink, and if they are unable to find the reason to refuse the toast, they have to drink. In this process, the emotional communication is achieved and enhanced.

(4) Daiyin

Daiyin is a way which not only avoids the toast but also does not make the guests and host disappointed without losing grace. If you cannot drink or have drunk too much, but the host or other guests still continue to propose a toast to you for respect, you can ask someone else to drink instead. The person who replaces you must have a special relationship with you. For example, at the wedding, the bridesman and bridesmaid are considered to be the ideal figures to drink instead of the new couple, so they must have a good capacity for liquor.

(5) Fajiu

Fajiu is a unique way of Chinese toasting. There are many reasons to be made to drink as a punishment. The most common one is probably for the late comers to a feast. They are usually penalized by being asked to drink three cups. Of course, usually it is just for fun.

第六章　中国传统婚俗文化

婚俗文化既是人类文明、人类文化中的一部分，又是人类文明、人类文化发展链条上的一个环节，一种特殊形态。经过几千年的发展和传承，婚礼习俗已经作为一种独特的文化现象植根于整个中华文化之中。

结婚是每个人都要经历的人生大事。虽然几千年来，中国的婚俗文化发生了许多变化，但是婚礼仍然是人们生活中的重要礼仪。

“婚”在古代是“昏”的意思。古人认为黄昏是吉时，所以会在黄昏行娶妻之礼。基于此原因，夫妻结合的礼仪称为“昏礼”。

一、汉族婚俗“三书六礼”

“三书六礼”是中国汉族的传统婚姻习俗礼仪。古代的结婚过程，与现代的意义有点不同。现代的结婚过程一般指结婚当日所举行的礼仪，“三书六礼”的结婚过程则包括了从谈婚、订婚到结婚等过程的文书和礼仪。

在古代，男女若非完成“三书六礼”的过程，其婚姻便不被承认为明媒正娶。嫁娶仪节的完备与否，直接影响婚姻的吉凶。

(一) 三　书

“三书”指在“六礼”过程中所用的文书，是古时保障婚姻的有效文字记录，包括聘书、礼书和迎书。

聘书是定亲的文书。在纳吉（男女订立婚约）时，男方家交予女方家的书柬。

礼书是在过大礼时所用的文书，列明大礼的物品和数量。

迎书是迎娶新娘的文书。是亲迎接新娘过门时，男方送给女方的文书。

（二）六　礼

“六礼”是结婚过程的六个礼法，指纳采、问名、纳吉、纳征、请期和亲迎。

纳采是当儿女婚嫁时，由男方家家长请媒人向物色好的女方家提亲。男方家在纳采时，需将大约三十种有象征吉祥意义的礼物送给女方家；女方家亦在此时向媒人打听男方家的情况。

问名是在女方家长接纳提亲后，女方家将女儿的年庚八字交由媒人带回男方家，以便卜问，决定成婚与否，吉凶如何。

纳吉（又称“过文定”）是指当接收庚帖后，将庚帖置于神前或祖先案上请示吉凶，以肯定双方年庚八字没有相冲相克。当得知双方并没有相冲相克之征象后，男方家委派媒人把订婚的聘书送到女方家，同时男方家要向女方家送订婚的彩礼。

纳征（又称“过大礼”）是指男方家把礼书送到女方家。在大婚前一个月至两周，男方家会请两位或四位女性亲戚约同媒人，把礼书和结婚礼品送到女方家。此时，女方家需回礼。

请期（又称“乞日”）是指男方家择定合婚的良辰吉日，并征求女方家的同意。

亲迎（或“迎亲”）是指在结婚吉日，穿着礼服的新郎会偕同媒人、亲友亲自把迎书送到女方家，并迎娶新娘。新郎在到女方家前需到女方家的祖庙行拜见礼，之后才用花轿将新娘接到男方家。在男方家完成拜天、地、祖先的仪式。

（三）拜　堂

在中国传统婚姻礼仪中，拜堂是婚礼过程中最后一个礼节，也是最重要的礼节。拜堂，又称拜天地、拜花堂、拜堂成亲。拜堂之后，新郎新娘即正式结为夫妻。因古代婚礼中的交拜礼都是在堂室举行，所以叫拜堂。古人认为，男女相交是从结婚开始，才有人伦之义，所以要拜天地；从结婚开始，女子才成为男方家族的一员，所以要拜列祖列宗；从结婚开始，才把男女的

个体合成一体，所以新婚夫妇一定要交拜，以示郑重其事。

二、维吾尔族婚俗

维吾尔族婚礼隆重、热烈，具有浓郁的民族特色，亲朋好友欢聚一堂，以歌舞庆贺，热闹非凡。

（一）尼　卡

婚礼第一天早晨，在女方家举行“尼卡”（证婚）仪式，由阿訇诵经，询问新郎新娘是否愿意结为夫妻，之后请新郎新娘吃用盐水浸泡过的馕，寓“同甘共苦，永结良缘”之意。

（二）招待来宾

“尼卡”仪式结束后，新郎回家做迎亲的准备。这天新郎和新娘两家同时在各自的家里设宴招待来宾。

（三）迎　新

下午，穿戴一新的新郎，在亲友的簇拥下去女方家迎娶新娘，一路上迎亲的小伙子们打起手鼓、吹着唢呐、弹着“热瓦甫”兴高采烈地唱《迎新娘歌》，整个迎亲队伍充满着欢乐的气氛。

（四）哭　别

新娘被接走前，新娘的父亲为女儿祝福，新娘与家人哭别。这时小伙子们唱着《劝导歌》：“莫哭泣，姑娘莫哭泣，这会儿你该是大喜，你和雄鹰般的小伙子结为伉俪。”

（五）拦道求礼

迎亲队伍簇拥着新娘、新郎坐上披红扎彩的迎亲车离家而去，沿途乡亲可以拦住迎亲队伍，迎亲队伍要送礼物给拦路者。

（六）抢“帕炎达孜”

当新娘来到婆家门口时，新郎的家人为新娘铺上了红色的“帕炎达孜”

（一块长布），新郎、新娘一走过，女宾们便扑上去抢那块布，又拉又扯，你抢我夺，扭作一团，场面甚是热闹，大家都力争抢到一块作为吉祥之物留作纪念。

（七）揭面纱

进屋后，青年男女唱歌跳舞进行揭面纱仪式。其中一人乘跳舞之机冷不丁将新娘的面纱揭去，然后客人们入席吃喜宴。晚上大家尽情地唱歌跳舞，尽情欢乐。

婚后第二天早晨，新娘、新郎在伴郎、伴娘陪同下，分别去给岳父母、公婆行礼问安。

三、佤族“做梦定姻缘”

佤族的男女十四五岁便开始“串姑娘”，谈情说爱了。夜幕降临时，男子便成群结伙到女孩家“串姑娘”了。女孩们成群结伙地在火塘边等待。当伙子们走进家时，姑娘的父母便起身回避。姑娘给小伙子们递上竹凳表示欢迎。伙子们坐在姑娘们身旁吹笛子，弹口弦，拉独弦胡，唱情歌，表示对姑娘的爱慕。姑娘们羞答答地低着头不停地忙手中的针线活计，暗地里却互相窥视和寻找着自己喜欢的对象。

当姑娘和伙子互相都喜欢时，便彼此交换槟榔包，结成“包格勒”（异性朋友）关系。姑娘在“包格勒”中最后确定一个对象，伙子送给姑娘一件定情物，彼此的恋爱关系便确立了。

当火塘燃尽的时候，伙子和姑娘们便双双对对睡在火塘边。睡中若梦见大树林、芭蕉林、青竹树或汩汩山泉、鲜花盛开、果实累累等便认为是吉兆，婚后可以多生小孩，有吃有穿，彼此的爱人关系就可以确定下来。若梦见蜂子叮咬、山崩地裂、发洪水、虎豹追赶、走路摔跤等则认为是凶兆，彼此不能结合，必须立即斩断关系，另择爱侣。

四、苗族的山歌求爱

（一）山歌求爱

苗族的婚姻比较自由，青年男女婚前都享有充分的社交自由，父母一般

不干涉，每逢节庆、赶场的日子，他们便利用聚会的时机对唱情歌、谈情说爱、互诉衷情。

（二）抢　婚

苗族结婚形式除通常所流行的男家迎娶、女家陪送之外，还有抢婚习俗。

现在的抢婚是在男女双方恋爱成熟情况下的一种象征性的仪式，抢法是由男方事先选派几个青年好友到女方村寨旁等待姑娘出门，便把姑娘抢走，女方兄长一旦发觉，要作追赶，追至男家，男家便以酒饭款待追赶者，或赠与追赶者若干银钱礼物，便将之打发回家。

（三）捉　魂

姑娘被抢至男家后，在预先设置的姑娘住处，用一把纸伞将她象征性地罩住，然后由男子的伯母或其他女性长者用一只活公鸡在姑娘头上绕三圈，此举谓之“捉魂”，经过“捉魂”，姑娘便正式成为男家成员。约待两三日，男家正式聘请媒人告之女家，并向女家求婚，女方父母要做些形式上的吵架，事实上也唯有答应男方求婚。然后议定礼金，择日正式接亲。正式接亲之前，须将抢来的姑娘送回娘家。

（四）插花日

结婚之前一天叫“插花日”，此日女方家宾客齐集，男方必须在插花日派迎亲队伍去女方家。迎亲队伍由年轻的七到十一人单数组成。领队的男人叫“娶亲大哥”，女子叫“娶亲婆”，另外还跟随一班吹鼓手（乐队）。迎亲队到女方家寨外即鸣放鞭炮，女方紧闭大门，必待娶亲大哥送上开门礼红包，讲一番娶亲客套话，才准进门。

（五）打　粑

迎亲队坐席饮酒时。女方村中的姑娘们会向迎亲客人们劝酒，必将迎亲客人灌醉，姑娘们还借劝酒、上菜、上茶、盛饭等伺机向迎亲人脸上抹锅底灰，抹得娶亲人个个成为大花脸，名曰“打粑”。或用豆渣和荨麻叶对娶亲人围攻，打得娶亲人遍体都是豆渣。荨麻叶蜇得娶亲火焦辣疼，叫“打亲”“打发”，既越打越亲，越打越发。女方要待老年人出来制止才停。

（六）正　日

然后，晚上男女青年可以对唱山歌，通宵达旦。结婚日叫作“正日”，正日黎明，开始发亲，由女方送亲大哥（兄弟）背新娘从正门出，换新鞋，送入户门外的花轿中，抬去男家。若途中与别寨娶亲队伍相遇，则各抢先从高处绕过。到了男家门外就由娶亲大哥背新娘从门前火盆上走过，然后新郎新娘行礼拜堂，男方家大摆宴席三天，答谢亲朋好友等不在话下，过完三日后新郎陪新娘回娘家探亲小住几天。

五、侗族婚俗

（一）踩脚后跟试情意

“踩脚后跟”是侗族青年交往的一种活动。侗族小伙子若是看上了哪位姑娘，他就会在赶场的时候，悄悄地跟在对方身后，故意踩一下对方的脚后跟。对方被踩了，回过头来觉得这个小伙子自己中意，便会跟着对方走，一直走出场外，两人悄悄细谈。如果自己不中意，就假装不知道，不去理睬。踩的人发现对方不跟出来，也就作罢，再进场另觅对象。

（二）夜　娶

在中国侗族部分地区有“夜娶”“夜嫁”的习惯。娶亲一般都是深夜。男家三十多人的迎亲队伍，除吹鼓手外，每人举着一个松明火把，穿山过坳，越溪蹚水，火红一片，活像一条翻腾跳跃的火龙，再加上唢呐锣鼓的敲打和吹奏，在这寂静的偏乡僻寨，越发显得欢快和火热。

（三）歌　卡

夜行十余里，迎亲队伍到达新娘的团寨里，但团门紧闭（每个团有一张大门），原来这里不可轻易进门，设有道道“歌卡”。迎亲队伍每经一道“歌卡”，都要对歌。一盘一对应答如流，方许进去，进了团门，能否接出新娘，还要费力气突破最后一关，因为新娘屋里对歌手云集，即兴盘问。什么古往

今来，天文地理，时事政策，随意编成，脱口而出，这就需要迎亲的男家歌手随机应变，很快地巧妙地对答出来，方可发亲。这确实是件很不容易的事。

（四）换　喜

盘问对答毕，女家宣布发亲。新娘头戴侗帕，颈挂项圈，身着大襟花边盛装，由女伴陪同，右手举着桐油纸伞（据闻可避邪），在鼓手热烈欢快的吹奏下上路。如果在途中遇到另外一支迎亲队伍，新郎和新娘必须交换腰带，互相“换喜”。

（五）进门仪式

当迎亲队伍来到男家的门前，即鸣放鞭炮，新娘暂停门外片刻，以等待“进门仪式”。一位五十开外的老人负责举行迎亲仪式。

（六）吃“半夜饭”

这套为时十来分钟的仪式完毕，新娘才在鞭炮声中进入洞房，稍事歇息便吃“半夜饭”。饭后便开始对歌。新娘和一群女伴在房里，新郎和一群男伴在门外，互相对唱，一直唱到次日凌晨。

（七）不“坐家”

有意思的是，新娘新郎成亲，并不“坐家”（夫妻同居）。次日，新娘吃罢丰盛的“百盘宴”（来参加婚礼的人不带其他贺礼，各带一盘最有侗乡特色的腌鱼、腌鸭、腌肉之类的东西），便由女伴陪同回娘家。之后新郎去女家做客，一旦女方有了身孕，新娘才一边挑着稻草（男耕）一边挑着纺车（女织）来到男家定居。从这时候起，才算是真正的夫妇。

六、土家族哭嫁

用哭声来庆贺欢乐的出嫁，用歌舞来祭祀死去的亲人，看似不可思议，却充分反映了土家族独特的禀性及文化意识。哭嫁是土家人婚礼的序曲，他们认为“不哭不热闹，不哭不好看”。亲朋好友前来送别，哭是一种友好，哭是一种礼貌。对于那些坐在人群中不哭唱的，新娘认为是瞧不起她而不高兴。

新娘一般在婚前一个月开始哭嫁，也有在出嫁前两三天或前一天开始哭的。娘家人边为她置办嫁妆，边倾诉离别之情。

哭有哭的规矩，可分为母女哭、姑侄哭、姊妹哭、舅甥哭、姑嫂哭、骂媒人等。不仅要哭自己，还要哭祖先、哭爹妈、哭兄嫂、哭姐妹、哭媒人。

哭的主要内容有回忆母女情、诉说分别苦、感谢养育恩、托兄嫂照护年迈双亲、教女为人处世等。

哭的形式是以歌代哭，以哭伴歌。哭嫁歌一般为即兴作，见娘哭娘，见婶哭婶。哭词各不相同，也有固定哭词，如“比古人”“共房哭”“十画”“十绣”“十二月”等。

哭有曲调，抑扬顿挫，是一门难度很大的唱哭结合的艺术。嫁娘必在此前求师练习。哭时以“嗡”“蛮”“啊呀呀”等语气词，一泣一诉，哀婉动人。

哭嫁的高潮是在新娘出嫁的日子。在出嫁的前一天，亲朋乡邻都前来祝贺和哭别。新娘家要邀请新娘九位最好的未婚女伴，陪着新娘哭，叫“十姊妹会”。新娘家先是在吊脚楼闺房架一方桌，置茶十碗，邀亲邻九女依次围坐，唱起哭嫁歌来，新娘居中，叫“包席”，右女为“安席”，左女为“收席”。新娘起声，“安席”接腔，依次哭去。哭的内容主要是叙述姐妹友情，也有鼓励、劝慰的话语。哭到半夜，新娘家里摆上夜宵让十姐妹吃，新娘以此为题还要哭一段，以感谢九姐妹的相陪。

Chapter 6 Chinese Traditional Marriage Culture

Marriage culture is a part of human culture, and a link, or a special form, in the chain of the development of human culture as well. With the development and inheritance for thousands of years, marriage culture, as a unique cultural phenomenon, has already been rooted in the Chinese culture as a whole.

Getting married is a life-changing event which will be experienced by every person. Although Chinese marriage culture has undergone great changes for thousands of years, the wedding ceremony is still an important ritual in people's lives.

In the ancient time, the word marriage means dusk. The ancients considered the dusk as the auspicious time of the day, thus the ritual of the couple's getting together was called "ritual of the dusk".

1. Han People's Marriage Culture, "Three Letters and Six Etiquette"

"Three Letters and Six Etiquette" are the traditional wedding customs of the Han people in China. This wedding process of the past is a little different from the modern one, which generally refers to the etiquette of the wedding day. However, the wedding process of "Three Letters and Six Etiquette" includes all the letters and etiquette during the process of talking about the marriage, engagement and final getting married.

In the past, the marriage wouldn't be admitted as a right and legal one unless the couple finished the whole process of Three Letters and Six Etiquette. Whether the marriage etiquette are complete or not will determine the auspiciousness of the marriage.

(1) Three Letters

"Three Letters" refer to all the letters used during the process of "Six Etiquette". They, including the Betrothal Letter, the Gift Letter and the Wedding Letter, were the valid written records to safeguard the marriage in the past.

The Betrothal Letter is the document of engagement. It is presented to the bride's family by the groom's at the moment of *Naji* (the couple's engagement).

The Gift Letter, the document used in the betrothal gift exchange, lists the items and numbers of the process.

The Wedding Letter is the document of marrying the bride. The groom's family presents it to the bride's when he comes to pick up the new wife.

(2) Six Etiquette

"Six Etiquette" are the six etiquette of the whole wedding process. They are proposing (*Nacai*), birthday matching (*Wenming*), presenting betrothal gifts (*Naji*), presenting wedding gifts (*Nazheng*), and picking a wedding date (*Qingqi*), and the wedding ceremony (*Qinying*).

Proposing refers to the groom's parents' formal proposal. When their kids are at the age of marriage, the groom's parents will invite a matchmaker to propose a marriage to the parents of an identified bride-to-be. They need to send about 30 kinds of gifts with certain auspicious symbolic meanings to the girl's side, who will inquire about the condition of the boy's family as well.

Birthday matching refers to the process of giving the date and hour of the prospective bride's birth to the groom's side. If the girl's parents accept the proposal, they will give the date and hour of their daughter's birth to the boy's family, who later will practice divination to see whether the marriage is auspicious or not and then decide whether the boy and the girl will get married or not.

Presenting betrothal gifts (also called *Guo wending*, which means engagement

now) refers to the groom's family's placement of the birth dates and hours of the couple in front of the God or at the ancestral altar to inquire whether the marriage is with a good luck or not, and thus confirm their compatibility. When there is no symbol of conflicting and restraining, the bridegroom's family will then arrange the matchmaker to present the betrothal letter and betrothal gifts to the bridegroom's family.

Presenting wedding gifts (also called *Guo dali*) refers to the groom's side's sending the Gift Letter and the wedding gifts to the bride's. About two weeks to one month before the wedding ceremony, bridegroom's family will ask two or four female relatives of theirs, together with the matchmaker, to come to the bride's house with the Gift Letter and wedding gift. At this moment, the bride's parents need to return a set of gifts to the groom's family.

Picking a wedding date (also called "Selection of Date") refers to the groom's parents' selecting an auspicious day for the wedding ceremony and asking permission from the bride's side.

Wedding Ceremony (or called "Welcoming the Bride") refers to the action that the bride in full dress, escorted by the matchmaker, friends and relatives, goes to the bride's house to send the Wedding Letter and to fetch his new wife on the auspicious wedding day. The groom has to go to the bride's ancestral temple to worship, and then the bride, in a sedan, will be escorted to the groom's house, where the rituals of bowing to the Heaven, Earth and Ancestors will be carried out.

(3) Performing the Formal Wedding Ceremony

Among the traditional Chinese marriage rites, "performing the formal wedding ceremony" is the last step of the wedding ceremony, and the most important one as well. After the "performing the formal wedding ceremony", which is also called "bow to the Heaven and Earth" (as part of a wedding ceremony) "bow to the flower hall" or "bow to get married", the couple formally become husband and wife. Performing the formal wedding ceremony is called "bowing to the hall" because it is held in the hall in the ancient wedding. Chinese ancestors hold that only

after the marriage, the relation between a man and a woman become ethic and thus they need to bow to the Heaven and Earth. Only after the marriage, the woman becomes one of her husband's family, so they need to bow to the ancestors. Only after the marriage, the two individuals can compose as a whole. Therefore the newly-married couple needs to bow to each other to show that they are serious.

2. Uighur People's Marriage Culture

The Uighur wedding is grand, ardent, and full of national characteristics. Friends and relatives will get together happily. They sing and dance, making the wedding full of buzz and excitement.

(1) Nika

On the first morning of the wedding, the ritual called *Nika* (witnessing the marriage) will be held at the bride's home. The imam will chant sutras, ask the bride and groom whether they are willing to get married, and then invite the new couple to eat a kind of crusty pancake soaked in saline water, conveying the meaning of "sharing happiness and sorrow, and being united in wedlock forever".

(2) Serving the Guests

After the rite of *Nika*, the groom will go back home to get prepared for welcoming the bride. On this day, both the bride and groom will give a banquet at their home to serve their guests respectively.

(3) Welcoming the Bride

In the afternoon, dressed in new clothes and surrounded by his friends and relatives, the groom will come to the bride's home to fetch his new wife. On the way, rattling the hand-held drums, playing the *Suona* and the *Rawap*, those young men escorting the groom will sing the *Song of Welcoming the Bride* cheerfully, which makes the whole procession full of joy.

(4) Weeping Farewell

Before the bride leaves her home, her father will send his blessings to his daughter, and the bride will weep farewell to her family. At this time, those young men will sing a *Song of Persuasion*, "Don't cry. Girl, please don't cry. It is a joyful time for you, for you are getting married with a young man like a tercel."

(5) Blocking the Way to Ask for Gifts

Clustered by their fellow villagers, the bride and groom get on the festively-decorated wedding car and leave. On their way, those villagers will block the procession. They have to send a gift to the villagers, who are blocking the way.

(6) Grabbing "Payan Dazi"

When the bride comes to the door of her mother-in-law's, her husband's family will spread a red *Payan dazi* (a length of fabric) for her. And while the new couple walk by, the female guests will stand out to grab the fabric. Squawking and fighting among themselves, they will try hard to get one piece as an auspicious keepsake, making the bustling atmosphere unprecedented.

(7) Removing the Veil

After the new couple go into the house, young men and women will sing and dance to hold the rite of removing the veil. One of them will remove the veil abruptly while dancing and singing, and then the guests will take their seats to have the wedding banquet. In the evening, all the guests will sing and dance to their heart's content, and enjoy themselves to their heart's content.

On the next morning of the wedding ceremony, the bride and groom, accompanied by the bridesmaid and groomsman, will come to greet their parents-in-law respectively.

3. Wa People's "Dreaming to Decide the Marriage"

Wa people begin to "chase the girl" and have a date in their teens. When the evening comes, the young guys will come to the girl's in groups to "chase the girl". And the girls will also wait for them in crowds around the fireplaces. When the boys go into the house, the girl's parents will stand out to leave and the girls will give the boys a bamboo chair to show their welcome. Then, the boys, sitting beside the girls, will blow the flute, play the *Kouxianqin*, play the *Duxianhu* and sing love songs to express their love to the girl they love, while the girls, hanging their heads with their needle work shyly, will secretly peep at the boys to look for the one they love.

When a girl and a boy fall in love with each other, they will exchange their betel nut bags to establish their relationship as *Baogele* (friends of the opposite sexes). And as soon as the girl finally chooses one from her *Baogele* and the latter sends her a token of love. Then, their romantic relationship goes steady.

When the fire of the fireplaces goes out, the boys and girls will sleep beside the fireplaces in pairs. If they dream a large forest, a banana forest, bamboo trees or gurgling springs and blooming flowers, their love will be given a good omen, which symbolizes that they will have many children and a prosperous life after the marriage. At that time, their relationship as lovers can be made certain. But if they dream that the bees bite them, mountains fall and the earth splits, the flood flashes, tigers and leopards chase them, or they fall down while walking, an ill omen is received. They are not permitted to get married. Instead, they should end their love as soon as possible and try to find another partner.

4. Miao People's "Singing Folk Songs to Woo"

(1) Singing Folk Songs to Woo

The marriage of the Miao people is comparatively free, and the young men and women have sufficient freedom for their social intercourse without their parents' interruption. When it is time for the festival celebration or village fairs, they will make use of the get-together to sing love songs to each other, courting with each other and expressing their love to each other.

(2) Grabbing the Bride

Besides the popular steps as the groom's fetching the bride and the latter's giving as a dowry, the flow of the Miao wedding has another custom as grabbing the bride.

Nowadays, grabbing the bride has become a symbolic ritual when the romantic relationship between the young man and woman goes mature and steady. On such an occasion, several young men pre-chosen by the groom will go to the bride's village to wait for her, so that they can grab her as soon as she turns up. Once the brothers of the bride find them, they will chase them to the groom's, where they will be entertained or given some money as a gift before they finally go back home.

(3) Catching the Soul

After the girl's being grabbed to the boy's, in the place where the girl is going to live, she will be veiled with a paper umbrella symbolically, and then the boy's aunt or some other female senior will use a live cock to circle her head for three times, the process of which is called "catching the soul". After that, the girl becomes one of the members of the boy's family formally. About two or three days later, the boy's family will formally invite a matchmaker to tell the girl's and make the proposal. After the amount of the gift money is settled among the two sides, they will choose an auspicious date to fetch the bride formally. However, before the formal welcoming ceremony, they need to send the grabbed girl back to her parents.

(4) The Day of Flower Arrangements

The day before the wedding ceremony is called "the Day of Flower Arrangements". On that day, the guests will gather at the bride's house, and the groom must send the wedding procession to the bride's to welcome her. The procession consists of seven to eleven members, and the number must be odd. The leading man is called "Escorting Brother" and the leading woman is called "Escorting Lady". They are followed by a group of trumpeters (band). As soon as they arrive at the bride's, the procession would let off firecrackers, but the girl's

door will not be opened until the Escorting Brother sends the door-opening red pocket and makes a few polite remarks.

(5) Daba (Making a Kind of Cake)

When the wedding procession sit down and begin to drink the wine, girls from the bride's village will urge them to drink, so as to make them drunken. The girls will also take chance of urging to drink, serving the dishes and the tea, and filling the bowls to smear some bottom ash on those guests' faces, and make all of their faces painted. This kind of action is called *Daba*. In addition, they would use the bean dregs and nettle leaves to lay siege on the wedding procession. As a result, those escorting procession would be covered with bean dregs and the nettle leaves would sting them severely. This kind of custom is called *Daqing*, *Dafa*, which means the more and harder they beat, the closer and richer they will become. The girls won't stop until the senior from the bride's side stands out to ask them to do so.

(6) Zhengri

Then, in the evening, the young men and women will begin to sing folk songs to each other for the whole night. The wedding day is called *Zhengri*. At dawn, the bride's family will start the ceremony. The bride-see-off brother will bear the bride to go from the main door to change a pair of new shoes, and then send her to the bride's sedan which is waiting outside the door. If the wedding procession meets another on their way, they will try to detour from the above respectively. When they arrive at the groom's, the escorting brother will carry the bride on his back and walk over the fire baskets. Thereafter, the bride and groom will bow and vow to each other, and the groom's family will hold a banquet for three days to thank their friends and relatives. After the three days, the groom will accompany his new wife to go back to his parents-in-law's home to stay for several days.

5. Dong People's Marriage Culture

(1) Step on the Heel to Test Love

Stepping on the heel is one activity of the young Dong people's intercourse. If a young Dong boy falls in love with a girl, he would follow her secretly on the village fair, and then step on her heel on purpose. Turning around, the stamped one will follow the boy to go outside of the fair and talk with each other in details if the guy hits her fancy. If not, the girl will pretend that she doesn't sense any stepping-on and just ignore the boy. And the boy, who finds that there is nobody follows him, will give up and come into the fair again to find another girl.

(2) Getting Married at Night

Some Dong people in China have the custom of getting married at night. They usually hold the wedding ceremony at night. The escorting procession from the groom's side, which consists of more than 30 people will walk over the mountain, past the valley and across the brook to fetch the bride. The whole procession, except for the trumpeter, will carry a pine torch, which makes the place they go to a piece of fire-like red, just like a jumping and rolling fire dragon. The fire, together with the beating and blowing of gongs and trumpets, makes this silent remote village full of happiness and passion.

(3) Border of Songs

After touring for more than five kilometres, the procession finally gets to the bride's village group, but the gate (each of the village group has a gate) is closed. Actually the gate will not be opened easily, for the villagers have set several "borders of songs". Every time when the procession passes a "border", they have to sing in antiphonal style. And only when they, one to one, can answer as quickly as the flowing of the water, they are permitted to go into the gate. However, whether they can fetch the bride successfully still depends on the troublesome final step,

because singing experts gather at the bride's. Their songs involve the past and the present, astronomy and geography, and current affairs and politics as well. They can improvise randomly with any careful thought, so the escorting singers from the groom's side need to make immediate and wise responses so that they can fetch the bride successfully. This is really not an easy task.

(4) Exchanging Happiness

After the question-and-answer section, the bride's family will announce to send out the bride. Wearing the Dong handkerchief, necklace and being dressed up with laced garment, the bride, accompanied by her maids and with a Tung-oiled paper umbrella in her right hand, will start off with the warm and joyful rhythms of the trumpeters. If they meet another escorting procession on the way, the bride and groom will exchange their belts to "exchange their happiness".

(5) The Rite of Entering the Door

When the escorting procession comes to the door of the groom's, they will let off firecrackers, whereas the bride will stand there for a while to wait for "the rite of entering the door". A senior in his or her 50s will take charge of the welcoming ceremony.

(6) Having Dinner of the Midnight

The previous rite will last for more than ten minutes. After that, the bride will go into the bridal chamber with the sound of the firecrackers, where she would rest for a moment. Then, the new couple and their friends will "have dinner of the midnight", after which they will sing songs to each other. While the bride and her maids stay inside, the groom and his friends will stay outside. They sing to each other, and their singing will last till the next dawn.

(7) Not Living Together

What's meaningful is that the new couple will not live together after the

wedding. The next day, after having the "hundred-dish banquet" (without any other gifts, the guests to the wedding will bring a dish of food with the most distinctive Dong features, such as salted fish, salted duck and salted pork), the bride will go back home with the company of her maids. Then, the groom will come to visit his new wife. Once the girl becomes pregnant, she will come back to settle at the boy's, with straws on one of her shoulders (symbolizing men's farming) and spinning wheels on the other (symbolizing women's weaving). And from that time on, the boy and girl become a real couple.

6. Tujia People's Crying to Get Married

It seems amazing to cry to celebrate the cheerful marriage and to sing and dance to worship the dead relatives, but these customs sufficiently inflect the unique characters and cultural consciousness of Tujia people. Crying to get married is the prelude of a Tujia wedding ceremony, for the reason that they hold the thought that "the ceremony is not bustling without the crying and the bride is not beautiful without the crying". When friends and relatives come to see off the bride, they cry to show their friendliness and politeness. The bride will think that those who don't cry within the crowd look down upon her and thus feel unhappy.

Normally speaking, the bride begins to cry for her marriage one month before the wedding ceremony, and some of them may start to do so two or three days or even one day before the ceremony. Her family will pour out their sense of departure while prepare the dowry for her.

There are also different kinds of crying, including the crying of mother and daughter, of aunt and niece, of sisters, of uncle and nephew, of sisters-in-law, scolding the matchmaker, and so on. The bride will not only cry for herself, but also cry for her ancestors, parents, brothers and sisters-in-law, sisters and the matchmaker.

The main contents of their crying include recalling the love between mother and daughter, talking about the bitterness of departure, expressing gratitude to parents' maintenance, asking brothers and sisters-in-law to take care of their old parents,

teaching the daughter to behave, and so on.

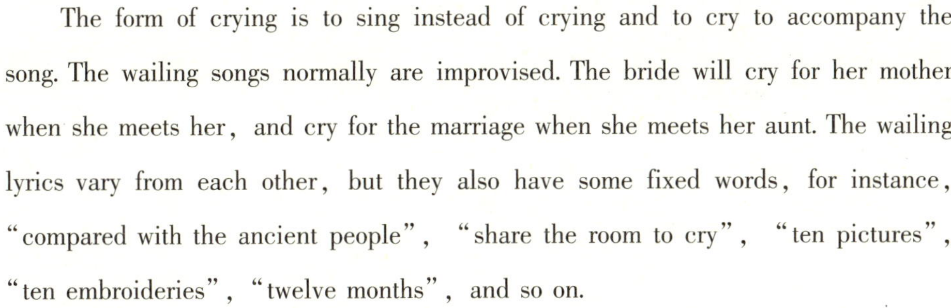

The form of crying is to sing instead of crying and to cry to accompany the song. The wailing songs normally are improvised. The bride will cry for her mother when she meets her, and cry for the marriage when she meets her aunt. The wailing lyrics vary from each other, but they also have some fixed words, for instance, "compared with the ancient people", "share the room to cry", "ten pictures", "ten embroideries", "twelve months", and so on.

Crying also has its different tones, rising and falling in cadence. It is a kind of art which is quite hard and mixed up with singing and crying. Before the marriage, the bride will invite a teacher and practice frequently. While they are crying, modal particles such as "Weng", "Man" and "Ayaya" will be employed. Crying for a while and speaking for a while, the bride makes herself pathetic.

The climax appears on the day of the wedding ceremony. On the previous day, friends, relatives and neighbors will come to congratulate and cry for departure. The bride's family will invite nine of her best single maids to accompany her to cry, which is called "get-together of ten sisters". They will also set a square table in the boudoir of the stilted building, on which there are ten bowls of tea. The nine close sisters will be invited to sit around the table and begin to wail the song. The bride sitting in the middle is called *Baoxi*, the sisters on the right *Anxi*, and those on the left *Shouxi*. The bride starts the crying, and then the *Anxi*. The three of them continue to cry one by one. They will mainly cry to narrate the friendship between them, and sometimes their crying may include some encouraging and comforting words. Their crying will last till the midnight, when the bride's family invites them to have some night snacks, which also can be one topic of the bride's crying to thank the company of the other nine sisters.

第七章　中国人的忌讳文化

忌讳是"避讳"和"顾忌"的意思，是社会与文化的产物，是中国的一大长期而普遍的民俗，是一种神秘的文化现象，取决于民众的自我认同，存在于社会的每个角落，影响着人们的生活。

一、数字禁忌

数字是人们在日常生活的言语交际中经常使用的文字。各民族在对数的运用过程中，认为数字是神秘莫测的，因而也就把数字神秘化，赋予其神圣的性质。于是在人们的观念里，数字也就有了吉凶之分。

（一）忌讳的数字

给结婚、庆寿的人家送礼，忌讳单数，因为这与"好事成双"的愿望背道而驰。给病人和丧家送礼，就忌双数，因为谁也不希望坏事成双。

因"三"与"散"谐音，做寿和结婚忌这个日子，祝寿、贺喜送礼也忌"三"这个数字。

"四"和"死"谐音，不吉利，所以门牌号、汽车牌号、电话号码、手机号码等忌讳用这个数字。

"五"谐音"无"，五日忌晒席垫，忌盖屋，认为不吉利。古时忌农历五月五日生人，据说，因为在古人的观念中，每年农历五月五日是恶月中的恶日，是一年中毒气最盛的一天，就连此日出生的孩子，也可能会克父母，故或弃而不养，或另改出生日。

旧时对妇女有"七出"之条，犯了七条，男人就要休妻。所以嫁女时，

尽量避免“七”这个数字。

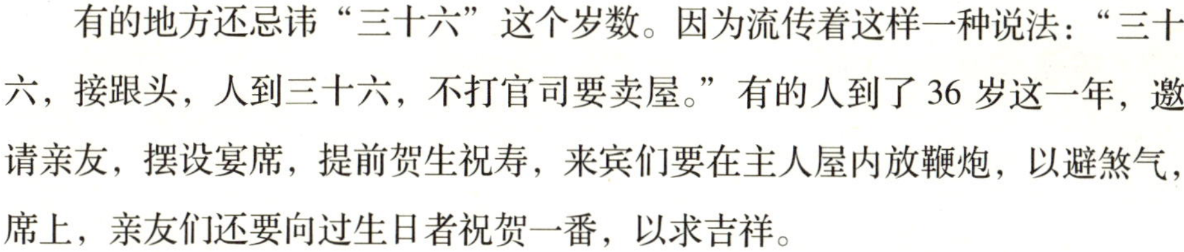

有的地方还忌讳“三十六”这个岁数。因为流传着这样一种说法：“三十六，接跟头，人到三十六，不打官司要卖屋。”有的人到了 36 岁这一年，邀请亲友，摆设宴席，提前贺生祝寿，来宾们要在主人屋内放鞭炮，以避煞气，席上，亲友们还要向过生日者祝贺一番，以求吉祥。

古人很忌讳 45 岁这个年龄。因为流传着这样一种说法：“人到四十五，庄稼去了暑。”即使到了这个年龄，他们也会多说一岁或少说一岁，有意地避开。有的还让家人做一件红色的裤头或是红色的腰带，避避 45 岁的邪气。

有的地方还忌讳“六十六”，认为 66 岁是老年人的一个“坎”，因为流传着这样一种说法：“年纪六十六，阎王要吃肉”，所以就形成了很多与此有关的习俗。

有的地方还忌讳“七十三”“八十四”。因为流传着这样一种说法：“七十三、八十四，阎王不请自己去。”还有另外一种说法是相传圣人孔子享年 73 岁，孟子则 84 岁去世。人家就认为连孔孟这样的圣人都难逃“七十三”“八十四”，一般人就更不用说了。所以人们认为这两个数字是人生的一大关口。过了 73，便闯过了一道难关，可以活到 84 岁；84 岁又过一关，则可活到百岁。

有的地方忌讳说“八十一”，因为流传着这样一种说法：“九九八十一，财数算尽，后代穷败”，所以很多地方忌讳 81 岁这个岁数。

有的地方忌讳“九”，这是因为，古代的数理观念中，一、三、五、七、九为阳，二、四、六、八为阴；九为阳数之极，物极必反，故有由盈而亏、由盛转衰的不吉寓意，所以就忌讳岁数逢“九”，认为岁数逢“九”是关口。

（二）吉祥的数字

吉祥的数字一般是双数，结婚时忌讳选单日子，一方面是有好事成双的愿望，另一方面是怕有鳏寡之灾。

人们对“六”和“八”这两个数字特别的偏爱。因为在中文里面，“八”与“发”是谐音，“发”就是“发财”的意思。过去商人远行，一般选在逢“八”的日子出门。至今还流传着一句“要得发，不离八”的吉言。在中文里，“六”是顺的意思，“六”和“六”连着更好，有“六六大顺”之意。因

此，在选电话号码和楼层的时候，人们非常愿意要“八”与“六”。

二、节日禁忌

（一）正月初一

正月初一忌出嫁之女回娘家，传说嫁出去的女儿回娘家过年，会把娘家吃穷，因此只能在初二或者初三回娘家。忌喝米汤或吃稀粥，据说出门会遇大雨。忌洒水、扫地、倒垃圾，因为会把家中的财运扫出去。忌打骂孩子，因为会伤了家庭和气。忌用针，怕会“断线”，进而影响后代。忌打破碗、碟、杯、盘等，会有破运，如人破、家破、财破等。忌食荤腥，只用素菜，因为食肉就要杀生，而杀生必见血光，会引起血光之灾。忌说不吉利的字眼，凡是“破”“死”“病”“输”“穷”等不吉利的字在这一天要小心避免出口。如果不慎犯忌，则一年内可能会发生不吉利的事。

（二）初一、初二

初一、初二忌洗衣，传说，水神的生日在初一、初二，因此这两天不能洗衣服。

（三）正月初一至十五

正月初一至十五，忌到田园耕作，因为会冲犯神灵，一年做事都会不顺。

（四）冬　至

冬至节夫妇忌宿娘家，因古来有谚语说：“娘家住个冬，夫家失去公。”

三、吃饭时的禁忌

（一）碗

忌扣碗，因病人服药后常将碗倒扣于桌上，以示今后不再生病吃药。忌以筷子击碗，因乞丐常以筷子击碗，以求人施舍，故“以筷子击碗”被视为不祥之兆。忌端碗时手心朝上，因为乞丐要饭的姿势就是这样的，所以这也

是端碗的禁忌。

(二)筷　子

忌将筷子竖插在饭中，因为在中国，祭祀亡灵时会把筷子直接竖插在饭中，所以这一动作被视为不吉利。忌筷子放在杯子两侧，一双筷子要放于碗或杯子的同一侧，而不能一边放一只筷子，因为在汉语里，这与“快（筷）分开了”谐音，不利于家人感情，所以视为不吉利。

(三)说　话

忌吃饭时说不吉利的话，吃饭时说出不吉利的言语，也是犯忌讳的，所以，吃饭时候忌讳提到伤、亡、病、灾、祸等凶事。

(四)饭　后

忌饭后洗澡、剃头，因为民间有“饭饱不洗澡，酒醉不剃脑”“肚饱不剃头”等说法。忌吃饭时剩饭，因为民间有“小孩剩碗底，长大娶麻妻”“吃不光，好生疮”等说法。

四、招待客人的禁忌

(一)忌狗肉

忌用狗肉来办酒席或宴请客人。因为自古以来狗肉被视为不洁之物，用狗肉来办酒席或宴请客人会被视为不吉和不敬，故有“狗肉不上席”之说。

(二)忌勺子往外翻

招待客人吃饭时，主人要亲自给客人布菜、敬酒，以示对客人的尊重，但是盛饭时忌勺子往外翻，因为有一种说法是，牢房内给犯人盛饭时候才勺子外翻。宴客时忌茶壶、酒壶壶口向人，因为这样对别人不礼貌。

(三)忌讳提前离席

在吃饭时，主人应该始终陪坐，忌讳提前离席，以免客人吃得不安心。

（四）忌讳将空碗、空碟收走

客人还在吃饭时，忌讳将空碗、空碟收走，会让客人认为这是“赶客”的举动。

（五）忌第一顿饭给客人吃饺子

忌第一顿饭给客人吃饺子。民间有“送客的饺子迎客的面”的说法，所以在喜欢吃饺子的中国北方，当家里有客人来时，第一顿饭吃水饺，会让客人以为自己不受欢迎，是主人家逐客呢。

五、做客的忌讳

去别人家中做客或赴宴时，在言谈举止方面也有许多忌讳，一定要注意，以免给双方带来尴尬。

喝酒时，忌转动酒杯或将酒弃泼；吃饭时忌脱衣和松裤带；忌谈论饭菜不好；忌站起身来，夹远处的菜；忌将菜盘里的菜食光；忌主动要求添菜、添饭；吃鱼时，忌主动把鱼翻转过来，在中国有“客不翻鱼”的说法；忌不道别就离席而去；等等。

六、生活中的禁忌

（一）谐音带来的忌讳

梨不能分着吃，因为在汉语里“分梨”和“分离”是谐音。送礼不能送钟表、伞、扇和杯子，因为“送钟”的谐音是“送终”，“伞”和“扇”的谐音是“散”，杯的谐音是“悲”，不吉利。

（二）传统带来的忌讳

不能用红笔写人名，因为在古代，对死刑犯问斩的时候，要在押号上用鸡血写上犯人的名字，后来演变为用红色的笔写了，所以用红颜色的笔写别人的名字，会被认为是对别人的冒犯。正月里不能理发，在民间有“正月理发会死舅”的说法。长辈睡在床上，晚辈不能在床前跪拜。因为这是跪拜死人的做法。

（三）传说带来的忌讳

晚上走路，头不能向左右看，因为这样会吹灭肩灯，那么鬼就会跟来。日落后忌看病人，因那时阴盛阳衰，容易招惹鬼神。女人裤子不能晒在过道上，据说人从下面走过去，便会晦气。夜间不能露天晒衣服，特别是小孩子衣服，传说会招来夜游神。床不能对着镜子，传说会摄人魂魄。人外出，忌鸟屎落在头上，传说鸟屎落在头上会很不吉利，回家要吃太平面，以驱晦气。

七、颜色禁忌

（一）贵色忌

中国人以黄色、紫色、香色等为贵色。这些颜色曾经一度是皇室或权贵人士的专用色，在民间中国百姓很忌讳用黄色、紫色、香色做衣服。在中国封建社会，黄色是皇室专用色，如果百姓用黄色衣料做衣服，会被砍头。

（二）贱色忌

民间常以绿色、碧色、青色为贱色，因为元代、明代、清代时，只有娼妓、歌妓等人才会用绿色、碧色、青色做服饰。

（三）凶色忌

中国人以白色、黑色等为凶色，在服饰方面都有所忌讳。因为，举办丧事，要么戴黑纱，要么穿白色孝服。所以在婚嫁、做寿、满月、过年、过节等喜庆日子里忌讳穿纯白、纯黑的衣裳。

（四）艳色忌

浓妆艳抹，穿着华丽，在中国民间也是犯忌讳的。因为在中国传统文化里，人们认为服饰的色彩是应当与人的年龄、职业、品行相匹配的。女人过分浓妆艳抹会被视为轻浮，男人穿着过于鲜亮，会被视为轻薄。

八、儿童禁忌

（一）满　月

婴儿满月忌不沐浴剃头。传说，婴儿的头发带有母体秽气，满月如果不沐浴剃头，就会触犯神明。

（二）睡　觉

小孩睡觉时灵魂会出窍，不能在脸上涂抹，否则灵魂归来时，认不得自己躯体，会长眠不醒。

（三）上　学

儿童忌8岁上学，因为在中国传统文化里有“七上八下”之说，因此，8岁入学的孩子学习不能上进。

九、婚配禁忌

（一）相　克

在中国传统文化里，青年男女若要通婚，要将生辰八字请看命先生推算，看看是相生还是相克。如相克，则视为不合婚。自古以来就有“白马怕青牛”“猪猴相伴不到头”之说。

（二）相　生

有相克也有相生，如相生视为合婚，自古以来就有“红蛇白猴满堂红，福寿双全多康宁”“青兔黄狗古来有，万贯家财捉北斗”之说，这些都是好姻缘，可以通婚。

（三）六　害

男女相差6岁者，古人谓之“六害”，忌通婚。

（四）迎亲禁忌

迎亲路上忌与丧葬相遇，如遇到，要摔物件或互换礼物，双方均取吉利。新婚之日忌穿白衣服的妇女进屋，忌孕妇和寡妇入洞房。

十、生育禁忌

孕妇忌拿剪刀剪东西，据说会伤害胎儿。孕妇忌看戏、忌进入寺庙，忌接触丧事，忌夜间外出，忌参与祭祀和他人的婚礼，忌食狗肉。产妇生产时，忌肖虎、穿丧服、带雨伞和携金属器皿的人入产房。

十一、礼仪禁忌

忌在人背后泼水、吐痰；忌直呼长者的名字。老人病逝忌说“死”，应说“老了”或“过后了”。

Chapter 7 Chinese Taboo Culture

Taboo means the thing that should be prohibited or excluded from use or practice, which is the product of our society and culture. As one of long-standing and prevalent Chinese folk customs, taboo is a kind of mysterious cultural phenomenon which depends on public self-identity, exists everywhere and influences people's lives.

1. Taboos in Numbers

Numbers are frequently used during verbal communication in people's daily life. During the process of using them, numbers are believed to be unpredictable, so they are mystified and are considered to have some holy attributes. Thus in people's views, numbers can be lucky or unlucky.

(1) Tabooed Numbers

When giving presents or celebrating for wedding or birthday, odd numbers should be avoided since it disobeys the wish that "happiness comes in twos". However, when giving presents for the patients or giving gifts at the funerals, even numbers should be avoided because nobody expects "misfortune comes in twos".

Because 3 ([Sān]) and seperated ([Sàn]) have similar pronunciations in Chinese, When celebrating birthdays or choosing wedding dates, people tend to avoid the dates which are related to 3. Besides, when sending birthday presents or wedding gifts, number 3 should be avoided.

Number 4 ([Sì]) has the similar pronunciation with death ([Sǐ]), which means unlucky, thus, when choosing house numbers, car numbers, telephone numbers and cell phone numbers, number 4 are always avoided.

Number 5 ([Wǔ]) has the similar pronunciation with nothing ([Wú]), so on dates, which are related to 5, sunning mats or building houses are often avoided because they are believed to be unlucky. In ancient time, persons, who are born on May the fifth in lunar calendar, are often resented. It's said that in the ancients' views, May the fifth in lunar calendar is the evil day in the evil month so it's the worst day in a year. Even the children born on this day will do harm to their parents. So the parents will either abandon the child or change the baby's birthday.

In the old days there are the rule of *Qichu* (seven reasons for divorce) aiming at women. If they commit seven sins, their husbands will divorce them. Therefore when people marry off daughters, number 7 are always tried to be avoided.

In some places, the age of 36 is also avoided as a taboo. There is an old saying which goes like this, " When a person is 36, he or she will encounter trip and fall. A person at 36 will be either engaged in lawsuit or being forced to sell his house. " At the age of 36, some people will make a feast and invite their relatives and friends to celebrate his birthday ahead of time. Visitors will set off firecrackers in host's house to drive bad luck away. At the dinner table, they also should send their congratulations to the host or the hostess to pray good luck for him or her.

The age of 45 is also avoided as a taboo by the ancients. As the old saying goes, "when people reach the age of 45, they are just like the limp crops lacking of sunshine. " Thus people will pretend to be one year older or younger than 45 deliberately. Some people will ask the family to make red underpants or waist belts for them to drive away evil spirits in the year of 45.

In some places, the age of 66 is also avoided as a taboo. It's believed that the age of 66 is a tough period for the elderly. A legendary saying goes as follows, "at the age of 66, the God of Death wants to kill you. " Therefore, many customs related to it have grown up.

Moreover, number 73 and 84 are avoided as a taboo because of the old saying,

"reaching at the age of 73 or 84, you will go to hell even God of Death doesn't invite you." There's another legend saying that two of Chinese sages, Confucius passed away at the age of 73 while Mencius at 84. Even the sages like Confucius and Mencius couldn't escape from the curse of 73 and 84, let alone the normal people. So these two numbers are regarded as the critical junctures of life. If you can live through 73, you pull through difficult times and you can at least survive till 84; if you can live through 84, you can live as long as 100 years.

Number 81 is avoided as a taboo according to the saying, "nine by nine we get a one, the good fortune on wealth has run out and the descendants will be poor forever." So in many places number 81 is avoided.

In some places, number 9 is avoided as a taboo for that in ancient mathematical idea, number 1, 3, 5, 7 and 9 are regarded as Yang while 2, 4, 6 and 8 as Yin and number 9 is the extreme of Yang. There is an old saying which goes like this, "Things always reverse themselves after reaching latan extreme." which indicates that profit will turn into loss and ups will turn into downs. So ages related to 9 are also avoided as a taboo by people, because they believe those will bring them bad luck.

(2) Lucky Numbers

Lucky numbers are usually even numbers. Therefore, when choosing the wedding dates, odd numbers are avoided as a taboo. For one thing, people wish "happiness comes in twos". For another, they don't want to suffer the widowed disasters.

People tend to show preference for the number 6 and 8 for the reason that, in Chinese, 8 ([Bā]) has the similar pronunciations with "发" ([Fā]), which means making a fortune in Chinese. In the past, merchants always choose the days related to 8 to go on a long trip. Till now the lucky saying, "if you want to become rich, you should depend on number 8." In Chinese, number 6 ([Liù]) has the similar pronunciations with "溜" ([Liū]) which means things will go on smoothly. If a six goes after another six, it is even better, because two sixes mean "liuliu da shun",

which means everything goes smoothly. So when choosing the telephone number or the number of floor levels, people prefer to choose numbers related to 8 and 6.

2. Taboos in Holidays

(1) First Day of Chinese Lunar Year

On the first day of Chinese lunar year, married daughters should not go back to her parents' home because it is said that if they do so, they will eat their parents out of house and home. So daughters can only go back on the second or third day of the lunar New Year.

On the first day of the lunar New Year, people should not eat the rice water, water in which rice has been cooked, or gruel because it is said that if you do so it will encounter heavy rain when they are out. What's more, watering, sweeping and dumping are also forbidden because it is said that the luck for fortune will be swept out . On that day, people should not beat or scold children because it is said that it will break the harmony among the family members. Besides, needle and thread should not be used because "broken thread" in Chinese is pronounced as *Duanxian* ([Duànxiàn]) which means dying without descendants.

People ought to be careful and not to break bowls, dishes, cups, and so on, or the evil things such as "people getting separated", "family member suffering death" and "suffering financially loss", and so on. Eating meat or fish is avoided for the reason that you have to kill living beings if you eat meat or fish and their blood will cause bloody disaster. Unlucky words are also avoided on that day, for example, words about breaking, death, disease, failure, poverty should not be mentioned. If people accidentally commit a taboo, something unlucky may happen within the coming year.

(2) First and Second Day of the Lunar New Year

On the first and second day of the lunar New Year, washing clothes is avoided because it is said that the birthday of the Water God is on these two days.

(3) First Day to the Fifteenth Day of the Lunar New Year

From the first day to the fifteenth day of lunar year, working in the field is avoided because it will offend the gods, and nothing will go smoothly in the whole year.

(4) Taboos on Winter Solstice

On the Winter Solstice, couples should not stay overnight in the woman's parents ' home according to the old saying "staying in married woman's parents' on Winter Solstice, her father-in-law will be cursed to death. "

3. Taboos at Table

(1) Bowl

At the dinner table, bowls are avoided being put upside down because after patients take medicine they usually turn the bowl upside down to express the best wishes that they will not be ill and take medicine any more. Knocking the bowl with chopsticks is also avoided since the beggars usually do that to beg for charity, so this action is regarded as the unlucky sign. When holding the bowl, palm is avoided being up since the beggars beg in the same gesture, so that's the taboo when holding bowl.

(2) Chopsticks

Sticking chopsticks upright in the rice bowl is avoided because in China when worshiping the dead, chopsticks are usually put upright in the rice, which is treated as unlucky. A pair of chopsticks are avoided to be set on two sides of a bowl or cup since in Chinese that symbolizes "will soon be (Kuai, the homophone of chopsticks) separated", which hurts the family's feelings thus it is regarded unlucky.

(3) Speech

Unlucky words are avoided during dinner. Unlucky words at dinner table are

avoided as a taboo, so the words about injury, death, disease, disaster and accident are avoided to be mentioned when dining.

(4) After Dinner

Taking a shower or cutting his hair immediately after dinner is avoided because there is an old saying in Chinese folk which goes, "no shower after dinner; no hair cut when drunk" and "do not shave your head when you are full". Leaving over food from a meal are avoided because there is an old saying in Chinese folk which goes, "if a child leave over food from dinner, he will marry an ugly wife when he grows up", and "leftovers result in canker".

4. Taboos on Entertaining Visitors

(1) Avoiding Dog Meat

Dog meat should be avoided at feast when hosting guests. Since the ancient time, dog meat has been believed to be a dirty thing. People feel unlucky and insulted when dog meat is served on dinner table. Hence the saying of "no dog meat at feast" came into existence.

(2) Avoid Spoon Facing Outer Side

When entertaining guests for dinner, the host will serve them food and propose a toast personally to express the respect for the guests. But the spoon is avoided to face the outer side when serving guests bowls of rice. It is believed that only when prisoners were served for rice, the spoon faces the outer side. Also spout of the teapot or flagon can't face the others because it's rude for the guests.

(3) Avoid Leaving Early from Feast

When hosting the guest for dinner, the host should sit there with the guests from beginning to the end and avoid leaving early from feast to make the guests feel uneasy.

(4) Avoid Taking Away the Empty Bowls during Feast

When the guests are still at dinner, the empty bowls or dishes are avoided to be taken away because that will make the guests feel they are driven.

(5) No Dumplings on the First Meal for the Guests

Dumplings are avoided to be served to the guests for the first meal. In the folklore, there's a saying of "dumplings for leaving guests and noodle for receiving guests", so in the northern part of China where the dumplings are popular, when there are visitors, dumplings are avoided to be served to host the guests for the first meal, which will make guests feel unwelcome and want to leave.

5. Taboos for the Guest

When visiting other's home or going to the dinner party, there are also many taboos in the guest's manner which should be paid attention to in order to avoid embarrassment.

When drinking wines, twisting the wineglass or spiltting the wine should be avoided. When having a meal, taking off clothes or loosening belt are avoided. In addition, giving negative comments on the food, standing up to pick the dish in the distance, and eating up the whole dish volunteering for more rice or dishes are avoided. When eating a fish, volunteering to turn the fish over should be avoided when one side is finished, because there is an old saying in China, which goes, "guests can not turn over fish by themselves." When leaving, it is avoided to leave the feast without farewell, and so on.

6. Taboos in Life

(1) Taboos Caused by Homophony

A pear can't be split between two people because in Chinese "splitting pear" ([Fēnlí]) and "separated" ([Fēnlí]) sound the same. When exchanging gifts,

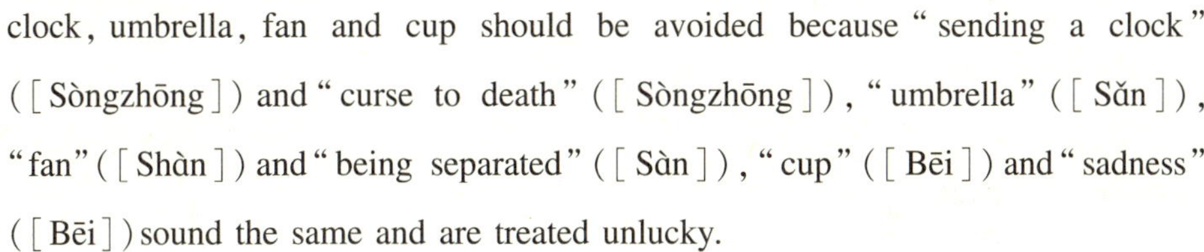

clock, umbrella, fan and cup should be avoided because "sending a clock" ([Sòngzhōng]) and "curse to death" ([Sòngzhōng]), "umbrella" ([Sǎn]), "fan" ([Shàn]) and "being separated" ([Sàn]), "cup" ([Bēi]) and "sadness" ([Bēi]) sound the same and are treated unlucky.

(2) Taboos Brought by Traditions

Writing a person's name in red ink should be avoided because in the ancient time, when a criminal is carried out the death sentence, the criminal's name is written in chicken blood on his confession. Later it turns out to use the red ink instead of chicken blood. So writing a person's name in red ink is regarded as being offend. In the first month of Chinese lunar calendar, cutting hair is avoided because there is an old saying which goes, "haircut in the first month of lunar year will curse your uncle to death." When the elders lie in bed, kneeling before the bed is avoided because that's the way to kneel to the death.

(3) Taboos from Legends

When walking at night, looking left and right is avoided because it is said that the shoulder light will be blown out and the person will be followed by ghost. After the sunset, visiting the patients is avoided because of excess of Yin and shortage of Yang at that time and the ghosts and gods are easily offended. Hanging women's trousers in the passageway is avoided. It's said that people who walk under them will be brought bad luck. Hanging clothes especially those for children outdoor at night is avoided because it is said that it will attract God on Patrol at Night. Setting the bed opposite the mirror is avoided because it is said that people's soul will be sucked into the mirror. Birds' droppings falling on the head is avoided because it will bring you bad luck. In order to drive bad luck away, it is better to go back home to eat Taiping noodle.

7. Taboos about Colors

(1) Avoid Elegant Colors

Chinese people classify yellow, purple, champagne color into elegant colors. These colors used to be exclusively used for the royal and noble family, so civilians are forbidden to dress in yellow, purple or champagne color. In Chinese feudal society, yellow is used only for the royal family and if the civilian who wears yellow clothes will be decapitated.

(2) Avoid Humble Colors

In the Chinese folk, green, verdurous and cyan are considered to be the humble colors because in Yuan, Ming and Qing Dynasties, only prostitute and singing girls dress in these colors.

(3) Avoid Evil Colors

In Chinese culture, white, black are considered to be evil colors so there are taboos in clothing because in the funeral, people wear black armbands or white mourning garments. So in the happy days, such as wedding, birthday, kid's first month, New Year, festivals, and so on, white or black clothes should be avoided.

(4) Avoid Bright Colors

Among the people, excessive make-up and splendid dressing should also be avoided. In Chinese traditional culture, people believe that dress colors should match people's age, career and behavior. Women with excessive make-up will be seen as flirtatious and men in bright colors will also be considered as superficial.

8. Taboos for Children

(1) Baby's Completion of Its First Month

On the day of the completion of its first month, the baby must be given a

shower and cut hair. It is said that the baby's hair is full of its mother's mephitis. If the baby isn't given a shower or haircut, God will be offended.

(2) Sleep

It is said that when the child is sleeping, the soul will be out of the body. So the child's face can't be smeared otherwise when his soul goes back, it will not recognize his own body and will sleep for ever.

(3) Going to School

Children can't go to school at eight, because in Chinese traditional culture there's a saying of "seven up, eight down", so a child, who goes to school at the age of eight, will not work hard.

9. Taboos in Marriage

(1) Restriction

In Chinese traditional culture, before the young people get married, they bring their birth time to the fortune teller to reckon whether they mutually inter-promote or restrict each other. If they restrict each other, they are not suitable for marriage. Since the ancient time, there have been sayings such as "the horse person is not suitable to get married with the ox person", and "the pig person and the monkey person cannot live together for life".

(2) Inter-promote Each Other

Opposite to restriction, the young people who inter-promote each other are suitable to get married. Since the ancient time, sayings such as "if the snake person and the monkey person get married, they can enjoy both happiness and longevity."

(3) Avoid Six-year's Age Gap

If there is an age gap of six years between a man and a woman, it is called that

Liuhai and these two people are forbidden to get married.

(4) Taboos about Picking the Bride

On the way to pick the bride, if wedding greeter chances to meet the funeral procession, they should break something or exchange presents for luck. On the wedding day, woman in white should not get in the bridal chamber and pregnant woman and widow can not get in the bridal chamber.

10. Taboos in Childbirth

Pregnant woman should not use scissors to cut things because it is said that it will do harm to the baby. For a pregnant woman, going to the theater or temple, attending funerals, taking part in the sacrificial ceremony or wedding and eating dog meat should be avoided. When giving birth to a child, people, who were born in the Chinese tiger year, or wear mourning suit, or take umbrella and metal containers with them, could not get in the delivery room.

11. Taboos of Etiquette

Splashing water or spitting behind other's back and addressing anyone by the elder's name are avoided. Sending others clock because "clock" ([Zhōng]) and "end" ([Zhōng]) sound the same. When the elder died, rude words such as *Si* (dead) can't be mentioned, but *Lao le* or *Guohou le* (pass away).

第八章　中国汉族传统服饰文化

中国传统服饰是中国传统文化的重要组成部分，是中华各民族创造的宝贵财富。从史前到明清，中华各民族在长期的生产实践中，创造了无数精美绝伦的服饰。服饰作为人类生活的重要组成部分，是一种文化载体。在各个朝代、各个领域、各民族、各阶段有其不同的特点。中国服装款式的发展和演变、面料和色彩的选用和搭配、着装的特定场合和等级规定，反映着特定时期的社会制度、经济生活、民俗风情，也承载着人们的思想文化和审美观念。本章简要介绍一下中国各个时期的服饰，以便读者朋友对中国的服饰文化有一个简要的了解。

一、原始服饰

上古时期人类的服饰是以毛皮围系于下腹部，或许为了御寒，或许为了遮羞又或许为了装饰。但是不论出于何种原因，原始服装已经开始出现。由此，揭开了中国服饰文化的序幕。

二、商周服饰

商周时期的服饰采用了上衣下裳式，是中国最早的衣裳制度的基本形式。上身穿“衣”，衣领开向右边；下身穿“裳”，裳就是裙。在腰部束着一条宽边的腰带，肚围前再加一条像裙一样的“韨”，用来遮蔽膝盖，所以又叫做“蔽膝”。

中国的冠服制度始于周代，周代对服饰中的衣冠等级有了严格的区分，把衣服分为五大类，分为祭服、朝服、军服、吉服、凶服等。

三、春秋战国服饰

（一）深　衣

春秋战国之际，又出现一种服装，将上衣、下裳合并为一体，连为一件，这种服装被称为深衣。深衣是一种上下相连的服装，制作时上下分裁，然后在腰间缝合，衣式采用短领，衣长到脚跟。深衣既被用作礼服，又可日常穿着，是一种非常实用的服饰。

（二）胡　服

胡服，指胡人（历史上称北方的民族为“胡”）所穿的衣服，即鞑靼人或西北地区少数民族的服装，与当时中原地区宽大博带式的汉族服装有较大差异。一般为短衣、长裤和革靴，衣身紧窄，活动便利。胡服第一次被汉族人民所接受，是在公元前300多年的战国时期，赵武灵王为了加强军队的作战能力，把胡服引入到了中原一带，废弃传统的上衣下裳。

四、秦汉服饰

（一）袍　服

当时的男子多以袍服为贵，袍服的样式以大袖收口为多，一般都有花边。百姓、劳动者或束发髻，或戴小帽、巾子，身穿交领长衫，窄袖。

西汉男女服装仍沿袭深衣形式。汉代的男子的服装样式，大致分为曲裾、直裾两种。

曲裾　曲裾其实是战国时期流行的深衣。汉代仍然沿用，但多见于西汉早期。汉代曲裾深衣不仅男子可穿，同时也是女服中最为常见的一种服式。这种服装通身紧窄，长可曳地，下摆一般呈喇叭状，行不露足。衣袖有宽窄两式，袖口大多镶边。衣领部分很有特色，通常用交领，领口很低，以便露出里衣。如穿几件衣服，每层领子必露于外，最多的达三层以上，时称“三重衣”。

直裾　到东汉，男子穿曲裾者已经少见，一般多为直裾之衣，但并不能

作为正式礼服。礼服仍为曲裾之衣。

（二）汉代直裾女服

汉代除了穿深衣，穿襦裙。所谓襦裙就是上面是襦，下面是裙。一般上襦极短，只到腰间，而裙子很长，下垂至地。

（三）颜色的限制

汉代规定，百姓一律不得穿各种带颜色的服装，只能穿本色麻布。直到西汉末年（公元前13年）才允许平民服青绿之衣。

五、魏晋南北朝服饰

在魏晋南北朝时期，宽衣博带是这时期的流行服饰。男子穿衣敞胸露臂，衣服披肩，追求轻松、自然、随意。

女子服饰则长裙拖地，大袖翩翩，饰带层层叠叠，优雅而飘逸。

六、隋唐五代

隋代女子穿窄袖合身的圆领或交领短衣，高腰拖地的长裙，腰上还系着两条飘带。

唐高祖李渊于621年正式颁布《武德令》，对皇帝、皇后、群臣百官、命妇、士庶等各级各等人士的衣着、色彩、佩带诸方面都作了详细的规定，唐朝的衣冠制度正式确立。黄色只有皇帝和皇室亲臣、贵臣才可穿用，其他人穿用则为犯罪，因此黄色为皇权的特殊象征。另外，还以服装的颜色区分官职品级：三品以上为紫色，五品以上为朱色，六品为绿色，七品为青色。

（一）唐代官吏常服

唐代官吏，除穿圆领窄袖袍衫之外，在一些重要场合，如祭祀典礼时仍穿礼服。礼服的样式，多承袭隋朝旧制，头戴介帻或笼冠，身穿对襟大袖衫，下着围裳，玉佩组绶等。

（二）唐代平民常服

平民男子一般着圆领□衫，戴软角幞头。

女子一般着艳丽大袖衫，袒胸、裸臂、披纱、大袖、长裙是唐代妇女最典型的着装形象。

最时兴的女子衣着是襦裙，即短上衣加长裙，裙腰以绸带高系，几乎及腋下。

七、宋代服饰

宋朝的服装一改唐朝服饰旷达华贵、恢宏大气的特点，服装造型封闭，颜色严肃淡雅，色调趋于单一。

（一）女　装

宋代的女装是上身穿窄袖短衣，下身穿长裙，通常在上衣外面再穿一件对襟的长袖小褙子，很像现在的背心，褙子的领口和前襟都绣上漂亮的花边。

（二）男　装

宋代的男装大体上沿袭唐代样式，一般百姓多穿交领或圆领的长袍，做事的时候就把衣服往上塞在腰带上，衣服是黑白两种颜色。

八、元朝服饰

蒙古人多把额上的头发弄成一小绺，像个桃子，其他的就编成两条辫子，再绕成两个大环垂在耳朵后面，头上戴笠子帽。

（一）男装（质孙服）

元代人的衣服主要是“质孙服”，它是较短的长袍，比较紧、比较窄，在腰部有很多衣褶，这种衣服很方便骑射。

（二）女　装

元代的贵族妇女，常戴着一顶高高长长，看起来很奇怪的帽子。她们穿的袍子，宽大而且长，走起路来很不方便，常常要两个婢女在后面帮她们拉着袍角。

一般的平民妇女，多是穿黑色的袍子。

九、明朝服饰

（一）平民袍衫

朱元璋称帝后，为了恢复汉族的礼仪，便制定了以周汉、唐宋为准则的新服饰制度。以袍衫为主要服饰。

（二）补　服

官员以补服为常服，头戴乌纱帽，身穿圆领衫。所谓补服，是指在袍衫前有一块方形刺绣图案的官服，文官图为飞禽，武官图为猛兽。用袍衫颜色和图案的分别来区分官阶品位。平常穿的圆领袍衫则凭衣服长短和袖子大小区分身份，长大者为尊。

（三）儒生文士服

明朝的儒生文士男子服饰大多穿圆领或斜领的青布直身的宽袖长衣，头戴四方平定巾。

（四）女　装

明代的贵妇多是穿红色大袖的袍子。

一般妇女只能穿一些浅淡的颜色。裙子宽大，样式很多。

十、清代服饰

满族入关后，强迫汉人穿满人服装，渐渐形成了一套有别于明代的服饰体系。清朝是中国服装史上变化最大的一个朝代，清代是个满汉文化交融的时代，尤其是服装文化，也是在进入中原后保留原有服装传统最多的非汉族王朝。

满服改变了几千年来形成的中国古代服饰的基本形式，清服是中国古服与近代服装的交接点，它的存在是以后发展到近代男士的马褂长袍、女士的旗袍的前提。

（一）男子长袍马褂

长袍马褂是清朝男子最常穿的服饰。马褂是穿在长袍外面的短褂子，长度只到腰际，袖仅掩肘，短衣、短袖便于骑马，所以叫“马褂”。平日所戴的便帽就是瓜皮小帽，颜色是外面黑，里面红。

（二）女子服饰

妇女服饰在清代可谓满、汉服饰并存。满族妇女以旗袍为主，旗袍衣身修长，衣袖短窄，与历时数千年的宽袍大袖，拖裙盛冠，潇洒富丽，纤细柔弱的中国服装形成鲜明的对比。旗装以它用料节省，制作简便和穿着方便的优点取代了古代的衣裙，这是后人易于接受的主要原因。

Chapter 8 Chinese Traditional Costume

China's traditional costume is one of essential parts of Chinese traditional culture, which is one of the most precious wealth created by all ethnic groups of China. From prehistory to Ming and Qing Dynasties, the Chinese people, in the long course of productive practice, have made innumerable exquisite costumes which are beyond comparable. As an important part of human life, clothing is the embodiment of culture. It has its own unique characteristics in different dynasties, areas, nationalities and stages. The development and the evolution of Chinese clothing styles, the selection of fabric and color, the rules for dress occasions and grading, can all reflect social system, economic activities, and folk customs of the specific period, which is conveying the people's ideological culture and aesthetic ideas. This chapter will briefly introduce the Chinese costume in various periods of China in the hope that readers could gain a brief understanding about China's clothing culture.

1. Costumes in the Primitive Society

In ancient times, human beings are clothed with furs which are worn around the lower abdomen, perhaps in order to keep out the coldness or perhaps to hide the nakedness or even to embellish themselves. But no matter what the reason is, the original clothing starts to appear, which, thus, opens a prelude to China's clothing culture.

2. Costumes in Shang and Zhou Dynasties

People at that time often wear *Yi* (shirt) on the upper part of their bodies, whose collar opens to the right and wear *Chang* (skirt) on the lower of their bodies. *Chang* is actually the skirt. The waist is tied with a broad beam of the belt, coupled with a piece of *Fu* in the belly, which was like a skirt, to cover the knees, so *Fu* was also called the *Bixi*, which means "knee shelter".

China's costume system dates from Zhou Dynasty, which has a strict distinction in the clothing. The clothing is divided into five categories, which are royal robes, vestments, military uniforms, wedding dress and funeral dress, etc.

3. Costumes in the Spring and Autumn Period and the Warring States Period

(1) Shenyi

During the Spring and Autumn and the Warring States Period, there appears a type of Chinese clothing, which is also called *Shenyi*, a type of Han Chinese clothing in which the *Yi* and *Chang* are sewn together into one-piece garment at the waist. Shenyi has a short collar with a length to the heel with a *Xuren*, which means connecting two pieces of lappets to make up the front of a Chinese jacket, and *Goubian*, which means a kind of edge lining. *Shenyi* is a very practical dress which can be used as both ceremonial robe and daily dress.

(2) Hufu

Hufu refers to the garments worn by Tartars or those northwest minorities who lived in the Northwestern Regions. Compared with Han costume's broad shirt, long skirt and tunic, *Hufu* has a great change, which consists of narrow sleeved shirt, long trousers and boot. One of the most important characteristic of *Hufu* is that it is narrow and suitable for sport. *Hufu* is first accepted by the Han people, is around 300

B. C. in the Warring States Period. In order to enhance the army's strength, King Wuling of Zhao State introduces *Hufu* into Central Plain and abandons the *Yi*(shirt) and *Chang*(skirt) system.

4. Costumes in Qin and Han Dynasties

(1) The Robe

At the period of Qin and Han Dynasties, it is honorable for a male to wear a robe, which has wide sleeves with narrow laced cuffs. The ordinary people either bundle their hair, or wear a hat or a kerchief. They often wear a gown which is characterized in a crossed collar and narrow sleeves.

The costume in Western Han Dynasty follows *Shenyi* style, which is roughly divided into *Quju* and *Zhiju*.

Quju *Quju*, in fact, is the *Shenyi*, which is popular in the Warring States Period and is still worn in Han Dynasty, but it is more common in the early Western Han Dynasty. In Han Dynasty, *Quju* is not only worn by men but also by women. *Quju* is tight and narrow in the body part, with a horn-shape in the lower hem. With a length to the floor, when walking it can hide a person's feet. The *Quju* have two types of sleeves, the wide one and the narrow one mostly with edged cuffs. The collar part of *Quju* is quite distinctive, usually with a crossed collar, which is low enough to expose the coats worn inside. For example, if a person wore a few pieces of clothes, each layer of the collar would be exposed to the outside, sometimes, up to a maximum of three layers, which was called *Sanchongyi*(three folds of clothes).

Zhiju In Eastern Han Dynasty, wearing *Quju* for a man has been rare. It is common for a person to wear *Zhiju* but *Quju* also serves as a formal dress.

(2) Ruqun

In Han Dynasty, in addition to wear *Shenyi*, people wear the so-called *Ruqun*, a type of skirt which has *Ru*, a short coat, in the upper part and *Qun*, a skit, in the lower part. Generally the *Ru*, a short coat, is very short, only to the waist, and the

Qun, the skirt, is very long, drooping to the ground.

(3) The Color Limit

There is a regulation in Han Dynasty that ordinary people will not be allowed to wear various colored clothing. Ordinary people just can only wear clothes which are made of linen with natural color. It was not until the end of Western Han Dynasty (13 B. C.) that the ordinary people are allowed to wear dark blue and green clothes.

5. The Costumes in Wei and Jin Dynasties and the Period of Nanbeichao

In the period of Wei and Jin Dynasties and the period of Nanbeichao, the loose garment is one of the most important characteristic of the fashion of the clothes. Men's garment is so loose that it will expose naked chest and arms. The style of dressing in the period of Wei and Jin Dynasties and the period of Nanbeichao is easy, natural, and casual.

The women, in the period of Wei and Jin Dynasties and the period of Nanbeichao, are often dressed in the skirt with big sleeves, drooping to the ground. There are layers upon layers of laces decorated on the women's skirt, which is graceful and elegant.

6. Costumes in Sui and Tang Dynasties and Five Dynasties

Women in the Sui Dynasty wear tight cutty sarks with round or cross collars and a high-waisted long skirt with two ribbons streamers tied in the waist.

In 621 A. D. , the Emperor Gaozu of Tang, Li Yuan, officially promulgates the *Regulation of Clothes*, in which there are restrict and detailed provisions about the clothing style, color and adornments for the people in different positions, such as the emperor, the queen, ministers, officials, *Mingfu* (a woman in ancient China who was given a title or rank by the emperor) , gentry and civilian. Hence the dress system of Tang Dynasty dress system is officially established. Yellow, which is a special symbol of imperial power, can only worn by the emperor, queen, prince, princess, and members of the royal family. The rest of the people who wear yellow clothes are considered to commit a crime. In addition, the color of clothing is used to distinguish the rank of the officials, officials above the second rank wear purple clothes, officials above the fifth rank wear scarlet clothes, officials of sixth rank wear green clothes and officials of seventh rank wear cyan clothes.

(1) Offical's Clothing

The government officials in Tang Dynasty mostly wear robes with round collars and narrow cuffs. However, on such important occasions like rituals and sacrificial ceremony, they still wear ceremonial dress, the style of which is inherited from Sui Dynasty. They wear *Ze* (a headdress) or cage crown on the head, a front-opening large-sleeved shirt with buttons down the front on the upper part of the body, a *Weichang* (a kind of skirt) on the lower of the body decorated with jade and ribbons.

(2) Civilian's Clothing

Civilian men generally wear *Lanshan* (a kind of robe prevailed in Tang Dynasty) and wear soft angle scarf on the head.

Women generally wear right-colored and beautiful large-sleeved shirt and long dress. The topless, bared arm, veil, large sleeves, long dress is the most typical dressing image of women in Tang Dynasty.

The most fashionable women's clothing is *Ruqun*, which is the short shirt and long skirts, with a silk ribbon fastened on the upper part of waist which is almost to oxter.

7. Costumes in Song Dynasty

The clothing with a closed garment sculpts in Song Dynasty differs from those in Tang Dynasty. Furthermore, the color is serene and elegant and the tone of the color tends to be single.

(1) Women's Dress

Women's dress in Song Dynasty is made up of narrow sleeved short clothes and long skirt. A double-breasted *Beizi* which is quite similar to today's sleeveless sweater is usually put on outside the jacket. And the delicate lace is embroidered in the collarband and in the front part of the *Beizi*.

(2) Men's Clothing

The style of men's dress in Song Dynasty mostly follows that of Tang Dynasty. The populace usually wears a long gown with cross or round collars, and the clothes is often put into the waistband when people is laboring. There are only two colors, namely, white and black.

8. Costumes in Yuan Dynasty

The Mongols often tie their hair in the forehead up into a little lock, which is like a peach. The rest of the hair is braided into two pigtails coiling into two big rings and hanging behind ears. They often wear a Lizi cap (a traditional cap of Mongolian nationality in Yuan Dynasty) on the head.

(1) Men's Clothing (Zhisunfu)

A kind of clothes, which are called *Zhisunfu*, is the most common clothing in Yuan Dynasty. It is a short tight robe with a lot of smocking in the waist part, which is suitable of horsemanship and archery.

(2) Women's Clothing

The noblewomen in Yuan Dynasty often wear tall hats which look rather weird. Their robes are long and wide, which is not convenient for walking. As a result, two maids are needed to help them pull the hem of the robe in the back.

Generally, the civilian women wear black robes.

9. Costumes in Ming Dynasty

(1) Civilian's Clothing

After Zhu Yuanzhang takes the throne, he makes a new clothing regulation on the basis of those of the Zhou, Han, Tang, and Song Dynasties in order to restore the rites of Han Chinese people. The main clothing type is the gown shirt.

(2) Bufu

Officials usually wear *Bufu*, a kind of uniform for officals in Ming Dynasty, with a black gauze cap on the head. *Bufu* is a robe with a piece of squared embroidery pattern in its front part. A picture of a bird is embroidered in the civil officials' clothing, while a picture of a beast is embroidered in the military officers' clothing. The ranks and the grades of the officials can be seen from the color and pattern of the clothes. The superiority and inferiority can be differentiated from the length of the daily round-collar robe and its sleeve size. The people who wear longer robes with longer and larger sleeves are the people with superiority.

(3) The Scholar's Clothing

In Ming Dynasty, most of the Confucian scholars or scribes usually wear the long dress in black cloth, whose collars are either round or skew, with a cubic scarf on the head.

(4) Women's Clothing

The noblewomen in Ming Dynasty wear red robes, the sleeves of which are quite broad.

The common women only wear light-colored clothing. The skirts are wide, the types of which are varied.

10. Costumes in Qing Dynasty

After Man people intrudes into the inner land, the Han Chinese are forced to

wear the Man people's clothing. A clothing system, which is distinct from that of Ming Dynasty, takes shape. Qing Dynasty is a dynasty in which great changes have been made in clothing. Qing Dynasty is also an age in which the cultures of Man ethnic group and Han ethnic group are mixed together. Qing Dynasty also the only Non-Han dynasty that mainly preserves their original clothing customs after entering the Chinese Central Plains.

Man people's clothing changes the basic form of Chinese ancient costume. The clothing in Qing Dynasty is the turn-over point which connects China's ancient costume with modern costume, which is an essential prerequisite for men's *Magua* and women's cheongsam in modern society.

(1) Men's Long Robe and *Magua*

In Qing Dynasty a long robe with a *Magua*, which is a mandarin jacket worn over a gown, is the most favored clothing for a man. *Magua* is a short jacket worn outside the robe, which can only reach the waist. Its short sleeves can only cover the elbow. It is convenient to ride horses in this dress, so it's called *Magua*. The caps, people usually wear in their daily lives, are like watermelons with dark inside and red outside.

(2) Women's Clothing

The styles of Man clothing and Han clothing coexist in Qing Dynasty. Most Man women wear cheongsam, which forms a sharp contrast to the clothing styles of previous dynasties. Cheongsam, which replaces the ancient robes, not only saves the cloth but also is easy to make and wear. That is why it is widely accepted by the later generations.

第九章　中国八大菜系

中国地域辽阔，民族众多，因此饮食口味各种各样，但是都味美，令人垂涎。因为中国地方菜肴各具特色，总体来讲，中国饮食可以大致分为八大地方菜系，这种分类已被广为接受。

一、山东菜系

山东菜系由济南菜系和胶东菜系组成，清淡，不油腻，以其香、鲜、酥、软而闻名。胶东派擅长爆、炸、扒、熘、蒸，口味以鲜夺人，偏清淡。济南派则以汤著称，擅长爆、炒、烧、炸，口味以清、鲜、脆嫩为主。因为使用青葱和大蒜作为调料，山东菜系通常很辣。

名菜有九转大肠、糖醋鲤鱼、德州扒鸡等。

二、四川菜系

四川菜系，是最著名的中国菜系之一。四川菜以其香辣而闻名，味道多变，着重使用红辣椒，搭配使用青椒和花椒，产生出经典的刺激的味道。此外，大蒜、姜和豆豉也被应用于烹饪过程中。野菜和野禽常被选用为原料，油炸、无油炸、腌制和文火炖煮是基本的烹饪技术。川菜有“七滋八味”之说，“七滋”指甜、酸、麻、辣、苦、香、咸；“八味”是指鱼香、酸辣、椒麻、怪味、麻辣、红油、姜汁、家常。在国际上享有“食在中国，味在四川”的美誉。没有品尝过四川菜的人不算来过中国。

名菜有鱼香肉丝、宫保鸡丁、夫妻肺片、麻婆豆腐、回锅肉。

三、广东菜系

广东菜源自于广东省。由广州、潮州、东江三种地方菜组成。广东菜配料多，讲究鲜、嫩、爽、滑。以烹制海鲜见长，汤类、素菜、甜菜最具特色。广东人热衷于尝试用各种不同的肉类和蔬菜。不仅常用猛禽、走兽来烹饪出有创意的菜肴，还会使用很多来自世界其他地方的蔬菜，不大使用辣椒，而是烹饪出蔬菜和肉类自身的风味。广东菜系的基础烹饪方法包括烤、炒、煸、深炸、炖和蒸，其中蒸和炒最常用于保存天然风味。广东厨师也注重菜肴的艺术感。

名菜有烤乳猪、冻肉、冬瓜盅、大良炒牛奶等。

四、福建菜系

福建菜系由福州菜、泉州菜、厦门菜组成，以其精选的海鲜，漂亮的色泽，甜、酸、咸和香的味道而出名。烹调方法以清汤、干炸、爆炒为主，调味常用红糟，偏重酸甜，尤其讲究调汤，最特别的是它的“卤味”。

名菜有佛跳墙、醉糟鸡、糟汁氽海蚌、雪花鸡、菊花鲈鱼等。

五、江苏菜系

江苏菜由苏锡菜、南京菜和淮扬菜组成。以水产作为主要原料，注重原料的鲜味。烹饪技术包括炖、闷、蒸、烧、烤、炒、焙、煨等。其菜肴注重造型，讲究美观，色彩艳丽，其雕刻技术十分珍贵，其中瓜雕尤其著名。江苏菜的特色是淡、鲜、甜、雅。江苏菜以其精选的原料，精细的准备，不辣不温的口感而出名。

名菜有叫化鸡、狮子头、松鼠鳜鱼等。

六、浙江菜系

浙江菜系由杭州菜、宁波菜、绍兴菜组成，烹调方法以爆、炒、烩、炸为主，不油腻，以其菜肴的鲜、柔、滑、香而闻名。杭州菜是这三者中最出名的一个。

名菜有西湖醋鱼、东坡肉、家乡南肉、荷叶粉蒸肉、西湖莼菜汤、龙井

虾仁、杭州煨鸡等。

七、湖南菜系

湖南菜系由湘江地区、洞庭湖和湘西的地方菜肴组成。手法以熏、蒸、干炒为主，重酸辣。其制作精细，用料广泛，品种繁多，其特色是油多、色浓、味道极辣，讲究实惠。红辣椒、青辣椒和青葱是这一菜系中的必备品。

名菜有东安子鸡、红煨鱼翅、腊味合蒸、面包全鸭、油辣冬笋尖、板栗烧菜心、五元神仙鸡、麻辣仔鸡。

八、安徽菜系

安徽菜以徽州菜为代表。安徽菜注重烹饪过程的细节和原料的选择。擅长烧、煨、炖、蒸，注重油、色、火候，以烹调山珍野味著称。安徽厨师还会加入火腿和方糖来改善菜肴的口味。

名菜有火腿甲鱼、红烧果子狸、无为熏鸡、黄山炖鸽等。

Chapter 9　Chinese Eight Cuisine

China has a vast territory and diversified nationalities, which leads to the different food taste of different people in China. No matter how different the food taste is, the flavor of the food is always delicious and mouthwatering. Chinese food can be classified into eight local cuisine according to their characteristics, which has been widely accepted.

1. Shandong Cuisine

Shandong cuisine, mainly composed of Ji'nan and Jiaodong local food, which is light and oil free, is famous for its fragrant, fresh, crisp and soft. Jiaodong local food is characterized by quick-frying, deep frying, stewing and braising, the taste of which is fresh and light. While the Ji'nan local food is known for its soup and is characterized by quick-frying, stir-frying, roasting and frying, the flavor of which is clear, fresh, crisp and tender. In general, Shandong cuisine is spicy due to the adoption of green onion and garlic as seasoning ingredients.

Famous dishes of Shandong cuisine are "Braised Intestines in Brown Sauce", "Fried Carp with Sweet and Sour Sauce" and "Dezhou Braised Chicken", etc.

2. Sichuan Cuisine

Sichuan cuisine, which is famous for its flavor, spicy and various tastes, is one of the most famous Chinese cuisine in the world. Red chili, together with green pepper and Chinese red pepper, is widely applied in the cuisine, which can produce

classical and stimulating taste. In addition, garlic, ginger and fermented soya beans are also used in the cooking process. Edible wild herbs and wildfowl are always adopted as raw materials. Frying, non-frying, being salted and stewing with soft fire are the basic cooking methods of Sichuan cuisine. There are "Seven Tastes" and "Eight Flavors" in Sichuan cuisine. "Seven Tastes" are sweet, sour, tingle, spicy, bitter, savoury and salty, "Eight Flavors" are sweet and sour flavor, sour and hot, spicy and tingling, multi-flavor, pungent and spicy, red camphor oil, ginger juice and home style flavor. Sichuan cuisine enjoys the title of "food in China, taste in Sichuan" in the world. He, who does not taste the Sichuan cuisine, has not been really in China.

Famous dishes in Sichuan cuisine are "Shredded Pork with Garlic Sauce", "Saute Diced Chicken with Peanuts", "Pork Lungs in Chili Sauce", "Mapo Bean Curd", "Stir-fried Boiled Pork Slices in Hot Sauce".

3. Cantonese Cuisine

Cantonese cuisine, which originates from the southern province of Guangdong in China, is made up of the local dishes of Guangzhou, Chaozhou and Dongjiang. Cantonese cuisine is characterized by multiple ingredients and is particular about fresh, tender, cool and smooth of the dishes. Cantonese dish is famous for cooking seafood, soups, vegetables and sweet foods. Cantonese are keen on trying different meat and vegetables in their dishes. They not only choose raptors and beasts to produce originative dishes, but also apply vegetables from other places in the world to their dishes. They seldom adopt chilly in their dishes in order to get the original flavor of vegetables and meat. The basic cooking methods of Cantonese cuisine include baking, frying, stir-frying, deep frying, stewing and braising, among which frying and braising are frequently used to preserve the natural flavor. Meanwhile, Cantonese chefs are attaching importance to the artistic sense of the dishes.

Famous dishes in Cantonese cuisine include "Roast Suckling Pig", "Frozen Meat", "Wax Gourd Soup", and "Daliang Fried Milk".

4. Fujian Cuisine

Fujian cuisine is made up of Fuzhou cuisine, Quanzhou cuisine and Xiamen cuisine, which is distinguished for its choice of seafood, beautiful color and magic taste of sweet, sour, salty and savory. Light soup, deep frying, and quick frying are the main cooking methods. Red rice sauce is widely used as seasoning ingredients. The flavor of Fujian cuisine is sweet and sour with great emphasis on the ingredients of the soup in particular. The specialty of Fujian cuisine is braised food.

Famous dishes in Fujian cuisine include *Fotiaoqiang* (Steamed Abalone with Shark's Fin and Fish Maw in Broth), "Wined Chicken", "Sea Clam Quick Boiled with Red Rice Sauce", "Snowflakes Chickens", and "Fried Perch with Chrysanthemum".

5. Jiangsu Cuisine

Jiangsu cuisine, which is made up of Suxi cuisine, Nanjing cuisine and Huaiyang cuisine, adopts aquatic product as its principal raw materials and pay much attention to the delicate flavor of the raw materials. Stewing, braising, steaming, roasting, baking and stir-frying are the cooking methods of Jiangsu cuisine. Jiangsu cuisine pays great attention to the modeling of the dishes, which are always with beautiful appearance and colors. Its carving techniques are delicate, of which the melon carving technique is especially well known. The characteristics of Jiangsu cuisine are light, fresh, sweet and elegant. Therefore, Jiangsu cuisine is well known for its careful selection of ingredients, its meticulous preparation methodology, and its not-too-spicy, not-too-bland taste.

Famous dishes in Jiangsu cuisine include "Beggars' Chicken", "Braised Meatball", "Sweet and Sour Mandarin Fish".

6. Zhejiang Cuisine

Zhejiang cuisine is made up of Hangzhou cuisine, Ningbo cuisine and

Shaoxing cuisine. The cooking methods of Zhejiang cuisine are mainly quick-frying, frying, braising and deep frying. The Zhejiang cuisine is oil free and well known for its fresh, tender, smooth and fragrant. Hangzhou cuisine is the most famous among the Hangzhou cuisine, Ningbo cuisine and Shaoxing cuisine.

Famous dishes in Zhejiang cuisine include "West Lake Fish in Vinegar Gravy" "Dongpo Pork" "Hometown Salted Pork" "Steamed Pork with Rice Flavor in Lotus Leaves" "West Lake Soup" "Longjing Shrimp" and "Hangzhou Stewed Chicken".

7. Hu'nan Cuisine

Hu'nan cuisine is made up of Xiangjiang cuisine, Dongtinghu cuisine and Xiangxi cuisine. Hu'nan cuisine, which is characterized by its sour and spicy, adopts the way of smoking, steaming and deep frying. The cuisine is produced with careful making, wide ingredients and great varieties. The characteristics of the Hu'nan cuisine are oily, colory, and extremely spicy and pay attention to consumers' material benefit. Red chili, green chili and green onions are the essential seasoning materials in Hu'nan cuisine.

Famous dishes in Hu'nan Cuisine include "Dong'an Chicken" "Stewed Fins" "Steamed Multiple Preserved Ham" "Bread Duck" "Fried Tips of Bamboo Shoots with Chilly" "Roast Flowering Cabbage with Chestnut" "Immortal Chicken with Five Elements" and "Spicy and Hot Chicks".

8. Anhui Cuisine

Anhui cuisine is famous for its Huizhou cuisine, which pays great attention to the details of cooking process and the selection of the raw materials. It is characterized by roasting, braising, stewing and steaming and the Anhui cuisine attaches great importance on oil, color, duration and degree of heating and known for cooking delicacies from mountains and sea. Sometimes, the chefs add some ham and cube sugar in the cuisine for the taste.

Famous dishes in Anhui cuisine include "Ham Stewed Turtle" "Stewed Civet Cats" "Smoked Chicken" and "Mount Huangshan Braised Pigeon".

第十章　中国茶文化

茶，是中华民族的举国之饮，它发于神农，闻于鲁周公，兴于唐朝，盛于宋代，在漫长的岁月中，中华民族在茶的培育、品饮、应用以及对茶文化的形成和发展上，为人类文明留下了绚丽光辉的一页。

中国是茶的故乡，制茶、饮茶已有几千年历史。茶有健身、治疾之药物疗效，又富欣赏情趣，可陶冶情操。品茶、待客是中国人高雅的娱乐和社交活动。

中国人饮茶，注重一个“品”字。“品茶”不但是鉴别茶的优劣，也带有神思遐想和领略饮茶情趣之意。

在百忙之中泡上一壶浓茶，择雅静之处，自斟自饮，可以消除疲劳、涤烦益思、振奋精神，也可以细啜慢饮，达到美的享受，使精神世界升华到高尚的艺术境界。

中国茶文化的形成是在魏晋南北朝，在唐宋达到鼎盛期。茶文化是指人类在社会历史过程中所创造的有关茶的物质财富和精神财富的总和，包括了茶史、茶诗、茶词、茶道、茶艺、茶的栽培及加工等。茶文化的核心为茶道和茶艺。

茶文化是中国文化的特有现象，在中国古代的社会文化发展体系中长期占有重要地位，尤其是中国古代众多的文人雅士和士大夫对茶和茶文化的倾心与投入，在一定程度上给塑造中国茶文化的内在品性带来了极大的影响。古代文人“七件宝”指的就是琴、棋、书、画、诗、酒、茶。茶通六艺，是中国传统文化艺术的载体。

在中国，凡是来了客人，沏茶敬茶的礼仪是必不可少的，以茶待客、以

茶代酒历来是中国人的传统习俗，上至帝王将相、文人墨客，下至挑夫小贩、平民百姓，莫不以茶为礼，无不以茶为好。茶文化已经渗透到了中国人的方方面面，与婚礼、祭祀、宗教、歌舞、戏曲、美术、小说等有着千丝万缕割不断的联系。于是，茶成为了中国传统文化艺术的载体。

一、茶的起源

传说神农氏在野外以釜锅煮水时，刚好有几片叶子飘进锅中，煮好的水，其色微黄，喝入口中甘甜止渴、提神醒脑，神农以过去尝百草的经验判断它是一种药，从而发现了茶。这是有关中国饮茶起源最普遍的说法。

另外一种传说是：神农氏有个水晶肚子，由外观可得见食物在胃肠中蠕动的情形，当他尝茶时，发现茶在肚内到处流动，查来查去，把肠胃洗涤得干干净净，因此神农称这种植物为“查”，再转成“茶”字，而成为茶的起源。

二、茶的分类

（一）红　茶

红茶是一种全发酵茶（发酵程度大于 80%），其名字得自其汤色的红。功夫红茶是中国特有的红茶品种。

（二）绿　茶

绿茶是中国产量最多的一类茶叶，其花色品种之多居世界首位。绿茶是不经过发酵的茶，即将鲜叶经过摊晾后直接下到二三百度的热锅里炒制，以保持其绿色的特点。

（三）白　茶

白茶是中国特产，它加工时不炒不揉，只将细嫩、叶背满茸毛的茶叶晒干或用文火烘干，而使白色茸毛完整地保留下来。白茶主要产于福建的福鼎、政和、松溪和建阳等县，有“银针”“白牡丹”“贡眉”“寿眉”几种。

（四）青　茶

青茶属半发酵茶，即制作时适当发酵，使叶片稍有红变，是介于绿茶与红茶之间的一种茶类。它既有绿茶的鲜爽，又有红茶的浓醇。因其叶片中间为绿色，叶缘呈红色，故有“绿叶红镶边”之称。

（五）黄　茶

黄茶是在制茶过程中，经过闷堆渥黄，因而形成黄叶、黄汤。分“黄芽茶”（君山银芽）、“黄小茶”（沩山毛尖）和“黄大茶”（霍山黄大茶）。

（六）黑　茶

黑茶原料粗老，加工时堆积发酵时间较长，使叶色呈暗褐色。是藏族、蒙古族、维吾尔族等兄弟民族不可缺少的日常必需品。云南的普洱茶和湖南的安化黑茶是中国传统的经典黑茶。

三、茶叶评定

茶业的评定是通过人的感官（视觉、嗅觉、味觉和触觉）对茶叶的形状、色泽、香气、滋味、汤色、叶底六个因素进行综合评定。评定方法是“干看外形”和“湿评内质（冲水开泡）”这两个程序。外形看嫩度、条索、色泽、整碎、净度和干香。湿评品质是指茶叶经沸水冲泡后鉴别其香气、汤色、滋味和叶底。

四、茶　具

茶具是因人们饮茶的需要而产生的，随着历史的演变，它成了高雅的艺术品和世俗生活用品的统一体。作为历史产物的茶具，因其满足了人们不断变化的需求，不断发展，每个时期的茶具呈现出了鲜明的个性。历史上每个时代遗留下来的茶具能使人焕发精神，并帮助人们深刻了解每个时期的茶文化特性。透过茶具，我们可以窥视当时的社会文化。

茶具按其狭义的范围是指茶杯、茶壶、茶碗、茶盏、茶碟、茶盘等饮茶用具。中国的茶具，种类繁多，造型优美，除实用价值外，也有颇高的艺术

价值，因而驰名中外，为历代茶爱好者所青睐。

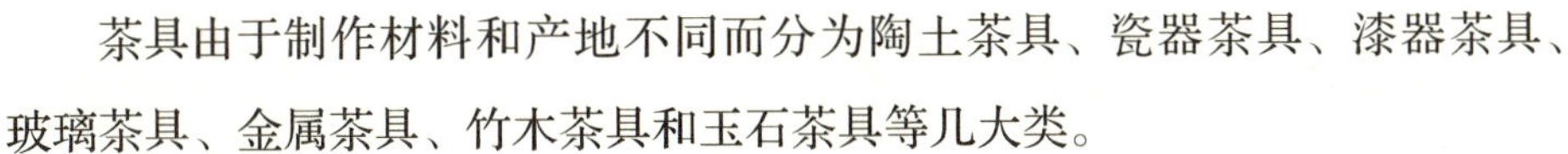

茶具由于制作材料和产地不同而分为陶土茶具、瓷器茶具、漆器茶具、玻璃茶具、金属茶具、竹木茶具和玉石茶具等几大类。

（一）陶土茶具

陶器中的佼佼者首推宜兴紫砂茶具。紫砂壶和一般陶器不同，其里外都不敷釉，采用当地的紫泥、红泥、团山泥抟制焙烧而成。由于成陶火温较高，烧结密致，胎质细腻，既不渗漏，又有肉眼看不见的气孔，经久耐用，还能汲附茶汁，蕴蓄茶味。传热不快，不致烫手；若热天盛茶，不易酸馊。即使冷热剧变，也不会破裂，如有必要，甚至还可直接放在炉灶上煨炖。艺人们采用传统的篆刻手法，把绘画和正、草、隶、篯、篆各种装饰手法施用在紫砂陶器上，使之成为观赏和实用巧妙结合的产品。

（二）瓷器茶具

因为瓷器茶具导热较慢、保暖适中，所以与茶不会发生化学反应，沏茶能获致较好的色、香、味。并且这类茶具造型好看、质感浩博、扮饰洒脱，极具欣赏价值。

（三）漆器茶具

漆器茶具始于清代，主要产于福建福州一带。漆器茶具通常是一把茶壶连同四只茶杯，存放在圆形或长方形的茶盘内，壶、杯、盘通常呈一色，多为黑色，也有黄棕、棕红、深绿等色，并融书画于一体，饱含文化意蕴。漆器茶具轻巧美观，色泽光亮，明镜照人，又不怕水浸，能耐温、耐酸碱腐蚀。脱胎漆茶具除有实用价值外，还有很高的艺术欣赏价值，常为鉴赏家所收藏。

（四）玻璃茶具

玻璃质地透明，光泽夺目，外形可塑性大，形态各异，用途广泛。玻璃杯泡茶，茶汤的鲜艳色泽、茶叶的细嫩柔软、茶叶在整个冲泡过程中的上下蹿动、叶片的逐渐舒展等，可以一览无余，可说是一种动态的艺术欣赏。特别是冲泡各类名茶，茶具晶莹剔透，杯中轻雾缥缈，澄清碧绿，芽叶朵朵，

亭亭玉立，观之赏心悦目，别有风趣。

（五）金属茶具

金属用具是指由金、银、铜、铁、锡等金属材料制作而成的器具，它是中国最古老的日用器具之一。金属贮茶器具的密闭性要比纸、竹、木、瓷、陶等好，具有较好的防潮、避光性能，更有利于散茶的保藏。

（六）竹木茶具

竹木茶具来源广，制作方便，对茶无污染，对人体又无害，因此，自古至今，一直受到茶人的欢迎。但是不能长时间使用，无法长久保存，只是到了清代，四川才出现了一种竹编茶具。竹编茶具由内胎和外套组成，内胎多为陶瓷类饮茶器具，外套用精选慈竹，经劈、启、揉、匀等多道工序，制成细如发丝的柔软竹丝，经烤色、染色，再按茶具内胎形状、大小编织嵌合，使之成为整体如一的茶具。这种茶具，不但色调和谐，美观大方，而且能保护内胎，减少损坏；同时，泡茶后不易烫手，并富含艺术欣赏价值。

（七）玉石茶具

玉石做的茶壶，还有一定的保健作用，用玉茶壶装一般清水数小时后，水中便含有大量对人体有益的微量元素，经常饮用能调节人体新陈代谢，具有抗氧化，防衰老及消石、防石的作用。据说用玉制成的茶壶在酷暑季节，具有泡茶五天内仍可保持茶水的色、香、味不变的神奇特点。因玉石材质很少，价格高昂，所以一般很少有。

五、喝茶礼仪

当今社会，客来敬茶成为人们日常社交和家庭生活中普遍的往来礼仪。当别人给自己倒茶时，为了表示感谢和敬意，用自己的手指轻叩桌面数下，称为“叩手礼”。

（一）叩手礼

正规的扣手礼（客人专用回礼）是这样的：右手握拳，因为是回礼，你

就是左撇子也得用右手的，大拇指的指尖对食指的第二指节，伸直屈着的食指和中指，用食指和中指的第二节的面，轻轻点击你面前的茶桌的桌面三下。

这种“叩手礼”或称“叩指礼”的来历，还有一个传说，据说是跟乾隆微服私访有关。传说当年乾隆皇帝带着两个太监微服私访下江南，来到松江，到一间茶馆店里喝茶。茶店老板拎了一只长嘴茶吊来冲茶，端起茶杯，茶壶“沓啦啦、沓啦啦、沓啦啦”一连三洒，茶杯里正好浅浅一杯，茶杯外没有滴水溅出。乾隆皇帝不明其意，忙问：“掌柜的，你倒茶为何不多不少齐巧洒三下？”老板笑着回答：“客官，这是我们茶馆的行规，这叫‘凤凰三点头’。”乾隆皇帝一听，夺过老板的水吊，端起一只茶杯，也要来学学这“凤凰三点头”。

这只杯子是太监的，皇帝向太监倒茶，这不是反礼了吗。在皇宫里太监要跪下来三呼万岁，可是在这三教九流罗杂的茶馆酒肆，暴露了身份，是有性命之虞的。当太监的当然不是笨人，急中生智，忙用手指叩叩桌子表示以“叩手”来代替“叩首”。“以手代叩”的动作一直流传至今，表示对他人敬茶的谢意。

（二）饮茶方式

汉族的饮茶方式大致可以分为品茶、喝茶、吃茶。古人重在“品”，近代多为“喝”，至于“吃”，则为数不多、范围不广。

品　重在意境，以鉴别茶叶香气、滋味和欣赏茶汤、茶姿为目的，自娱自乐。要细品缓啜，“三口方知真味，三番才能动心”。

喝　以清凉解渴为目的，大碗急饮，或不断冲泡，连饮带咽。

吃　连茶带水一起咀嚼咽下。

（三）喝茶时的禁忌

喝茶忌“一口闷”或者“亮杯底”。另外，第一泡的第一口茶汤，千万不可当着主人的面吐了出来，这个被视为极大的失礼，甚至是一种挑衅。

Chapter 10 Chinese Tea Culture

As a national drink of China, tea originates from Shennong (patron of agriculture) , becomes famous at the time of Duke Zhoulu, and flourishes in Tang Dynasty and prevails Song Dynasty. In the long process of history, Chinese people have made great contributions to the cultivation, drinking, appliance of the tea, as well as the formation and development of the tea culture in human civilization.

Tea originates from China, in which planting tea and drinking tea have lasted for thousands of years. Tea has a curative effect of health-keeping and medical treatment as well as appreciation and mental cultivation. Tea tasting and entertaining guests with tea are elegant entertainment and social activity in China.

When drinking tea, Chinese people put emphasis upon tasting tea which is not only about justification of the quality but meditation and tasting as well.

Making a pot of strong tea in a busy schedule, securing a serene space to absorb yourself in solitude, and pouring yourself a cup of tea and drinking it off, you will get rid of fatigue, refresh your mind and inspire your spirits. When sipping the tea, you can transcend yourself to aesthetics and reach the noble artistic realm.

Chinese tea culture has formed its shape between Wei and Jin Dynasties, and the period of Nanbeichao, and has prevailed in Tang and Song Dynasties. Tea culture is the total material and spiritual fortune created by human beings in the history of society, which includes the history, poems, sonnets, ceremonies, arts, cultivation and manufacturing of tea with tea ceremony and arts as its core.

As a special cultural phenomenon in Chinese culture, tea culture plays an

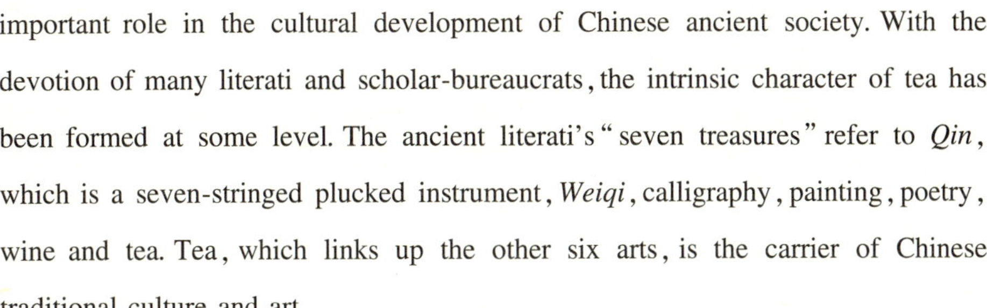

important role in the cultural development of Chinese ancient society. With the devotion of many literati and scholar-bureaucrats, the intrinsic character of tea has been formed at some level. The ancient literati's "seven treasures" refer to *Qin*, which is a seven-stringed plucked instrument, *Weiqi*, calligraphy, painting, poetry, wine and tea. Tea, which links up the other six arts, is the carrier of Chinese traditional culture and art.

In China, when a guest comes to visit you, the etiquette of making a tea and offering a tea is essential because it is Chinese tradition to entertain the guests with tea, and to offer guests with tea instead of wine. From the emperors, military or political leaders and literati to porters, hawkers and common people, tea serves as a gift and hobby as well. Tea culture has soaked into every aspect of Chinese life, which has linked with marriage, god-worshipping, religion, singing and dancing, operas, arts and novels. Hence, tea has become the carrier of Chinese traditional culture and arts.

1. The Origins of Tea

It is said that when Shennong once is cooking water in a pot outside, several leaves happen to drop into his pot, which makes the boiled water become slightly yellowish. When drinking it, the water became sweet and refreshing. Judging by his past experience of testing a hundred varieties of herbs, Shennong concludes that it's some kind of herb and thus the most common believe about the origin of tea.

Another legend about the origin of tea is also related with Shennong. It is said that he has a transparent belly in which the moving of food digestion can be seen in his intestines and stomach. When trying tea, the liquid is moving along to wash the intestines and stomach thoroughly, so he called this plant *Cha* which means "to check". Then *Cha* (to check) was translated as *Cha* (tea), which is another origin of today's tea.

2. The Classifications of Tea

(1) Black Tea

Black tea is fully fermented (above 80%) which is named from the dark-reddish soup. Gongfu black teas are one of China's specialties.

(2) Green Tea

Green tea is the most productive in China with the most varieties among the teas in the world. Green tea is not fermented. When the fresh leaves are spread and suntanned, they are stir-fried in hot pot with a temperature of 200℃ - 300℃.

(3) White Tea

White tea is also China's specialty without stir-frying or rubbing during the process of manufacturing. To completely reserve its white fuzz, the tender and fuzzy leaves will only be suntanned or dried over slow fire. White tea is mainly produced in Fuding, Zhenghe, Songxi, Jianyang counties in Fujian Province with varieties as Yinzhen (Silver needles), *Baimudan* (White poeny), *Gongmei* (Tributes eyebrows), and *Shoumei*(Eyebrows of longevity).

(4) Qingcha

Qingcha, which is also called Oolong tea, is half fermented with a little bit reddish color in its leaves during the manufacturing of proper ferment, so the color is between green tea and black tea. *Qingcha* contains the refreshing flavor of green tea and the mellow of black tea which is called "green leaves with a red edging".

(5) Yellow Tea

During the manufacturing of yellow tea, leaves and soup become yellowish because of the smouldered piling, therefore product has the yellow leaf and yellow tea soup. The varieties are *Huangyacha*(Silver sprouts in Junshan), *Huangxiaocha*

(Fuzzy sprouts in Weishan), *Huangdacha*(Big-leaved tea in Huoshan).

(6) Heicha

Heicha, which is a post-fermented tea, is made from rough and old tea leaves with long time fermenting which makes the tea leaves become darkened. *Heicha* is a daily necessity for such ethnic groups as Tibetan nationality, Mongolian nationality, Uighur nationality and other fraternal nationalities. Traditional representatives of *Heicha* are Pu'er tea in Yunnan Province and Anhua Heicha in Hu'nan Province.

3. The Evaluation of Tea

The Evaluation of tea includes shapes, colors, fragrance, tastes, soup and leaves in the bottom through feelings (eyesight, smell, taste and touch). The Basic two procedures are "examining the shape when it's dry" and "evaluating the quality when it is brewed". Shape judging means the tenderness, tissue organization, color, integrity, clearness and flavor, when it is brewed, the quality of tea will depend on the fragrance, soup, taste and leaves in the bottom.

4. Tea Sets

Tea sets are created with people's needs, changing with history evolving, and becomes a unity of elegant arts craft and earthly supplies. As a historical legacy, tea sets satisfies people's varying needs and develops itself with distinguished characteristics in every period. Tea sets in each period of Chinese history inspire us to understand characteristics of tea culture in each period profoundly. Through tea set, we can get to know the social culture of that period.

In its narrow scale, tea sets include cups, kettles, bowls, saucers and plates, etc. Chinese tea sets is various and beautiful. Besides its practical function, it enjoys high artistic value and reputation domestically and abroad, cherished by tea fans in history.

According to its materials and manufacturing place, tea sets can be classified

into earthenware tea sets, porcelain tea sets, lacquer tea sets, glass tea sets, metal tea sets, bamboo tea sets and jade tea sets.

(1) Earthenware Tea Sets

The most outstanding earthenware tea sets is Yixing purple clay tea sets. Different from common tea sets, Yixing purple clay tea sets are not glazed inside and outside but calcinated from local purple mud, red mud and Tuanshan mud. The high firing temperature makes intense and exquisite texture of the wares with no leaks and invisible blowholes which make them durable. These blowholes can absorb tea soup and maintain flavor and with a slow hot-transfer rate, which makes the ware not be very hot. When in summer, the tea soup does not easily become sour and rotten. Besides, when there is abrupt exchange from cold to hot temperature, the ware will not crack. If necessary, purple clay wares can be heated over fire directly. Craftsmen adopt traditional engraving skills, and apply Chinese painting and various calligraphy styles on the tea sets, which makes their products not only for application but also for appreciation.

(2) Porcelain Tea Sets

The slow thermal conductivity of porcelain wares leads to moderate warm-keeping, which makes the chemical reaction with the tea not occur. When making tea with the porcelain set, the shape of tea leaves, the fragrance and flavor will be well maintained in its nice model and delicate texture, which is highly appreciated by audience.

(3) Lacquer Tea Sets

Lacquer tea set, which originates from Qing Dynasty, are mainly made in Fuzhou City in Fujian Province. The common lacquer set is one kettle with four cups in a round or square plate which is usually presented as a whole black set. Besides, yellowish brown, reddish brown and dark green are common colors of these tea sets, which are embodied with calligraphy and painting for literacy

appreciation. Lacquer tea sets are characterized by the slight weight, bright color and shinning surface, good qualities of water-proofing, high temperature-resistance, and acid and alkali corrosion-resistance. Bodiless lacquer tea sets not only have practical functions but also have some high artistic value for appreciation, which are favored by collectors.

(4) Glass Tea Sets

With a transparent texture, bright color, and various shapes, glass tea sets are widely used. When making a tea with glass wares, the soup is clear with tender and soft tea leaves dancing up and down, extending out gradually in the glass as dynamic artistic show in a panorama. If famous teas are made with crystal tea sets, jade green soup is covered with mist and tea buds are vivid and tender, which presents a special feast to the eye.

(5) Metal Tea Sets

Metal tea sets, which are made of gold, silver, iron and tin, are one of the oldest wares in China. Metal wares enclose teas much better than paper, bamboo, wood, porcelain and earthen-wares as well as moisture proof. It keeps teas out of the sun and better for tea leaves.

(6) Bamboo and Wooden Tea Sets

These tea sets are convenient to make for their wide sources and do not contaminate to tea and our health. Bamboo and wooden tea sets are cherished by fans from ancient until now with a fault that can't be used for a long time, not mention of preserving as collection. Until Qing Dynasty, there appears a bamboo waved tea set in Sichuan Province which is made of inner tube and outside wrap. The inner tube is earthen and outside wrap is by Cizhu bamboo, with very complex processes of cutting, opening, rubbing and evening, etc. Bamboo is made into even and soft hairs, then the bamboo hairs are baked and dyed to wave according to the shapes and sizes of the inner tube. After those processes, a whole

tea set is accomplished. These tea sets are not only harmonious in color but beautiful. Its inner tube is protected from damage and hot-proofing with exuberant artistic value.

(7) Jade Tea Sets

Kettles made from jade are heath-keeping for lots of micro-elements produce in the water automatically after clear water is contained in a jade kettle for several hours. Being drinked frequently, the water can regulate body metabolism reduce and prevent calculi, which is anti-aging. It is said that in the hottest summer, tea soup, which remains in a jade kettle for five days will still be as fragrant and tasty. Even for this magic function, jade is pricy and rare because lack of material.

5. Etiquette of Tea Drinking

In nowadays society, tea etiquette has become rites in daily communications and family lives. When others make tea for you, to show your gratitude and respect, you can knock gently at the table several times and it's "knocking etiquette".

(1) Koushouli

A formal *Koushouli*, etiquette for returning hospitality to host, is to fist your right hand even if you are left-handed because it's returning hospitality. The tip of thumb turns directly to the second knuckle of index finger and the index finger and middle finger extend straightly. Knock slightly at the table three times with the pulp of second knuckle of the index finger and middle finger.

There is a legend of this *Koushouli* which is related with Emperor Qianlong, who wears plain clothes to experience the public life in the area of south China around the Yangtze River in Qing Dynasty. When the emperor is visiting Songjiang County in south China in plain clothes, he also brings two eunuchs with him to drink in a tea house. The owner of the tea house makes tea with a long-spout kettle, holding cup and filling hot water three times with gurgling. When the tea is

done, the tea soup is just reach the edge of the cup and does not splash out. Emperor Qianlong does not understand and ask, "Why do you fill water three times?" The owner replies, "My dearest guest, this is our rule called Three Nods of Phoenix." Emperor Qianlong grabs the kettle and holds a cup to imitate the owner's interesting motions.

The cup is used by one of the eunuchs. If emperor has ever made tea for a servant, it will be a great violation to loyal authority. If it were in the Forbidden City, eunuchs would knee down in front of emperor and call "Long Live the King!" three times. But in a tea house with people of all sorts, it will be dangerous if Qianlong's real identity is revealed. The eunuch is not a jerk, and quick-wittedly. He knocked his fingers at the table to show his respect in stead of bow. Until now, knocking with fingers as substation of kneeling is custom for returning other's tea.

(2) Ways of Tea Drinking

There are three basic ways of Han people's tea drinking, appreciating, drinking and eating. Ancient people emphasize appreciating, but in modern times, the way is usually drinking. As far as eating, it's seldom seen.

Tea Appreciation Artistic conception is most cherished by the drinkers who entertain themselves with identifying the tea leaves' fragrance, flavor, soup and shape. Only sipping and appreciating for several mouthfuls you are touched.

Tea Drinking To drink tea is to drink anxiously in big tea wares in order to relieve thirsty and cool. With repeating brewing, tea soup is swallowed.

Tea Eating To eat is to chew and swallow the tea leaves together with soup.

(3) Taboos for Tea Drinking

To avoid one big swallow and show the bottom of your tea cup. Besides, the first soup of the first brewing should never be spat out from your mouth in front of your host because this is regarded as huge impoliteness or even provocation.

第十一章　中国酒文化

酒是用高粱、大麦、米、葡萄或其他谷物和水果经发酵制成的含乙醇的饮料。在中国饮食文化中，酒与菜总是主题，美酒和佳肴的组合构成了中国传统饮食文化的基本元素。酒不仅仅是饮的艺术，也是调味人生的艺术。在古人眼里，酒是圣物，中国的饮酒艺术更是庄严的、神圣的，有着一整套远古酒事活动的俗尚和风格。中华民族5 000 年历史长河中，酒和酒类文化一直占据着重要地位。酒文化作为一种特殊的文化形式，在传统的中国文化中有其独特的地位。在几千年的文明史中，酒几乎渗透到社会生活中的各个领域。无论喜宴、庆功、接风、饯别，还是祭奠、祈福、消愁、解闷，甚至医疗、养生、健美、长寿，几乎都离不开酒。

中国的酒文化十分发达，中国人的饮酒，不仅饮人、饮时、饮地，还糅合了诗歌、书画、风俗、游戏，把物质享乐的酒升华为更高级的精神享乐；通过饮酒来影响人们的观念、感情、行为、人际关系，从而创造出了颇具浪漫色彩的生活意境和文化氛围。

一、酒的起源

中国是酒的故乡，也是酒文化的发源地，是世界上酿酒最早的国家之一。中国酒源远流长，品种繁多，名酒荟萃，享誉中外。酒的酿造，在中国已有相当悠久的历史。在中国数千年的文明发展史中，酒与文化的发展基本上是同步进行的。中国酒的历史，可以追溯到上古时期。中国酒的兴起，已有5 000 年的历史了。

关于酒的起源，大致有上天造酒说、猿猴造酒说、仪狄造酒说、杜康造

酒说四种传说。这些传说都颇有意趣，有文学渲染的成分，有人们想象的成分，全都是源于人们对酒的敬意和赞美。

二、酒的分类

（一）按酿造工艺分

酒按酿造工艺分，可以分为酿造酒、蒸馏酒和配制酒。

酿造酒　酿造酒是将水果、谷物等原料发酵后直接提取或采取压榨获得的酒。其酒精含量不高，一般不超过15%，刺激性较弱。除含有酒精外，还有酿酒原料中所含有的营养成分或分解产物，营养价值较高，如黄酒、啤酒、葡萄酒等。

蒸馏酒　蒸馏酒是将水果、谷物等原料先进行发酵，然后将发酵液进行蒸馏而制成的酒。蒸馏酒的酒精含量较高，通常在30%以上，如白酒。

配制酒　配制酒是以原汁酒或蒸馏酒作基酒，与酒精或非酒精物质进行勾兑，兼用浸泡、调和等多种手段调制成的酒。这类酒种类最多，食用价值依选用酒基和添加辅料不同而异，如杨梅烧酒、竹叶青、三蛇酒、人参酒、利口酒、味美思等。

（二）按酒精含量分

酒按酒精含量分，可以分为高度酒、中度酒、低度酒。

高度酒　高度酒是指酒精含量在40%以上的酒，如茅台酒和五粮液等。

中度酒　中度酒是指酒精含量在20%～40%之间的酒，如竹叶青、米酒、黄酒等。

低度酒　低度酒是指酒精含量在20%以下的酒，如葡萄酒、桂花陈酿、香槟酒等。

三、酒品的风格

任何一种酒品都有其独特的风格，不同的酒品风格各异，甚至同一品种的酒风格也会不同。酒品的风格是由很多因素共同形成的，这些因素包括酒品的色、香、味和体等。

（一）色

酒液的色泽来源有酿酒原料、生产过程（生色或退色）、陈酿和调色等。

（二）香

酒品香气形成的原因十分复杂，酒香的来源有酿酒原料、发酵过程和陈酿。

中国白酒的酒香风格有清香型、浓香型、酱香型、米香型、复合香型。清香型白酒以汾酒为代表。浓香型白酒以五粮液和泸州老窖为代表。酱香型白酒以茅台酒为代表。米香型白酒以桂林三花酒和广东长乐烧为代表。复香型（混香型）白酒以西凤酒为代表。

（三）味

酒味的好坏基本确定了酒的身价。酒的味道主要有甜、酸、苦、辣、涩。

（四）体

体是酒品风格的综合表现。在中国专指酒的色、香、味的综合表现，而国际酒界许多专家所说的“体”，专指口味的抽象表现。

四、酒器类型

酒器是随着酒的发明而产生的。酒器是酒文化的重要载体，通过各代的酒器，可以了解传统文化，研究中国悠久的历史。中国古代酒器的品类极多，功用各异，质料多种多样。从用途上大体分成盛储器、温煮器、饮用器等。就质料来说，从古至今有陶器、瓷器、漆器、玉器、青铜器、金银器、玻璃器、象牙器、兽角器、蚌贝器、竹木器等。

盛酒器主要有尊、卣、瓶等。

煮酒器主要有爵、角、斝等。

饮酒器主要有觥 、觚 、杯等。

五、酒的作用

酒以其特有功能和风格存在于社会并渗透到社会生活的各个方面。早在商周之际，酒已盛行，之后便与政治、经济、军事、医药、文学、艺术、礼仪结下不解之缘。酒的功能很多，日常生活中的贺喜、祝捷、感恩、谢师、遣忧、浇愁、解闷、压惊、赠别、团聚、访友、待客、迎宾等，都离不开酒，所以生活因酒而更加丰富精彩。所以有“无酒不成席”“无酒不成礼”“无酒不成俗”之说，形成了中国特有的酒文化。概括地讲，酒可以提神、御寒、治病、交友、解忧等等。

（一）酒与社会交际

人只要在社会上生活，就离不开交往，而酒就成了交际的媒介，酒在人际交往方面有着重要作用，它是沟通思想、构建友谊的桥梁，是密切关系、联络感情的纽带。在人类社会中，人们常以酒为媒介进行各种各样的交往活动。诸如以酒祭祀、以酒祝寿、以酒宴婚、以酒待客、以酒会友、以酒言志、以酒壮行、以酒为乐、以酒解愁、以酒祛病等，古今皆然。

中国人的好客，在酒席上发挥得淋漓尽致。人与人的感情交流往往在敬酒时得到升华。中国人敬酒时，往往都想让对方多喝点酒，以表示自己尽到了主人之谊，客人喝得越多，主人就越高兴，说明客人看得起自己；如果客人不喝酒，主人就会觉得有失面子。

（二）酒与中国文学创作

酒能刺激神经中枢，扩张血管，加快心律，促进血液循环。这种刺激能在一定条件下，作用于有某种才能的人，产生意想不到的神奇作用，成了才智和胆略的催化剂，造就了无数英雄豪杰和文学家、艺术家，使他们的功绩和作品名流后世。

东晋书法家王羲之被后人称为“书圣”，其代表作《兰亭集序》就是在酒酣之际，乘兴挥毫而作。全文“之”字最多，无一雷同，酒醒后他自己都不信能写出这样俊逸绝伦的字。后来他曾多次再写《兰亭集序》，却再也未达到那次酒兴正浓时所作。

“李白斗酒诗百篇”形象地说明了酒与诗的关系，王维、孟浩然、李白、杜甫、贺知章、韩愈、柳宗元、刘禹锡、白居易、杜牧、李商隐等无一不饮酒，无一不写酒。

（三）酒与医药保健

酒是一种祛寒提神的药。李时珍说“酒是百药之长”。适量饮酒对身体有调适作用，酒能疏通经脉、行气活血、蠲痹散结、温阳祛寒，疏肝解郁、宣情畅意，适量饮酒能增加唾液和胃液的分泌，促进胃肠的消化和吸收，促进血液循环；起兴奋精神、强心提神、消除疲劳、促进睡眠等作用。

（四）酒与政治

与酒有关的政治家、英雄豪杰很多，例如秦穆公酒送盗马人，楚庄王擅用酒谋，越王勾践投醪鼓士气，刘邦醉唱《大风歌》，曹操煮酒论英雄，隋炀帝临死要酒喝，赵匡胤杯酒释兵权，朱元璋以酒试大臣，项羽大摆“鸿门宴”，荆轲酒后刺秦王，霍去病倾酒入泉，关云长温酒斩华雄、单刀赴会，王安石叹“酒逢知己千杯少”，等等。

六、饮酒礼仪

饮酒作为一种饮食的文化，在远古时代就形成了一种礼节。中国古代饮酒有以下一些礼节：

主人和宾客一起饮酒时，要相互跪拜。晚辈在长辈面前饮酒，叫侍饮，通常要先行跪拜礼，然后坐入次席。长辈命晚辈饮酒，晚辈才可举杯；长辈酒杯中的酒尚未饮完，晚辈也不能先饮尽。

古代饮酒的礼仪约有四步：拜、祭、啐、卒爵。即先做出拜的动作，表示敬意；接着把酒倒出一点在地上，祭谢大地生养之德；然后尝尝酒味，并加以赞扬令主人高兴；最后，仰杯而尽。

在酒宴上，主人要向客人敬酒（叫“酬”），客人要回敬主人（叫“酢”），敬酒时还有说上几句敬酒辞。客人之间相互也可敬酒（叫“旅酬”）。有时还要依次向人敬酒（叫“行酒”）。敬酒时，敬酒的人和被敬酒的人都要“避席”，起立。普通敬酒以三杯为度。

七、酒　令

酒令，是酒席上的一种助兴游戏，一般是指席间推举一人为令官，余者听令轮流说诗词、联语或玩其他类似游戏，违令者或负者罚饮，所以又称“行令饮酒”。最早诞生于西周，完备于隋唐。

总的说来，酒令是用来罚酒。但实行酒令最主要的目的是活跃饮酒时的气氛。

（一）雅　令

先推一人为令官，或出诗句，或出对子，其他人按首令之意续令，所续必在内容与形式上相符，不然则被罚饮酒。它是酒令中最能展示饮者才思的项目。

（二）通　令

通令又称“俗令”，行令方法主要是掷骰、抽签、划拳、猜数等。通令很容易造成酒宴中热闹的气氛，因此较流行。但通令掳拳奋臂、叫号喧闹，有失风度，显得粗俗、单调、嘈杂。

（三）筹　令

筹令，即使用酒筹的酒令。行令时轮流抽取酒筹，按酒筹上的要求进行活动或饮酒。酒筹须事先制好，一般用纸签、竹签、纸牌等制成，讲究的还用骨头、象牙等制成。

八、中国各地代表性的酒

贵州：茅台酒、董酒。

四川：五粮液、泸州老窖、剑南春、郎酒、沱牌曲酒，合称“五朵金花”。

山西：汾酒、竹叶青。

陕西：西凤酒。

湖南：武陵酒。

湖北：黄鹤楼酒。

河南：宝丰酒、宋河粮液。

广西：桂林三花酒。

福建：沉缸酒。

江苏：洋河酒、双沟酒。

浙江：绍兴加饭酒。

安徽：古井酒。

Chapter 11 Chinese Wine Culture

Wine is an alcoholic beverage made from fermented sorghum, barley, rice, grapes or other grain and fruits. In Chinese food culture, wine and cuisine are the two major themes. Excellent wine and delicious foods are the basic elements of Chinese traditional food culture. Wine is not only about the art of drinking but also the art to enrich our lives. According to the ancients, wine is holy and Chinese drinking art is venerable which has a set of customs and styles for ancient drinking activities. In China's 5,000 years of history, wine and wine culture have always played important roles. As a special cultural form, wine culture occupies a unique position in traditional Chinese culture, in which wine almost has come to pervade every aspect of social life. Wine is necessary for not only wedding ceremony, celebration dinner, welcome party, farewell dinner, but also for memorial ceremony, praying, driving trouble away, pastime even for medical treatment, keeping in good health, bodybuilding and longevity.

Wine culture is highly developed in China. When drinking, people not only take interest in persons drinking together, drinking time, and drinking place but also mix poetry, painting, customs and games together to turn drinking for enjoying physical pleasure into advanced spirit pleasure. Through drinking, people's views, emotions, behaviors and interpersonal relationship are influenced thus the romantic life situation and cultural atmosphere are created.

1. The Origin of Wine

As one of the countries where the earliest winemaking started, China is the

hometown of wine and also birthplace of wine culture. Chinese wine has a long history and many varieties. In China, there are many famous kinds of wines which gain renowned reputation in the world. Winemaking also has a long history. In the several thousand years of development of civilization, wine and wine culture are mainly developing along with each other. The history of Chinese wine can be dated back to antediluvian period. So the rise of Chinese wine started from 5, 000 years ago.

About the origin of wine, there are mainly four legends, winemaking starts from God, winemaking starts from ape, winemaking starts from Yidi and winemaking starts from Dukang. These legends are full of interest and charm along with the parts of exaggeration and imagination which are all derived from the respect and praise for wine.

2. The Classification of Wine

(1) Classified by Brewing Process

According the brewing process, wine can be classified into brewed alcoholic beverage, distilled liquor and blending type.

Brewed Alcoholic Drink It's the wine extracted or pressed from the raw materials such as fermented fruit or grain. Usually this kind of wine is not strong. Alcohol degree is no more than 15% with weak pungency. Apart from containing alcohol, raw materials also have nutritional ingredients and decomposition products with high nutrition value. Yellow rice wine, beer and grape wine all belong to brewed alcoholic drink.

Distilled Liquor Distilled liquor is the wine made from the fermented raw materials such as fruit or grain and distilled fermented liquor. Distilled liquor usually is comparatively strong which degree is more than 30%. White wine belongs to distilled liquor.

Blending Wine The base wine of blending wine is normal juice wine or distilled wine, which is blended with alcohol or non-alcohol materials. After soaking

and mixing, the blending wine is obtained. This kind of wine has the most abundant species with different edible values according to the selected wine base and auxiliary materials. For example, *Yangmei shaojiu* (Waxberry aquavit), Zhuyeqing liquor, Sanshe wine (made from three kinds of snakes), ginseng liquor, liqueur and Chinese vermouth all belong to the blending types.

(2) Classified by Alchol Types

According to the alcohol content, wine can be classified into strong wine, moderate wine, and mild wine.

Strong Wine Strong wine refers to the wine with alcohol content more than 40%, for example, Maotai liquor and *Wuliangye*.

Moderate Wine Moderate wine is the wine with alcohol content between 20% ~ 40% such as Zhuyeqing liquor, rice wine and yellow rice wine.

Mild Wine Mild wine is the wine with alcohol content lower than 20% such as grape wine, sweet olive aged wine and champagne.

3. The Style of Wine

Each of wine has its unique style. Not only different wine but also wine of the same kind has different styles. Style of wine is the product of many factors, such as color, flavor, taste and body.

(1) Color

The wine color comes from raw materials in liquor-making, production process (adding color or fading in color), ageing color, blending color, and so on.

(2) Flavor

The formation of wine flavor is very complicated. The win flavor comes from liquor-making raw materials, fermentation process and ageing.

The flavor styles of Chinese spirit include Fen-flavor, Luzhou-flavor, Maotai-flavor, rice-flavor and multiple-flavor. Fen-flavor liquor is represented by

Fenjiu. Luzhou-flaovr liquor is represented by *Wuliangye* and *Luzhou laojiao*. Maotai-flavor liquor is represented by Maotai liquor. Rice-flavor is represented by Guilin Sanhua liquor and Guangdong Changleshao. Multiple-flavor liquor is represented by Xifeng liquor.

(3) Taste

The taste of wine basically determines its value. The main tastes include sweet, sour, bitter, hot and astringent.

(4) Body

Body refers to the comprehensive aspect of wine style, which in China specifically means the comprehensive reflection of color, flavor and taste while according to many experts from international wine industry, which only refers to the abstract aspect of taste.

4. The Types of Drinking Vessel

The drinking vessels, which are an important carrier of the wine culture, are born with the invention of wine. Through the drinking vessels of different dynasties, we can not only learn the traditional culture, but also study the long history in China. The types of drinking vessel in ancient times are in abundance with different functions and manufacturing materials. Drinking vessels are mainly used for storage, warming and drinking. In terms of the manufacturing materials, from ancient to now, there have been many materials, such as pottery, china, lacquer, jade, bronze ware, gold, and silver, glass, ivory, horn, clam shell and wood and bamboo.

Wine containers mainly have *Zun*, *You*, *Ping*, and so on.

Wine-warming vessels mainly have *Jue*(爵), *Jue*(角), *Jia*, and so on.

The main drinking vessels are *Gong*, *Gu*, *Bei*, and so on.

5. The Influences of Wine

With its unique function and style, wine exists in the society and its impact

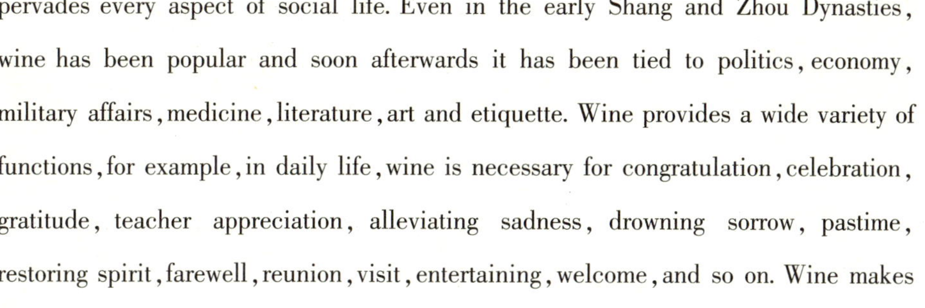

pervades every aspect of social life. Even in the early Shang and Zhou Dynasties, wine has been popular and soon afterwards it has been tied to politics, economy, military affairs, medicine, literature, art and etiquette. Wine provides a wide variety of functions, for example, in daily life, wine is necessary for congratulation, celebration, gratitude, teacher appreciation, alleviating sadness, drowning sorrow, pastime, restoring spirit, farewell, reunion, visit, entertaining, welcome, and so on. Wine makes our lives more colorful, hence there are sayings, which goes "no wine, no banquet" and "no wine, no folk custom", which lays the foundation of unique spirits culture of China. In general, wine can be used to refresh ourselves, protect us from cold, cure our disease, help us to make friends, distract our grief, and so on.

(1) Wine and Social Communication

As long as we live in the society, social communication is necessary. Then as a medium of communication, wine plays an important role in interpersonal interaction. Wine is the bridge to exchange ideas and build friendship, and the bond to greater closeness and acquaintance between people. In human society, wine is used frequently as the medium in varieties of intercourse activities. For instance, from ancient to now, wine has widely been used in sacrificing, celebrating birthday, organizing wedding party, entertaining people, making friends, speaking of ambitions, encouraging, enjoying, driving grief away, curing disease, and so on.

Chinese hospitality is especially prominent in the feast. Affection between people is sublimated when they propose a toast. When Chinese people propose a toast, they all urge others to drink more to do the honors. The more guests drink, the happier the host becomes, because he feels being respected. If the guests don't drink, the host will feel losing face.

(2) Wine and Chinese Literature

Wine can stimulate the nerve centers, dilate blood vessels, increase the heart rate and promote the blood circulation. In specific circumstances, this kind of stimulation on talented people will bring about unexpected magical result. Wine, as

the catalyst of intelligence and courage, has encouraged the emergence of numerous heroes, litterateurs and artists and has helped their achievements and works to be immortal.

Wang Xizhi, one of the greatest calligraphers in Eastern Jin Dynasty, is known as "saint of calligraphy". His masterpiece *Lantingji Xu* is done when he was comfortably drunk and wrote at ease. A lot of"Zhi" (之) are used in the whole passage, neither of which are the samely written. After Wang Xizhi sobered up, he himself can't believe that such a brilliant work is his own. Afterwards, he rewrites *Lantingji Xu* more than once, but never reaches the perfection as the one written during drunk.

"Li Bai drinks a *Dou* of wine then can write a hundred poems" vividly expresses the relationship between wine and poem. Famous poets in China such as Wang Wei, Meng Haoran, Li Bai, Du Fu, He Zhizhang, Han Yu, Liu Zongyuan, Liu Yuxi, Bai Juyi, Du Mu, Li Shangyin all drink and write about wine.

(3) Wine and Medical Care

Wine is the remedy for treating a cold and refreshing oneself. According to Li Shizhen, an ancient medical scientist in China in Ming Dynasty, wine heads the list of medicines. Sensible drinking can play an adjustment function for the body. Wine can dredge the channels, promoting blood circuation and remove blood stasis eliminate stagnation, warm *Yang* and dispel cold, disperse stagnated liver *Qi* for relieving *Qi* stagnation, enable people to express themselves freely. Sensible drinking can increase saliva and gastric juices secretion and promote primary digestion and absorption and blood circulation. Wine can also work for spiriting up, refreshing, relieving stress and facilitating sleep, and so on.

(4) Wine and Politics

There are plenty of politicians and heroes being related to wine. For instance, Qinmugong, a duke of Qin State, offers wine to people who stole his horse. Chuzhuangwang, a duke of Chu State, is good at wine strategy. Goujian, a king of Yue State, pours the wine into river and asks his soldiers to drink their fill to

enhance troop morale. Liu Bang, the first emperor of Western Han Dynasty, sang *Song of the Big Wind* when drunk. Cao Cao, the founder of Wei Regime in the Three Kingdoms Period, invited Liu Bei to drink together and discussed who the hero is. Yang Guang, the emperor of Sui Dynasty, asks for drinking when dying. Zhao Kuangyin, the first emperor in the Song Dynasty, removes from military position by means of cups of wine. Zhu Yuanzhang, the first emperor of the Ming Dynasty, uses wine to sound his ministers. Xiang Yu, the king of Western Chu, arranges Hongmen Banquet; Jing Ke, a warrior, wants to kill King Qin after drunk. Huo Qubing, a famous general in Western Han Dynasty, pours wine into spring. Guan Yunchang, a famous general of Shu Regime in the Three Kingdoms Period, kills Huaxiong, a famous general in Wei Regime, before the warm wine became cold and started a solo run. Wang Anshi, a famous prime minister in Western Song Dynasty, sighs, "a thousand cups of wine are not too many when drinking with close friends", and so on.

6. The Drinking Etiquette

As a kind of diet culture, drinking has had a serried of etiquette that everyone should abide by since ancient time. In ancient China, the etiquette are as follows.

When host and guests are drinking together, they should kneel down mutually. When drinking in front of the elders, young people should serve and accompany the elders to drink. Usually young people should make prostration and then take a secondary seat. Only when the elders asked them to drink, they can raise their glasses and they can't drink off the whole glass before the elders finish his wine.

There are four procedures in ancient drinking etiquette, *Bai*, *Ji*, *Cui and Zujue*. First, a guest makes a courtesy call to express respect. Then he spills a little wine to the ground to thank the earth for its virtue of breeding. Next he tastes and praises the wine to please the host. Finally drain off the whole glass.

In the banquet, the host should propose a toast to the guest (known as *Chou*) and in turn the guest should also propose a toast to the host (known as *Zuo*) and exchange their best wishes for each other. Guests also can propose a toast mutually (known as

Lvchou). Sometimes people should propose a toast one by one(known as *Xingjiu*). When proposing a toast, people should *Bixi*, stand up. In general, three glasses of wine are appropriate.

7. Jiuling(A Drinkers' Wager Game)

Jiuling is the game in banquet to make fun. Usually one person is elected as *Lingguan*(commander) and the rest will follow his order to read poems, supply the antithesis to a given phrase or play other similar games. People who disobey the order or lose in the game will be punished for drinking. So it is also called "play game and drink" which appears in Western Zhou Dynasty and develops in Sui and Tang Dynasties.

To sum up, *Jiuling* is used to penalize people to drink. But the main purpose is to provide a lively atmosphere when drinking.

(1) Yaling

First, one person is chosen as the commander to offer verses or antithetical phrases, then another people should supply the rest parts based on orders. The following part should conform to the given one in content and form, or the person will be punished for drinking. It's the part in which people can show their intelligence and talent.

(2) Tongling

Tongling, which is also called *Suling*, mainly includes playing dice, drawing lots, finger-guessing and number-guessing games. *Tongling* can easily warm up the atmosphere in the banquet so it has been relatively popular. But when playing *Tongling*, people always shake fists, swing arms, make noises that sometimes seem to lack of grace and be vulgar, dull and noisy.

(3) Chouling

Chouling is the *Jiuling* with playing chips. People should draw the chips in turn, and act and drink based on the orders on the chips. Chips should be prepared beforehand and they are usually made by paper, bamboo, card even bone and ivory.

8. The Representative Wines from Different Provinces in China

Guizhou Province Maotai liquor, *Dongjiu*.

Sichuan Province Five golden flowers (*Wuliangye*), *Luzhou laojiao*, *Jiannanchun*, *Langjiu* and Tuopai Yeast liquor.

Shanxi Province Fenjiu, Zhuyeqing liquor.

Shaanxi Province Xifeng liquor.

Hu'nan Province Wuling wine.

Hubei Province Huanghelou wine.

He'nan Province Baofeng wine, Songhe liquor.

Guangxi Province Guilin Sanhua liquor.

Fujian Province Chen'gang wine.

Jiangsu Province Yanghe liquor, Shuanggou wine.

Zhejiang Province Shaoxing rice wine.

Anhui Province Gujing wine.

第十二章　中国传统节日文化

一、春　节

春节又叫阴历（农历）年，俗称“过年”。是节日体系中的核心大节，是中国民间最隆重、最热闹，持续时间最长、内容最丰富的一个古老传统节日。

春节喜庆气氛要持续一个月。正月初一前有扫尘、祭灶、贴春联、贴福字、贴窗花、贴年画等活动；除夕夜有吃年饭、守岁、吃饺子、放鞭炮等活动。节中有给儿童压岁钱、亲朋好友拜年等活动。节后半月又是元宵节，其时花灯满城，游人满街，盛况空前，元宵节过后，春节才算结束。

春节蕴含了丰富的文化。春节蕴含的辞旧迎新、合家团圆的意义，成为凝聚民族情感的重要力量，也使它成为中华民族自我认同的一个文化符号。

春节原名为元日，相关的庆祝活动在夏代已经开始。它作为岁首大节的地位，在汉朝时得以确立。汉太初元年（前 104），汉武帝颁行《太初历》，确定以夏历的正月初一为岁首。每年的最后一天，就是除夕。

（一）祭　灶

中国春节，一般是从祭灶揭开序幕的。祭灶，是一项在中国民间影响很大、流传极广的习俗。旧时，差不多家家灶间都设有“灶王爷”神位。人们称这尊神为“司命菩萨”或“灶君司命”，传说他是玉皇大帝封的“九天东厨司命灶王府君”，负责管理各家的灶火，被作为一家的保护神而受到崇拜。

祭灶多在黄昏入夜之时举行。一家人先到灶房，摆上桌子，向设在灶壁神龛中的灶王爷敬香，并供上用饴糖和面做成的糖瓜等。

（二）春节的颜色

春节是红色的，红色是中国人的传统喜庆颜色，红色代表喜庆，它鲜艳、热烈，代表红红火火、吉祥如意。在春节中总也缺不了红色。红红的灯笼、红红的鞭炮、红红的春联和“福”字，洋溢着浓浓的节日气息，将春节变得红彤彤的。

（三）扫　尘

举行过祭灶后，便正式地开始做迎接过年的准备。每年从农历腊月二十三日起到除夕止，中国民间把这段时间叫作“迎春日”，也叫“扫尘日”。在春节前扫尘，是中国素有的传统习惯。扫尘就是年终大扫除，北方称“扫房”，南方叫“掸尘”。每逢春节来临，家家户户都要打扫环境，清洗各种器具，拆洗被褥、窗帘，到处洋溢着“欢欢喜喜搞卫生，干干净净迎新春”的气氛。

（四）贴“福”字

每逢新春佳节，家家户户都要在屋门上、墙壁上、门楣上贴上大大小小的“福”字。春节贴“福”字，是中国民间由来已久的风俗。故意把福字贴倒了，表示是“福到”的意思。“福”字现在的解释是“幸福”，而在过去则指“福气”“福运”。

（五）贴春联

每逢新春佳节，家家户户都要写春联、贴春联，这是上千年来流传下来的象征吉祥、表达人们向往美好生活的民族风俗。春联俗称“门对”“春贴”“对联”“对子”，雅称“楹联”。

春联的前身是桃符，桃符是用一寸宽、七八寸长的桃木做的。在桃木板上写上神荼、郁垒二神的名字，悬挂在门两旁以压邪。这就是春联的雏形。

早在2 000多年前的战国时期，在民间，春节到来之际，就悬挂“桃符”来压邪。

后来，人们逐渐用纸代替桃木板，并在上面写上一些工整、对偶、简洁、精巧的文字描绘时代背景、抒发美好愿望，这就是现在的春联。

春联的种类比较多，依其使用场所，可分为门心、框对、横批、春条、斗斤等。门心贴于门板上端中心部位；框对贴于左右两个门框上；横批贴于门楣的横木上；春条根据不同的内容，贴于相应的地方；斗斤也叫“门叶”，为正方菱形，多贴在家具、影壁中。

春节贴春联的民俗起于宋，并在明代开始盛行。

（六）贴门神

每逢新春佳节，家家户户除了要写春联、贴春联外，还要贴门神，汉代以前的门神通常是能捉鬼的神荼和郁垒。传说上古的时候，有神荼和郁垒两兄弟，他们住在度朔山上。山上有一棵桃树，树荫如盖。每天早上，他们便在这树下检阅百鬼。如果有恶鬼为害人间，便将其绑了喂老虎。后来，人们便用两块桃木板画上神荼、郁垒的画像，挂在门的两边用来驱鬼避邪。

真正史书记载的门神，却不是神荼、郁垒，而是古代的一个叫作成庆的勇士。在班固的《汉书·广川王传》中记载：广川王（去疾）的殿门上曾画有古勇士成庆的画像，短衣，大裤，配长剑。到了唐代，门神的位置便被秦叔宝和尉迟敬德所取代。

（七）贴年画

过年，人们除了贴春联，剪窗花，挂福字，还喜爱在客厅里、卧室中挂贴年画。年画是中国的一种古老的民间艺术，它反映了人民大众的风俗和信仰，寄托着人们对未来的希望。一张张新年画给家家户户平添了欢乐的节日气氛。年画中最常见的内容是莲花和鱼：莲花代表连年，是年年，每一年的意思；鱼代表富裕，生活有余，日子过得好。两者合起来就是年年有余的意思。

（八）贴窗花

新春佳节时，许多地区的人们喜欢在窗户上贴上各种剪纸。剪纸是一种非常普及的民间艺术，千百年来深受人们的喜爱，因它大多是贴在窗户上的，

所以人们一般称其为“窗花”。窗花不仅烘托了喜庆的节日气氛，而且也为人们带来了美的享受，集装饰性、欣赏性和实用性于一体。

（九）除夕和年夜饭

除夕是一年中最使人留恋的一晚。除夕是中国传统节日中最重大的节日之一。指农历一年最后一天的晚上，即春节前一天晚上，因常在阴历腊月三十或二十九，故又称该日为年三十。一年的最后一天叫“岁除”，那天晚上叫“除夕”。

除夕之夜，全家团聚在一起吃“年夜饭”，所以“年夜饭”也叫“团圆饭”。劳作了一年，全家人会把所有最好吃的东西搬上饭桌。丰盛的年菜摆满一桌，桌上有各式各样的大菜、冷盘、热炒、点心，但是，一般少不了两样东西——火锅和鱼。火锅沸煮，热气腾腾，温馨撩人，说明红红火火；“鱼”和“余”谐音，象征“吉庆有余”，也喻示“年年有余”。值得注意的是，吃团圆饭时，桌上的鱼是不能动的，因为这鱼代表“富裕”和“年年有余”，象征来年的财富与幸运，它属于一种装饰，是碰不得的。

据史书记载，至少在南北朝时已有吃年夜饭的习俗。

（十）守　岁

除夕守岁是最重要的年俗活动之一。中国民间在除夕有守岁的习惯。守岁从吃年夜饭开始，这顿饭要慢慢地吃，有的人家一直要吃到深夜。

除夕夜是指每年农历腊月的最后一天的晚上，它与春节（正月初一）首尾相连。“除夕”中的“除”字是“去，易，交替”的意思，“除夕”的意思是“月穷岁尽”，这一天人们都要除旧迎新，有“旧岁至此而除，来年另换新岁”的意思。守岁的习俗，既有对如水逝去的岁月含惜别留恋之情，又有对来临的新年寄以美好希望之意。

（十一）拜　年

拜年是中国民间的传统习俗，是人们辞旧迎新、相互表达美好祝愿的一种方式。正月初一，家长带领小辈们出门谒见亲戚、朋友、尊长，以吉祥语向对方祝颂新年，卑幼者并须叩头致礼，谓之“拜年”。主人家则以点心、糖

食、红包（压岁钱）热情款待之。

关于拜年习俗的由来：传说远古时有一种怪兽，头顶长独角，口似血盆，人们叫它“年”。每逢腊月三十晚上，它便窜出山林，吃人害人。人们只好备些肉食放在门外，然后把大门关上，躲在家里，相聚交谈，互壮胆气，直到初一早晨，“年”饱餐后扬长而去，人们才开门相见，作揖道喜，互相祝贺。而现在，人们拜年寄托了对新年美好的祝福！

（十二）放爆竹

在除夕夜，爆竹声响是辞旧迎新的标志、喜庆心情的流露。中国民间自古就有春节“开门爆竹”的习俗。在新的一年到来之际，家家户户开门第一件事就是燃放鞭炮，在“噼噼啪啪”的爆竹声中除旧迎新。爆竹声后，碎红满地，称为“满堂红”。

传说，古时候，有一种叫年的怪兽，凶猛异常，长年居海底，每年除夕才爬上岸，吞食牲畜，伤害人命。据说年最怕红色、火光和炸响。从此每年除夕，家家户户贴红春联，燃放爆竹，以驱除年兽。

（十三）发压岁钱

新年的初一，人们都早早起来，穿上最漂亮的衣服，打扮得整整齐齐，出门去走亲访友，相互拜年，恭祝来年大吉大利。春节拜年时，晚辈要先给长辈拜年，祝长辈长寿安康，长辈可将事先准备好的压岁钱分给未成年的晚辈（根据传统的观念，已婚者算成年），据说压岁钱可以压住邪祟，因为“岁”与“祟”谐音，晚辈得到压岁钱就可以平平安安度过一岁。

派发红包给未成年的晚辈，是表示把祝愿和好运带给他们。红包里的钱，只是要让孩子们开心，其主要意义是在红纸，因为它象征好运。请注意：在发放红包的长辈面前打开红包是不礼貌的做法。

二、元宵节

农历正月十五元宵节，又称为“上元节”或“春灯节”，是中国汉族民俗传统节日。

正月是农历的元月，古人称夜为“宵”，而元月十五日又是一年中第一个

月圆之夜，是一元复始，大地回春的夜晚，所以称正月十五为元宵节。道教称之为“上元节”，认为这是天官赐福的日子。老百姓也叫它“灯节”，因为元宵节的核心活动是夜游观灯。元宵节是春节之后的第一个重要的节日。人们对此加以庆祝，也是庆贺新春的延续。

（一）赏　灯

元宵节也叫灯节。按中国民间的传统，在这皓月高悬的夜晚，人们要点起彩灯万盏，以示庆贺。出门赏月、燃灯放焰、喜猜灯谜、共吃元宵，合家团聚、同庆佳节，其乐融融。

元宵燃灯的风俗起自汉朝，兴起于唐代。传说，东汉明帝时期，明帝提倡佛教，见佛教有正月十五日，僧人观佛舍利，点灯敬佛的做法，就命令这一天夜晚在皇宫和寺庙里点灯敬佛，令士族庶民都挂灯。之后这种佛教礼仪节日逐渐演变成了民间盛大的节日。汉文帝时，正式下令将正月十五日命名为元宵节。

（二）猜灯谜

“猜灯谜”又叫“打灯谜”，是元宵节的一项活动。灯谜最早是由谜语发展而来的，起源于春秋战国时期。它是一种富有讥谏、规诫、诙谐、笑谑的文艺游戏。灯谜悬之于灯，供人猜玩。灯谜既能启迪智慧又有乐趣，所以深受社会各阶层人民的欢迎。

（三）耍龙灯

耍龙灯，也称舞龙灯或龙舞。它起源于上古时代。传说早在黄帝时期，在一种叫“清角”的大型歌舞中就出现过由人扮演的龙头鸟身的形象，其后又编排了六条蛟龙互相穿插的舞蹈场面。中华民族崇尚龙，把龙作为吉祥的象征。现在，龙舞流行于中国很多地区。

（四）舞狮子

舞狮子是中国优秀的民间艺术，每逢元宵佳节或集会庆典，民间都以狮舞助兴。舞狮子始于魏晋，盛于唐，又称“狮子舞”“太平乐”。舞狮一般由

三人完成：二人装扮成狮子，一人充当狮头，一人充当狮身和后脚；另一人当引狮人。有抖毛、打滚、腾跃、蹬高、滚彩球等动作。

（五）吃元宵

民间过元宵节有吃元宵的习俗。“元宵”作为食品，在中国也由来已久。宋代，民间即流行一种元宵节吃的新奇食品。通俗地说，元宵就是汤圆，以白糖、玫瑰、芝麻、豆沙、黄桂、核桃仁、果仁、枣泥等为馅，用糯米粉包成圆形，有荤有素，风味各异。

烹制方法多样，可以汤煮、油炸、蒸食。这种食品，最早叫“浮圆子”，后来又叫“汤团”或“汤圆”，后称为“元宵”，生意人还美其名曰“元宝”。这些名称与“团圆”字音相近，取团圆之意，象征全家人团团圆圆、和睦幸福，人们也以此怀念离别的亲人，寄托了对未来生活的美好愿望。中国人吃元宵，有团圆美满之意。

（六）走百病

一些地方的元宵节还有“走百病”的习俗，又称“烤百病”“散百病”，参与者多为妇女，他们结伴而行，或走墙边，或过桥，或到郊外，目的是祛病除灾。

三、清明节

清明节是农历二十四节气之一，在仲春与暮春之交，大约在每年的公历4月5日前后。清明一到，气温升高，正是春耕春种的大好时节，故有“清明前后，种瓜点豆”之说。清明节大约始于周代，距今已有2 500多年的历史。

清明节是中国传统节日，也是最重要的祭祀节日，是祭祖和扫墓的日子。清明节的起源，据传始于古代帝王将相“墓祭”之礼，后来民间亦相仿效，于此日祭祖扫墓，历代沿袭而成为中华民族一种固定的风俗。

（一）扫　墓

扫墓俗称上坟，祭祀死者的一种活动。扫墓时，人们要携带酒食果品、纸钱等物品到墓地，剪除坟丘上所有的杂草，修理陵墓周围，往坟丘上添上

一些新土培护，折几枝嫩绿的新枝插在坟上，烧纸钱香烛、供奉酒肉饭菜，燃放鞭炮，叩头行礼祭拜，向祖先行跪拜礼，最后吃掉酒食回家。

（二）踏　青

清明节，又叫踏青节，古时叫探春、寻春等，现在习惯上叫春游。按阳历来说，它是在每年的 4 月 4 日至 6 日之间。在中国，四月清明，春回大地，自然界到处呈现一派生机勃勃的景象，春光明媚，草木吐绿，正是郊游的大好时光。人们告别蛰居生活，迎着春天的明媚阳光，呼吸着青青绿草的气息，脚踩着松软的土地，徜徉在姹紫嫣红、莺歌燕舞的原野上，心情该是多么轻快愉悦。自古以来，民间长期保持着清明踏青的习惯。

（三）荡秋千

这是中国古代清明节习俗。民俗相传，荡秋千可以驱除百病，而且荡得越高，象征生活过得越美好。

（四）拔　河

据说，在时值春耕春种的清明时节举行拔河，具有祈求丰收的意味，历代帝王自然非常重视。

（五）植　树

清明前后，春阳照临，春雨飞洒，种植树苗成活率高，成长快。因此，自古以来，中国就有清明植树的习俗。

（六）放风筝

放风筝也是清明时节人们所喜爱的活动。古人认为，放飞的风筝可以带走邪气与晦气。每逢清明时节，人们不仅白天放，夜间也放。夜里在风筝下或风筝拉线上挂上一串串彩色的小灯笼，像闪烁的明星，被称为“神灯”。过去，有的人把风筝放上蓝天后，便剪断牵线，任凭清风把它们送往天涯海角，据说这样能除病消灾，给自己带来好运。

（七）插　柳

清明节期间，家家户户都在门上插柳枝，柳枝上挂燕子状的食物。前往郊外扫墓时，人人都会在自己的衣物上插上柳枝，小孩将柳条编成帽子戴在头上，姑娘们则将柳枝斜插在鬓角，搭乘的车轿上也要插挂柳枝。

（八）射　柳

射柳是一种练习射箭技巧的游戏。据明朝人的记载，就是将鸽子放在葫芦里，然后将葫芦高挂于柳树上，弯弓射中葫芦，鸽子飞出，以鸽子飞的高度来判定胜负。

（九）斗　鸡

古代清明盛行斗鸡游戏，斗鸡由清明开始，斗到夏至为止。中国最早的斗鸡记录，见于《左传》。到了唐代，斗鸡成风，不仅是民间斗鸡，连皇上也参加斗鸡。如唐玄宗最喜斗鸡。

（十）蹴　鞠

蹴鞠是一种皮球，球皮用皮革做成，球内用羽毛塞紧。蹴鞠，就是用足去踢球。这是古代清明节时人们喜爱的一种游戏。相传是黄帝发明的，最初目的是用来训练武士。

四、端午节

端午节又称端阳节、重午节、盂兰节、蒲节等，是一个众多民族都拥有的古老的传统节日，时间为每年五月初五。端午节始于中国的春秋战国时期，至今已有 2 000 多年的历史。

围绕端午节的由来和习俗的传说很多，这些传说为端午节增添了新的习俗和文化内涵，较通行的解释是纪念伟大的爱国诗人屈原。

屈原是春秋时期楚国的大臣。公元前 278 年，秦军攻破楚国都城。屈原的政治理想破灭，对前途感到绝望，虽有心报国，却无力回天，只得以死明志，就在同年五月五日怀恨投汨罗江自杀。老百姓听到噩耗很悲痛，争先恐

后地来打捞他的尸体，结果一无所获。于是，有人用苇叶包了糯米饭，投进江中祭祀屈原，这种祭祀活动一年一年流传下来，渐渐成为一种风俗。

端午节习俗有吃粽子，赛龙舟，挂艾蒿，佩戴香包，喝雄黄酒等。现在“端午节”为中国法定节假日之一，并被列入“世界非物质文化遗产名录”。

（一）食粽子

端午节有吃粽子的习俗，这一习俗的形成跟纪念屈原相关。据说，屈原投汨罗江自杀后，老百姓用苇叶包了糯米饭，投进江中祭祀屈原，这种祭祀活动一年一年流传下来，渐渐成为一种风俗。

每年农历五月初，中国百姓家家都要浸糯米、洗粽叶、包粽子。粽子又称“角黍”“筒粽”，是端午节汉族的传统节日食品，由粽叶包裹糯米蒸制而成。

粽子最早出现在春秋时期，到晋代，端午食粽子成为全国性风俗，到了唐代，粽子已经成为端午节的必备食品。

（二）划龙舟

每年在长江流域及各地区都有赛龙舟的习俗。据说这一习俗的形成，跟纪念屈原有关。屈原投汨罗江后，当地百姓闻讯马上划船捞救，一直行至洞庭湖，终不见屈原的尸体。那时，恰逢雨天，湖面上的小舟一起汇集在岸边的亭子旁。当人们得知是打捞贤臣屈大夫时，再次冒雨出动，争相划进茫茫的洞庭湖。为了寄托哀思，人们荡舟江河之上，此后逐渐发展成为今天的龙舟竞赛。

（三）挂艾蒿和菖蒲

端午节有挂艾蒿和菖蒲的习俗。家家都洒扫庭除，将艾叶和菖蒲插入门缝间以驱鬼和辟邪。传说在先秦时代，普遍认为农历五月是个毒月，五日是恶日，相传这天邪佞当道，五毒并出。从那时开始，人们便认为此日为不吉之日。这样，在此日插菖蒲、艾叶以驱鬼，薰苍术、白芷和喝雄黄酒以避疫。

（四）佩戴香包

端午节小孩要佩香囊，传说佩香囊有避邪驱瘟之意。香囊内有朱砂、雄

黄、香料，外包以丝布，再以五色丝线弦扣成索，作各种不同形状，结成一串，形形色色，玲珑可爱。佩在胸前，清香四溢，有驱逐蚊虫之效。

（五）画　额

端午节有以雄黄涂抹小儿额头的习俗，以驱避毒虫。典型的方法是用雄黄酒在小儿额头画“王”字，一借雄黄以驱毒，二借猛虎（“王”似虎的额纹，又虎为兽中之王，因以代虎）以镇邪。

（六）饮雄黄酒

端午饮雄黄酒的习俗在长江流域地区极为盛行。雄黄酒是在白酒或自酿的黄酒里加入微量雄黄而成。雄黄是一种矿物质，俗称“鸡冠石”，主要成分是硫化砷，并含有汞，有毒，有杀菌驱虫解五毒的功效，中医还用来治皮肤病。

五、中秋节

中秋节，中国传统节日之一，为每年农历八月十五日，因其在一年秋季的八月中旬，故称“中秋节”。民间称为“过八月十五”，又称“秋夕”“八月节”“八月半”“月夕”“月节”。传说是为了纪念嫦娥奔月。因为这一天月亮满圆，象征团圆，人们仰望天空如玉如盘的朗朗明月，自然会期盼家人团聚。远在他乡的游子，也借此寄托自己对故乡和亲人的思念之情。所以，中秋节又称“团圆节”。

中秋节始于唐朝，盛行始于宋朝，至明清时，已与元旦齐名，成为中国的主要节日之一。

（一）“嫦娥奔月”传说

传说在远古时候，天上出现了十个太阳，大地被烤得生烟，海水干涸，世间万物都无法生存下去了。这件事惊动了一个名叫后羿的英雄，他登上昆仑山顶，运足神力，拉开神弓，一气射下九个多余的太阳。后羿立下汗马功劳，受到百姓的尊敬和爱戴，不少志士慕名前来投师学艺。不久，后羿娶了个美丽善良的妻子嫦娥。后羿除传艺狩猎外，终日和妻子在一起，人们都羡

慕这对郎才女貌的恩爱夫妻。有一天，后羿到昆仑山访友求道，巧遇由此经过的王母娘娘，便向王母求得一包不死药。据说，服下此药，能即刻升天成仙。然而，后羿舍不得撇下妻子，只好暂时把不死药交给嫦娥珍藏。嫦娥将药藏进梳妆台的百宝匣里，不料被后羿的徒弟蓬蒙看到了。三天后，后羿率众徒外出狩猎，心怀鬼胎的蓬蒙假装生病，轻而易举地骗过了后羿，留了下来。待后羿率众人走后不久，蓬蒙手持宝剑闯入内宅后院，威逼嫦娥交出不死药。嫦娥知道自己不是蓬蒙的对手，危急之时她当机立断，转身打开百宝匣，拿出不死药一口吞了下去。

嫦娥吞下药，身子立时飘离地面、冲出窗口，向天上飞去。由于嫦娥牵挂着丈夫，便飞落到离人间最近的月亮上成了仙。傍晚，后羿回到家，侍女们哭诉了白天发生的事。后羿既惊又怒，抽剑去杀恶徒，蓬蒙早逃走了。气得后羿捶胸顿足哇哇大叫。悲痛欲绝的后羿，仰望着夜空呼唤爱妻的名字。这时他惊奇地发现，今天的月亮格外皎洁明亮，而且有个晃动的身影酷似嫦娥。由于思念嫦娥，后羿每天都到月亮前观望爱妻，并派人到嫦娥喜爱的后花园里，摆上香案，放上她平时最爱吃的蜜食鲜果，遥祭在月宫里眷恋着自己的嫦娥。百姓们闻知嫦娥奔月成仙的消息后，纷纷在月下摆设香案，向善良的嫦娥祈求吉祥平安。

（二）吃月饼

每年八月半，人们都会吃着月饼品着茶，月饼是团圆的象征，是中秋祭的必备祭品。而中秋节吃月饼的习俗，是由元朝流传下来的。元朝末年，汉人打算起来反抗蒙古人的统治，却苦于无从传递消息。后来刘伯温想出一条计策，到处散布流言，说有冬瘟流行，除非家家户户都在中秋节买月饼来吃，才能避免。人们买了月饼回到家中，发现里面藏着纸条，上面写着：“中秋夜，杀鞑子，迎义军！”于是众人纷纷起义反抗统治者，中秋节吃月饼的习俗就是这样留下来的。

（三）拜　月

在古代有“秋暮夕月”的习俗。夕月，即祭拜月神。设大香案，摆上月饼及各种瓜果干品等祭品，其中月饼和西瓜是绝对不能少的，西瓜还要切成

莲花状。人们在月下将月亮神像放在月亮的那个方向，红烛高燃，全家人依次拜祭月亮，然后由当家主妇切开团圆月饼。拜月成为人们祈求团聚、康乐和幸福的习俗，以月寄情。

（四）玩花灯

中秋节，有许多的游戏活动，首先是玩花灯。中秋节是中国三大灯节之一，这一天要玩灯。当然，中秋没有像元宵节那样的大型灯会，玩灯主要只是在家庭成员、儿童之间进行。

Chapter 12 Chinese Traditional Festivals

1. The Spring Festival (The First Day of the Year in the Lunar Calendar)

The Spring Festival is the lunar New Year's Day in Chinese calendar, also known as *Guonian* by the Chinese people. It is the most important festival in China, which is also the nosiest, most joyous and longest festival of the year.

The happy atmosphere of the Spring Festival usually lasts for a whole month. The preparations and celebrations before the festival include sweeping the dust, Kitchen God worshipping, and putting on the Spring Festival couplets, Chinese character *Fu*(福), paper-cut for window decoration and New Year paintings.

On the eve of the Spring Festival, family members will get together to share a big meal, to staying up late for the coming of a new year, having *Jiaozi*, and setting off firecrackers. During the Spring Festival, seniors will give *Yasuiqian*, money given to children as a lunar New Year gift, to children, and people will visit their relatives and friends. 15 days after the Spring Festival, there comes the Lantern Festival, on which colorful lighted lanterns can be seen everywhere, and people can enjoy the bright lit night tremendously. After the Lantern Festival, the Spring Festival will come to an end.

The Spring Festival contains abundant cultural connotations for the Chinese people. It is a time to bid farewell to the old year, and also a time for family

reunion. The Spring Festival has already become a cultural symbol of self-indentification for the Chinese people all over the world.

The original name for Spring Festival is *Yuanri*, which means the first day of the year, and related celebrations began from Xia Dynasty. But it is not until Han Dynasty that it's settled as a formal festival for the whole country to celebrate. Hanwudi, the seventh emperor of Han Dynasty in China, issues *Taichu Calendar*, in which the first day of the first month in lunar calendar becomes the first day of the year, and the last day of the year is the New Year's Eve.

(1) Kitchen God Worshipping

In China, the Spring Festival begins with offering a sacrifice to the Kitchen God. It is a very influential and widely spread custom among the Chinese people. In ancient times, there is almost a spirit tablet of the Kitchen God hanging above the kitchen range in every household. It is said the Kitchen God is sent by the Jade Emperor, the supreme deity of Taoism, to each family to take charge of family affairs and make a report on what the family has done in the past year, so it is worshipped as the family's protection god.

Kitchen God worshipping often takes place at dusk, when family members go to the kitchen first, set the table, burn joss sticks piously, and put forth the sacrifice which is a lotus-like sticky cake made of a typical Chinese candy.

(2) The Color of Spring Festival

The color of the Spring Festival is red, which is the typical color for happy events in China over the years. Red stands for happiness and good luck. It is irreplaceable in such an important festival. The red lanterns, red firecrackers, red couplets, and red *Fu* character, all display a festival atmosphere.

(3) Sweeping the Dust

After Kitchen God worshipping, people begin preparing for the coming of the New Year. People call the days between the 23rd of the last lunar month to New

Year's Eve as "seeing the New Year in" or just "Sweeping the Dust Day". It's a tradition for Chinese people to sweep the dust before Spring Festival, and it's a kind of cleaning up at the end of year. In the North, it is called "cleaning the house", while in the South, it is called "sweeping the dust". Before the coming of the New Year, nearly every household will have a thorough cleaning, in order to have a tidy and refreshing festival atmosphere.

(4) Pasting the "Fu" Character

During the Spring Festival, it is a traditional custom for Chinese to paste the character *Fu* (福), big and small, on walls, doors and doorposts around the houses. Some people even purposely invert the character *Fu* to signify that blessing has arrived. *Fu* means happiness nowadays, while in the past it means good luck.

(5) Pasting Spring Festival Couplets

During the Spring Festival, every household will write and paste Spring Festival couplets, which is a folk custom preserved for thousands of years, which indicates people's yearning toward a good life. The Spring Festival couplets, is also called "couplet" or "a pair of antithetical phrases", or "poetic couplet".

Before the paper Spring Festival couplets appears, people use peach wood charms with the names of Shentu and Yulei, two gods in Chinese culture who can drive evil spirits, on them to drive evil spirits away.

Early in the Warring States Period, people begin to use the peach wood charms hung on the gate to ward off evil spirits during the lunar New Year's Day.

Gradually, people use paper to replace peach wood panel, with concise and antithetical matching sentences on them. These sentences often give a background of the day or convey people's good wish for the future.

People used to paste couplets on doorposts, door panels and lintel, as well as on furniture and screen wall.

The custom of pasting Spring Festival couplets starts in Song Dynasty (960 – 1279 A. D.), and becomes popular in Ming Dynasty (1368 – 1644 A. D.).

(6) Pasting the Door God

Besides pasting the Spring Festival couplets, every household will also paste Menshen pictures, the Door God. Before Han Dynasty, the pictures for Door Gods are Shentu and Yulei, who can get hold of the ghost. In ancient times. There are two brothers named Shentu and Yulei, who lived on Dushuoshan Mountain. There is a giant shady peach tree on the mountain. Every morning, Shentu and Yulei will inspect hundreds of ghosts under this tree. Whenever Shentu and Yulei discover a monster doing mischief, they tie it up and feed it to the tigers. Later on, people hang two pieces of peach wood boards with the figures of Shentu and Yulei to expel evil spirits.

The real Door Gods in history book are not Shentu and Yulei, but Chengqing, an ancient warrior. According to *The King Guangchuan's Biography in the History of Han*, written by Ban Gu, a famous historian in Eastern Han Dynasty, the king of Guangchuan County has the portrait of Chengqing with short jacket, long trousers and a long sword on his hall gate. In Tang Dynasty(581 –907 A. D.), Qing Shubao and Yuchi Jingde, two famous generals in Tang Dynasty, replace others as Door Gods.

(7) Pasting New Year Painting

Besides pasting Spring Festival couplets, making Paper-cuts, and hanging *Fu* character, people still like to paste New Year paintings in their living room and bed room. The New Year painting is an ancient folk art, which shows common people's custom and faith and contains their best wish for the future. A piece of brand-new painting gives a happy and joyous atmosphere to every household. A lotus flower represents every year, and the fish stands for abundance, and all together, they represent rich and happy life every year.

(8) Pasting the Paper-cuts

During Spring Festival, people in many areas like to decorate their windows with various kinds of paper-cuts. It is a very popular form of folk art, and deeply liked by

Chinese people. Paper-cuts can foil a lively festival atmosphere as well as bring the enjoyment of beauty to people. Paper-cuts combine the decoration, appreciation and practicability together.

(9) New Year's Eve and New Year's Eve Dinner

New Year's Eve is a night when most Chinese are unwilling to leave behind, and it is one of the most important festivals in all traditional Chinese festivals. It refers to the last evening of the 12th month in the lunar calendar. It often falls on the 29th or 30th of the last month in the lunar calendar, it also called the Spring Festival Eve. On New Year's Eve, the members of a family will get together to have dinner. For the reason that all the family members are present, it is also called family reunion dinner. After a year's hard working, all the best dishes are served on the table. Among the many delicacies, two are irreplaceable, the hot pot and fish. When the hot pot is boiling, it can really warm your heart and body, which symbolizes a flourishing year. Fish, which is pronounced [Yú] in Chinese, is homophonic with *Yu* (余) in Chinese, which means abundance and surplus. It is important to note that the fish on the table can not be moved, because it represents wealth and abundance, which is a kind of decoration that can not be touched.

According to history books, having a family reunion dinner is recorded as early as in Nanbeichao Period.

(10) Observe the Year Out on New Year's Eve

The tradition of observing the year out on New Year's Eve is one of the most important activities during the Spring Festival. New Year's Eve starts from having the family reunion dinner, which is taken very slowly, some even last deep into the night.

New Year's Eve refers to the night of the last day of the last month in lunar calendar, and the next day is New Year! New Year's Eve means bid farewell to the old year and usher in the new. This custom not only expresses people's unwillingness to part with the old days but also convey their best wishes for the coming New Year.

(11) Make a Ceremonial Call on New Year

Making a ceremonial call on New Year is a traditional custom among the people, and a time to exchange greetings. On the first day of the Chinese lunar year, seniors will take juniors to visit relatives, friends and elder relatives, and wishing them happy New Year, meanwhile juniors have to kowtow to seniors. The host family will treat the greeting people with candies, cakes, and red pocket(*Yasuiqian*).

Making a ceremonial call on New Year originates from a folk tale. In ancient times, there lives a monster with unicorn and bloody mouth named Nian(year). Nian always goes out from its burrow on New Year's Eve to devour people. Therefore people have to prepare some meat outside their closed gate. The family members inside will sit together, chatting and emboldening each other. Next morning, when Nian leaves after a big meal, people open the door and greet each other. But now making a ceremonial call on New Year entrusts people's best wished for the coming year.

(12) Setting off Firecrackers

On New Year's Eve, the sound of firecrackers is the symbol of biding farewell to the old year and usher in the new and an expression of delightfulness. On the first day of Spring Festival, the first thing, which every household must do after they open the door, is to set off firecrackers, it's a traditional custom. After the setting off, the remains of the fireworks are everywhere on the ground, it's called"full red".

According to a folk tale, in ancient China there lives a monster named Nian, who was very ferocious. It lives under the sea for most times, but on New Year's Eve it will go on shore and devour people and livestock. It is said Nian is afraid of red, light and the sound of explosion. From then on, every household will paste Spring Spring couplets and set off fireworks to drive Nian away.

(13) Yasuiqian

On the first day of the Chinese lunar year, everybody puts on their best clothes

and pays ceremonial calls on their relatives and friends, wishing them all the luck in the coming year. Juniors will greet seniors, wishing them health and longevity, while seniors will give juniors (those who are not married) some *Yasuiqian* (gift money). It is said the *Yasuiqian* can beat evil spirits. Those who get *Yasuiqian* can be safe and sound in the year.

Yasuiqian (usually wrapped in a red pocket) to unmarried juniors is a way to bring them luck. The important point is not the money in the pocket, but the red paper that wrap the money. The money is for children's sake. It's the red paper that matters, for it stands for good luck. Please note, it's impolite to open the red pocket in front of the person who gives it to you.

2. Yuanxiao Festival

The 15th day of the 1st lunar month is the Chinese Yuanxiao Festival, also called Shangyuan Festival or Lantern Festival. It's a folk festival of Han nationality in China.

The first lunar month is called "Yuan-month" (元月) in Chinese culture. In the ancient times the night is called "Xiao" (宵). The 15th day is the first night to see a full moon, which symbolizes the beginning of the year and the sign of the Spring comes back. So the day is called Yuanxiao Festival in China. In Daoism, it is called "Shangyuan Festival", on which Tian'guan, a god responsible for good fortune, will give bless to people. The common people also call it Lantern Festival, because the key activity on this festival is to appreciate colorful lanterns on the night. Yuanxiao Festival or Lantern Festival is the first important festival after the Spring Festival. The celebration of it is also an extension of welcoming the approaching Spring season.

(1) Enjoying the Colorful Lanterns

Yuanxiao Festival is also called Lantern Festival. According to the Chinese tradition, at the very beginning of a new year, when there is a bright full moon hanging in the sky, there will be thousands of colorful lanterns hung out for people to appreciate. At this time, people will try to guess the riddles on the lanterns and eat

yuanxiao, sweet dumplings, which can create an atmosphere of family reunion and great happiness.

The customs of lighting lanterns begins in Han Dynasty, and becomes popular in Tang Dynasty. It is said Buddhism is advocated during the reign of Emperor Mingdi in Eastern Han Dynasty. He observed that according to Buddhism practice, Buddhist monks will watch Buddhist relics, which are the remains from the cremation of Buddha's body, and light lanterns to worship Buddha on the 15th day of the first lunar month. So he orders his people to light lanterns in the imperial palace and temples to show respect to Buddha on this day. The government official's houses and common households must follow suit. Later on, this religious ritual gradually develops into a grand festival among the people. Emperor Wendi of Han Dynasty gives the official order to name this day as Lantern Festival.

(2) Guessing Lantern Riddles

Guessing lantern riddles is also known as "riddle solving", which is an important activity during Lantern Festival. Lantern riddles evolve from puzzles, originating from the Spring and Autumn Periods and the Warring States Period. It is a game of art which is rich in irony, precept, and humor. A lantern riddle is written on the lantern which is hung out for people to guess. It is interesting and inspiring, which is enjoyed by people from different social levels.

(3) Dragon Lantern Dance

The dragon lantern dance is also known as the dragon dance, which can be traced back to prehistoric times. According to legends, during the period of Huangdi, a legendary ruler in ancient China, there is a grand dance performance entitled *Qingjiao*, in which there appears the image with dragon's head and bird's body. Then the scene of six dragons dancing is also presented. The Chinese people think highly of dragons, and regard them as an emblem of good luck. Nowadays, dragon dance is very popular in many areas of China.

(4) Lion Dance

The lion dance is a brilliant folk art in China. During the Lantern Festival and other festivals, there is always the lion dance to bring luck and happiness to all. The lion dance starts in Wei and Jin Dynasties, which is flourishing in Tang Dynasty. The lion dance is usually composed of three people, two people act as a lion, one person moves the head and the other moves the body and tail, the third performer leads the lion. The actions which are to be performed include shaking the hair, rolling, jumping and rolling a colorful ball, etc.

(5) Eating Yuanxiao

It is a folk custom to eat *Yuanxiao*, sweet dumplings, on Lantern Festival or Yuanxiao Festival. As a kind of food, it has a long history. In Song Dynasty, there is a new food that is popular during Yuanxiao Festival. *Yuanxiao* is also known as *Tangyuan*, sweet dumplings, with fillings of sugar, rose petals, sesame, osmanthus flowers, bean paste or jujube paste and then cover them with glutinous rice flour in small round shapes. The fillings can be minced meat or vegetables, creating a different flavor. The cooking method is various, boiled, steamed, or fried. It is first called "floating ball", then "dumplings" or "glutinous rice ball", later *Yuanxiao*. Businessmen call it "gold ingot". These names are homophonic with *Tuanyuan* in Chinese, which means family reunion. People also take the occasion to miss their loved ones and express their wish for a better future life. For the Chinese, enjoying *Yuanxiao* together means a happy reunion.

(6) Dispelling Diseases

In some places, local women are encouraged to walk together along a section of a city's wall to dispel sickness on the day of the Lantern Festival.

3. The Qingming Festival

The Qingming Festival (Tomb-sweeping Day), which is one of the 24 seasonal

division points in China, occurs in the middle of Spring, and usually falls on April 4th – 6th of the Gregorian calendar each year. After the festival, the temperature will rise up, and it is the high time for Spring plowing and sowing. There is a saying, which goes, "before and after Qingming Festival, it is good time to plant melons and beans". Originating from Zhou Dynasty, Qingming Festival has a tradition stretching back more than 2,500 years.

Qingming Festival is a traditional Chinese festival as well as the most important day for people to offer sacrifices to their ancestors. It is said that the origin of the festival begins with the ritual of worshipping the deceased ancestors by emperors and top officials. Later on, the common people did the same. Therefore, it is passed down as a settled custom of Chinese people.

(1) Tomb-Sweeping

Tomb-sweeping is also called *Shangfen*, which means visiting the graves or burial grounds. It is an activity to remember and honor the deceased ancestors. During the activity, weeds around the tomb are cleared away. New soil is added. New branches are also inserted on the tomb. After sweeping the tombs, people offer food, flowers and favorites of the dead, then burn incense and paper money and bow before the memorial tablet.

(2) Taqing (Spring Outing)

The Qingming Festival is also called Taqing Festival. In ancient times, people also use "looking for Spring day" to refer to this festival. Now, it is usually known as Spring outing. It falls on April 4th – 6th of the Gregorian calendar each year. In April, Spring comes back again. The sun shines brightly. The trees and grass become green. The nature is again lively. It is a fine time to go out and to appreciate the beautiful scenes of nature. People say goodbye to the quite boring life, and it will be pleasant to hug the bright sunshine, breathe the refreshing air, and wander on the cheerful wild field. This custom of *Taqing* has been preserved since ancient times.

(3) Swinging

Swinging is an ancient folk activity performed at the Tomb-sweeping Festival. According to folk custom, swinging can dispel diseases, and the one who can swing the highest can lead a happy and prosperous life.

(4) Tug of War

It is said that carrying out this activity during Qingming Festival, which is a time for Spring plowing and sowing, has a significant meaning to pray for a bumper harvest in the coming year. Therefore, the emperors from ancient time all pay much attention to it.

(5) Trees Planting

Around Qingming Festival, the temperature rises up and rainfall increases, so the survival rate of saplings is high and trees grow fast. Since ancient times, people have the custom of planting trees during the Qingming Festival.

(6) Kites Flying

Flying kites is an activity favored by many people during the Qingming Festival. Little lanterns are tied to the kite or to the string that holds the kite. And when the kite is flying in the sky, the lanterns look like twinkling stars, which adds unique scenery to the sky during the night. In the past, people cut the string while the kite is in the sky to let it fly freely. It is said that it brings good luck and diseases can be eliminated by doing this.

(7) Willow-wearing

During the Tomb-sweeping Festival, people will insert willow branches on gates and front doors and hang festival food, which is made into the shape of a swallow on willow branches. On the way to sweep tomb in the suburb, everyone wear small willow branches on their clothes. Little kids wear garland made of willow twigs. Girls wear

willow in their hair. There will also be willow branches on the sedan chairs.

(8) Willow-shooting

Shooting the willow is a game that can practice archery skills. According to material from Ming Dynasty (1368 - 1644 A. D.), people first put pigeons into gourds before tying them on top of a willow tree. Several people then shoot the gourds with bows and arrows, which will set free the pigeons inside when they fall onto the ground. The winner is the one whose pigeon fly the highest on its release.

(9) Cockfighting

Cockfighting is a very popular game during Qingming Festival in ancient times. It begins at Qingming and ends at summer solstice. The earliest record about cockfighting is in *The Spring and Autumn Annals* (*Zuozhuan*). Cockfighting is rather prevalent in Tang Dynasty. Not only do the common people participate in this activity, but also the emperors do so. Emperor Xuanzong of Tang Dynasty likes cockfighting intensely.

(10) Cuju

Cuju refers to a kind of leather ball stuffed with feathers. Cuju means to kick a ball with feet. It is a game that ancient people like playing during Qingming Festival. It is said this game is invented by Huangdi, a legendry leader in ancient China, which is used to train warriors at first.

4. Duanwu Festival

Duanwu Festival, also known as Dragon Boat Festival, Duanyang Festival, and Yulan Festival, is celebrated by all ethnic groups as a traditional festival. It falls on the fifth day of the fifth lunar month. It started from the Warring States Period, and had a history of more than 2,000 years.

There are many legends about the evolution of this festival, which add new customs and cultural connotations to it. But the most popular saying about the Dragon

Boat Festival is to commemorate Qu Yuan, a great patriotic poet of Chu State in the Warring States Period.

Qu Yuan is a minister of the State of Chu during the Warring States Period (475 B. C. – 221 B. C.). In 278 B. C., Qu Yuan's political hopes are evaporated after hearing Qin troops have conquered Chu's capital. Disillusioned and disappointed, he plunges himself into the Miluojiang River on the fifth day of the fifth month. Nearby fishermen rush over to save him but they are unable to recover his body. Deeply grieved, the fishermen look for his body, but fail. People throw glutinous rice dumplings wrapped in reed leaves into the water as a sacrifice for Qu Yuan. Year after year, people do the same thing, so it gradually becomes a custom.

The customs on Duanwu Festival include eating *Zongzi* (glutinous rice dumplings wrapped in reed leaves), dragon boat racing, hanging mugwort, wearing sachets, and drinking realgar wine. Duanwu Festival is one of the national public holidays, and is inscribed on the Representative List of the Intangible Cultural Heritage of Humanity by UNESCO.

(1) Eating Zongzi

It is customary to eat *Zongzi* during Duanwu Festival. It is said that this custom is closely related to the commemoration of Qu Yuan. After Qu Yuan drowns himself in Miluojiang River, people throw into the water glutinous rice dumplings wrapped in reed leaves as a sacrifice for Qu Yuan. This sacrifice is passed down year after year, so it finally becomes a custom.

Every year in the fifth lunar month, every Chinese household will soak glutinous rice, wash reed leaves and wrap up *Zongzi* themselves. *Zongzi* is also called *Jiaoshu* or *Tongzong*, which is a traditional food of the Han nationality. It is made by steamed glutinous rice wrapped in reed leaves.

Zongzi first appears in Spring and Autumn Period. In Jin Dynasty, eating *Zongzi* at Duanwu Festival has already become a country wide custom. In Tang Dynasty, *Zongzi* is an indispensable part of the festival.

(2) Dragon Boat Racing

Dragon boat racing is held every year along the Yangtze River and other areas. It is said that this custom is closely related to the commemoration of Qu Yuan. After Qu Yuan leapt into Miluojiang River, local people immediately sail their boats up and down the river to look for his body, but they failed. It is raining, all the boats gather around a pavilion near the bank. When other people hear that they are looking for the upright Qu Yuan, they join the team and again sail to the direction of Dongtinghu Lake to look for Qu Yuan. This is how the dragon boat racing comes into being.

(3) Hanging Mugwort and Calamus

It is customary to hang mugwort and calamus during the Duanwu Festival. Every household will clean their yard, and hang mugwort and calamus on their door to ward off evil. It is said that during the Pre-Qin Period, the fifth month in the lunar calendar is an evil month, and the fifth day of this month is a bad day. Ghosts and evil spirits come out on this very day. From then on, this day is considered as an unlucky day. So people hang mugwort and calamus to ward off the evil. In this day, people light Chinese atractylodes and angelica dahurica and drink realgar wine to get rid of diseases.

(4) Wearing Sachets

It is said that wearing sachets children during Duanwu Festival can ward off evil and diseases. The sachets are made from silk cloth with cinnabar, spices, and realgar inside, wrapped with silk thread of five colors. The sachets can take various shapes. They are quite pretty and fragrant when wearing the sachets around the neck. What's more, the sachets can dispel the harmful pesticide.

(5) Painting the Forehead

It is customary to paint on little children's forehead with realgar wine to drive away the vermin during Duanwu Festival. The typical way of doing this is to paint the

Chinese character *Wang*(王) on the children's forehead with realgar wine. On the one hand, realgar wine can ward off the vermin, on the other hand, tigers (the character *Wang* resembles the lines on tiger's forehead, and tigers are the king of all animals) can expel the evil.

(6) Drinking Realgar Wine

The custom of drinking realgar wine during the Duanwu Festival is quite popular along the Yangtze River. Realgar wine is made by adding small amount of realgar into liquor or rice wine. Realgar is a kind of mineral, commonly known as *Jiguanshi*. Its main component is arsenic sulfide, and it also contains mercury. Being poisonous, realgar can kill bacteria and ward off the harmful insects, and detoxicate. Traditional Chinese Medicine used it to treat skin diseases.

5. Mid-Autumn Festival

Mid-Autumn Festival, which is one of Chinese traditional festivals, falls on the fifteenth day of the eighth month of the lunar calendar. For the reason that it is in mid-August, so people call it Mid-Autumn Festival. In Chinese folk, it is also called the "Fifteenth of the Eighth Moon", "Autumn Night", "August Festival", "Mid-August", "Night with Moonlight", or "August Day". It is said that this festival is to commemorate Chang'e's flight to the Moon. The full moon on this day represents reunion. As people look up at the full silver moon, they will naturally expect a family reunion. Those who are far away from home will also express their yearning towards relatives and family. So Mid-Autumn Festival is also called "Family Reunion Festival".

Mid-Autumn Festival starts from Tang Dynasties, and becomes very prevalent in Song Dynasty. During Ming and Qing Dynasty, it is as well-known as the New Year Festival as one of the most important festivities.

(1) The Legend of Chang'e's Flight to the Moon

In remote antiquity, it is said that there are ten suns rising in the sky, which

scorch all crops and drive people into dire poverty. Houyi, a hero in Chinese legend, is much worried about it. He ascends to the top of the Kunlunshan Mountain, and directing his superhuman strength to full extent, draws his extraordinary bow and shoots down the nine superfluous suns one after another. For this reason, he is respected and loved by the people. Lots of people of ideals and integrity came to him to learn martial arts from him. Before long, Houyi gets married with a beautiful wife named Chang'e. Besides tutoring and hunting, Houyi stay with his wife all day long; people all admire this pair of affectionate couple. One day on his way to the Kunlunshan Mountain to call on friends, he runs upon the Wangmu Niangniang (the Queen Mother of the West), the Queen Mother of the West, who is passing by. Wangmu Niangniang presents to him a parcel of elixir, by taking which, it is said, one will ascend immediately to the heaven and becomes a celestial being. Houyi, however, hates to separate with his wife. So he gives the elixir to Chang'e to treasure for the time being. Chang'e hides the parcel in a treasure box at her dressing table when, unexpectedly, it is seen by Pengmeng, a disciple of Houyi. Three days later, Houyi leads his disciples to go hunting. Pretending to be ill, Pengmeng does not go with them. After Houyi's departure, Pengmeng, sword in hand, rushes into the inner chamber and forces Chang'e to hand over the elixir. Knowing that she is unable to defeat Pengmeng, Chang'e makes a prompt decision at that critical moment. She turns round to open her treasure box, takes out the elixir and swallows it in one gulp.

As soon as she swallows the elixir her body floats off the ground, dashes out of the window and flies towards heaven. When Houyi returns home at dark, he knows from the maidservants what has happened. Surprised and furious, Houyi wants to kill Pengmeng, but he has already fled. Overcome with grief, Houyi looks up into the night sky and calls out the name of his beloved wife. To his surprise, he finds that the Moon is especially clear and bright and on it there is a swaying shadow that is exactly like his wife. Thinking of his wife day and night, Houyi then has an incense table arranged in the back garden that Chang'e loved. Putting on the table sweetmeats and fresh fruits Chang'e enjoys most, Houyi holds at a distance a memorial ceremony for Chang'e who is sentimentally attached to him in the palace of the Moon. When people hear of the story that Chang'e has turned

into a celestial being, they arrange the incense table in the moonlight one after another and pray kindhearted Chang'e for good fortune and peace.

(2) Eating Mooncakes

Every year during the Mid-Autumn Festival, people will enjoy mooncakes accompanied by tea. Mooncakes represent family reunion, and are indispensable during the festival. Eating mooncakes during the Mid-Autumn Festival is passed down from Yuan Dynasty. During the last years of Yuan Dynasty, the Han people attempt to overthrow the Mongolian rulers, but they are troubled by the message distribution. Liu Bowen, a military counselor for Zhu Yuanzhang of Ming Dynasty, then puts forward an idea that he has someone circulated a rumor that a deadly plague is spreading, and the only way to prevent it is to eat special mooncakes. People buy mooncakes and discover a secret message inside the cake which reads "kill the Mongolians and welcome the revolutionaries". People take part in the revolution and overthrow the rulers. From then on, the custom of eating mooncakes is passed down.

(3) Worshipping the Moon

In ancient time, people hold the custom of worshiping the Moon during the Mid-Autumn Day. A large incense table is set, on which there are mooncakes and various kinds of fruits and preserves. Mooncakes and watermelons are absolutely necessary, and what's more, the watermelon must be cut into the shape of lotus petals. The statue of the Moon Goddess will be put in the direction of the Moon in the sky, and red candles are lit. Then the family members worship the Moon in return. After that, the lady in charge of the family matters cuts the mooncake for the whole family to enjoy. Moon worship demonstrates people's wish to have family reunion and a welfare life.

(4) Enjoying the Lanterns

Among the celebrating activities during the holiday, the most important one is enjoying the various lanterns. The Mid-Autumn Festival is one of the three national

festivals related with lanterns. Therefore, people enjoy them intensely. However, the activities related with lanterns are usually held among families and children, for there is no large lantern fair as in the Yuanxiao Festival.

第十三章　中医文化

中医是中国的国粹，是建立在中国传统文化基础上的科学，它融汇了阴阳、五行学说以及辩证哲学等古老智慧，具有独特而神秘的东方意味。

中医药文化历史源远流长，博大精深，是中华三大瑰宝之一。

一、中医名医大家

在中国医学发展史上，出现过许多杰出的医学家，他们以自己高超的医术救死扶伤，治病救人，为人们所崇敬。

（一）神农尝百草，始有医药

炎帝种五谷，中华民族得以繁衍生息，故后人敬之为“神农”。神农为民尝食百草，始有医药。《神农本草经》是世界最早的药物学专著。

（二）“岐黄之术”开中医理论之先河

《黄帝内经》托名黄帝与岐伯所著，故称为“岐黄之术”。黄帝内经阐释了阴阳、五行、天人合一理论，并全面阐释人体生理、病理及疾病诊断、治疗与预防方面的知识，奠定了中医理论的基石。《黄帝内经》还反映出“药食同源”的养生思想，阐释了最早的食疗原则。

（三）扁鹊著《难经》，创中医“四诊”

扁鹊是中国中医理论的奠基者，他以自己的实践，首创了中医“四诊法”，也就是我们常说的望、闻、问、切，并在此基础上建立了一个比较完整

的科学诊断体系。扁鹊所著的《难经》被尊为中医四大经典著作之一，他被尊为“医祖”。

（四）“神医”华佗奠定中医外科基石

华佗因创麻沸散，行剖腹术，刮骨疗毒而闻名于世，奠定中医外科基石。华佗还创制五禽戏，是中医运动养生之开山鼻祖。

（五）“医圣”张仲景开辨证论治之先河

张仲景所著的《伤寒杂病论》是医学史上第一部从理论到实践的总结性的医学专著，确立了中医辨证论治原则，融理、法、方、药为一体。

（六）雷敩著《雷公炮炙论》奠基中药炮制法的基础

《雷公炮炙论》是中国第一部中药炮制学专著，奠定了中药鉴定、炮制、熬煮的理论基础，因此，后世才有了“术遵岐伯，法效雷公”的说法。

（七）“药王”孙思邈著《千金要方》

“药王”孙思邈著《千金要方》，是中国最早的医学百科全书。

（八）孟诜著《食疗本草》

孟诜著《食疗本草》，是世界上第一部食疗专著，书中收录百余种“药食两用”食材。后世多有引用，是一部研究食疗和营养学的重要文献。

（九）王惟一撰《铜人腧穴针灸图经》集宋以前针灸学之大成

王惟一撰成《铜人腧穴针灸图经》三卷，记载了657个腧穴。他还铸造针灸铜人两座，“以铜人为式，分脏腑十二经，旁注腧穴，集宋以前针灸学之大成”。

（十）李时珍著《本草纲目》

李时珍历27年著成《本草纲目》，收载药物1 892种，涵盖生物、化学、天文、地理、地质等多学科知识。

（十一）明周定王朱橚汇编《普济方》

明周定王朱橚倾举国之力编撰《普济方》是中国历史上最大的方剂专著。

（十二）张景岳倡“医易同源”

张景岳倡“医易同源”，是史上医易学的一次全面总结。

二、中医的阴阳五行学说

阴阳五行学说是中国古代朴素的唯物论和自发的辩证法思想，它认为世界是物质的，物质世界是在阴阳二气作用的推动下孳生、发展和变化的，并认为木、火、土、金、水五种最基本的物质是构成世界不可缺少的元素。这五种物质相互孳生、相互制约，处于不断的运动变化之中。这种学说对后来古代唯物主义哲学有着深远的影响，如古代的天文学、气象学、化学、算学、音乐和医学，都是在阴阳五行学说的协助下发展起来的。

中国古代医学家，在长期医疗实践的基础上，将阴阳五行学说广泛地运用于医学领域，用以说明人类生命起源、生理现象、病理变化，指导着临床的诊断和防治，成为中医理论的重要组成部分，对中医学理论体系的形成和发展，有着极为深刻的影响。

（一）阴阳学说

阴阳是中国古代哲学的一对范畴，是中国古代的一种宇宙观和方法论，具有对立统一的内涵。阴阳，是对自然界相互关联的某些事物和现象对立双方的概括。阴阳既可以代表两种相互对立的事物或势力，也可以代表同一事物内部所存在的相互对立的两个方面。阴阳可用来解释自然界两种对立和相互消长的物质势力，对立和消长是事物本身所固有的，是宇宙的基本规律。阴阳的最初含义是很朴素的，表示阳光的向背，气候的寒暖，方位的上下、左右、内外，运动状态的躁动和宁静等。阴和阳，既可以表示相互对立的事物，又可用来分析一个事物内部所存在着的相互对立的两个方面。

阴阳学说认为，世界是物质性的整体，自然界中的一切事物都存在着相互对立的阴阳两个方面，而对立的双方又是相互统一的。阴阳的对立统一运

动，是自然界一切事物发生、发展、变化及消亡的根本原因。

（二）“阴阳”的四个属性

两个条件 用“阴阳”来概括某些事物或现象的对立统一关系必须具备两个条件：对立事物或现象具有相关性和阴阳属性的规定性。

相关性 相关性是指这些事物或现象必须是属于同一统一体中的相互关联的事物或现象，而不是毫不相干的。例如，“水”与“火”乃是自然界中物质存在的不同状态和现象，两者是相互关联而又相互对立的。水性寒而下走，火性热而上炎，故水属阴，火属阳。实际上，阴阳学说中的阴阳，仅是抽象的属性概念，而非指互不相关的具体事物。

规定性 阴阳属性的规定性是指阴或阳不仅能概括事物或现象对立统一的两个方面，而且还代表着这两个方面的一定属性。也就是说，自然界相互关联的事物或现象对立的两个方面，本身就具有截然相反的两种属性。阳代表积极、进取、刚强等特性和具有这些特性的事物或现象；阴代表消极、退守、柔弱等特性和具有这些特性的事物和现象。

一般来说，凡是剧烈运动着的、外向的、上升的、温热的、明亮的，都属于阳；相对静止着的、内守的、下降的、寒冷的、晦暗的，都属于阴。以天地而言，天气轻清为阳，地气重浊为阴；以水火而言，水性寒而润下属阴，火性热而炎上属阳。

相对性 事物或现象相互对立的两个方面的阴阳属性是相对而言的，是由事物或现象的性质、位置、趋势等因素所决定的。

（三）阴阳学说的基本内容

阴阳学说的基本内容包括阴阳对立、阴阳互根、阴阳消长和阴阳转化四个方面。

阴阳对立 阴阳对立是指世间一切事物或现象都存在着相互对立的阴阳两个方面，如上与下、天与地、动与静、升与降等等。其中上属阳，下属阴；天为阳，地为阴；动为阳，静为阴；升属阳，降属阴。

阴阳互根 对立的阴阳双方又是互相依存的，任何一方都不能脱离另一方而单独存在。如上为阳，下为阴，而没有上也就无所谓下；热为阳，冷为

阴，而没有冷同样就无所谓热。所以可以说，阳依存于阴，阴依存于阳，每一方都以其相对的另一方的存在为自己存在的条件。这就是阴阳互根。

阳消阴长　阴阳之间的对立制约、互根互用并不是一成不变的，而是始终处于一种消长变化的过程中，阴阳在这种消长变化中达到动态的平衡。这种消长变化是绝对的，而动态平衡则是相对的。比如白天阳盛，人体的生理功能也以兴奋为主；而夜间阴盛，机体的生理功能相应的以抑制为主。从子夜到中午，阳气渐盛，人体的生理功能逐渐由抑制转向兴奋，即阴消阳长；而从中午到子夜，阳气渐衰，则人体的生理功能由兴奋渐变为抑制，这就是阳消阴长。

阴阳转化　阴阳双方在一定的条件下还可以互相转化，即所谓物极必反。可以说，阴阳消长是一个量变的过程，而阴阳转化则是质变的过程。阴阳消长是阴阳转化的前提，而阴阳转化则是阴阳消长发展的结果。

在中医学理论体系中，处处体现着阴阳学说的思想。阴阳学说被用以说明人体的组织结构、生理功能及病理变化，并用于指导疾病的诊断和治疗。

（四）五行学说

在中文里，“五”是指数，“行”是“运动”的意思。五行是指木、火、土、金、水五种物质的运动。中国古代人民在长期的生活和生产实践中认识到木、火、土、金、水是必不可少的最基本物质，并由此引申为世间一切事物都是由木、火、土、金、水这五种基本物质的运动变化生成的，这五种物质之间，存在着既相互孳生又相互制约的关系，在不断的相生相克运动中维持着动态的平衡，这就是五行学说的基本含义。

（五）五行学说的规定性

根据五行学说，“木曰曲直”，凡是具有生长、升发、条达舒畅等作用或性质的事物，均归属于木；“火曰炎上”，凡具有温热、升腾作用的事物，均归属于火；“土爰稼穑”，凡具有生化、承载、受纳作用的事物，均归属于土；“金曰从革”，凡具有清洁、肃降、收敛等作用的事物则归属于金；“水曰润下”，凡具有寒凉、滋润、向下运动的事物则归属于水。

（六）相生、相克、相乘、相侮

五行学说以五行的特性对事物进行归类，将自然界的各种事物和现象的性质及作用分别归于五行之中，五行学说认为，五行之间存在着相生、相克、相乘、相侮关系。

相生，指相互孳生和相互助长。相克，指相互制约和克制。相乘，指乘虚侵袭，即克制太过。相侮，指恃强凌弱，即相克的反相，又叫“反”克。

相生相克指的是事物之间的相互联系。相乘相侮指的是平衡被打破后的相互影响。

五行相生的秩序　五行相生的秩序是：火生土，土生金，金生水，水生木，木生火。火生土，因为火燃烧物体后，物体化为灰烬，而灰烬便是土；土生金，因为金蕴藏于泥土石块之中，经冶炼后才提取黄金；金生水，因为金若被烈火燃烧，便熔为液体，液体属水；水生木，因为水灌溉树木，树木便能欣欣向荣；木生火，因为火以木料作燃烧的材料，木烧尽，则火会自动熄灭。

五行相克的秩序　五行相克的秩序是：火克金，金克木，木克土，土克水，水克火。火克金，因为烈火能熔化金属；金克木，因为金属铸造的割切工具可锯毁树木；木克土，因为树根苗的力量强大，能突破土的障碍；土克水，因为土能防水；水克火，因为火遇水便熄灭。

（七）五行所主的事物

金主西方、秋天、燥、白色、鼻孔、皮毛、肺脏、大肠。木主东方、春天、风、青绿色、筋、眼睛、肝、胆。水主北方、冬天、寒、黑色蓝色、骨、耳朵、肾脏、膀胱。火主南方、夏天、暑、红色紫色、脉、舌头、心脏、小肠。土主中央、长夏、湿、黄色啡色、肉、嘴巴、脾脏、胃。

中医学应用五行学说来解释人体的生理功能，说明机体病理变化，用于疾病的诊断和治疗。

（八）阴阳与五行的关系

阴阳学说主要说明事物对立双方的互相依存、互相消长和互相转化的关

系；五行学说是用事物属性的五行归类及生、克、乘、侮规律，以说明事物的属性和事物之间的相互关系。在中医学里，二者皆以脏腑、经络、气血津液等为其物质基础；都是从宏观自然现象（包括人体）的变化规律，用取象比类的方法，来分析、研究、解释人体的生理活动和病理变化及人体内外的各种关系，并指导临床辨证与治疗。

三、中医的“天人合一”理论

中医认为人与自然界是一个统一的整体，即“天人合一”。人的生命活动规律以及疾病的发生等都与自然界的各种变化（如季节气候、地区方域、昼夜晨昏等）息息相关，人们所处的自然环境不同及人对自然环境的适应程度不同，其体质特征和发病规律亦有所区别。因此在诊断治疗同一种疾病时，注重因时、因地、因人制宜，并非千篇一律。

中医认为人体各个组织器官共处于一个统一体中，不论在生理上还是在病理上都是互相联系、互相影响的。因而从不孤立地看待某一生理或病理现象，头痛医头，脚痛医脚，而多从整体的角度来对待疾病的治疗与预防，特别强调“整体观”。

四、中医的“四诊”

中医的“四诊法”是指望、闻、问、切。

所谓“望诊”，就是观察病人的神、色、形、态的变化。“神”是精神、神气状态；“色”是五脏气血的外在荣枯色泽的表现；“形”是形体丰实虚弱的征象；“态”是动态的灵活呆滞的表现。这就是对病人面目、口、鼻、齿、舌苔、四肢、皮肤进行观察，以了解病人的“神”。

所谓“闻诊”，是指听病人说话的声音、呼吸、咳嗽、呕吐、呃逆、嗳气等的声动，还要以鼻闻病人的体味、口臭、痰涕、大小便发出的气味。

所谓“问诊”就是问病人起病和转变的情形，寒热、汗、头身感、大小便、饮食、胸腹、耳、口等各种状况。

所谓“切诊”，就是脉诊和触诊。脉诊就是切脉，掌握脉象。触诊，就是以手触按病人的体表病颁部分，察看病人的体温、硬软、拒按或喜按等，以助诊断。

五、中医的辨证施治

中医的辨证是运用“四诊”所获得的客观资料（即证候），用中医理论（三因、四诊、六经、八纲、脏腑、气血等等）分析辨证，从而提高对原因、病理、病机、病位的认识，同时注意病情的发展趋势与邪正盛衰。

中医的施治是在辨证的基础上，根据不同证候，而采用相应的治疗方法，潜方用药。因此辨证是施治的依据；施治是治疗的目的。辨证施治既不同于对症治疗，也不同于西医的辨病治疗，它把人体的内在联系，疾病的发展变化规律联系起来。辨证施治可以说是病因疗法。

六、中医养生

养生，古时又称“摄生”或“道生”，是在中医理论的指导下，研究增强生命力和防病益寿原理，并运用各种手段强身健体的传统保健方法。要平衡阴阳，调理气血，强壮脏腑，保养真气，扶正固本，从而达到减少或避免疾病的发生，维系机体身心健康，延缓人体衰老进程的目的。中医养生涉及的内容包括环境、情志、饮食、药物和运动等多个方面。

七、中医学典故

（一）岐黄之术

中医的医术往往又称为“岐黄之术”，黄指的是轩辕黄帝，岐是他的臣子岐伯。相传黄帝常与岐伯、雷公等臣子坐而论道，探讨医学问题，对疾病的病因、诊断以及治疗等原理设问作答，予以阐明，其中的很多内容都记载于《黄帝内经》这部医学著作中。后世出于对黄帝、岐伯的尊崇，遂用“岐黄之术”指代中医医术。

（二）悬壶济世

东汉时有个叫费长房的人。一日，他在酒楼喝酒解闷，偶见街上有一卖药的老翁，悬挂着一个药葫芦兜售丸散膏丹。卖了一阵，街上行人渐渐散去，老翁就悄悄钻入了葫芦之中，费长房看得真切，断定这位老翁绝非等闲之辈。

他买了酒肉，恭恭敬敬地拜见老翁，敬为师，习得医术，造福一方百姓。后世以此典故表达医术之精。

（三）杏林春暖

三国年间，董奉治病不收钱，只允病人种杏树以表心意，后成一山杏林。后人用此典故表达中医之大医精诚。

Chapter 13 Traditional Chinese Medicine Culture

As a quintessence of Chinese culture, traditional Chinese medicine (TCM) is a science, which is based on Chinese traditional culture and incorporates such ancient wisdoms as the theory of Yin-Yang, Five Elements Theory and Dialectics Philosophy, which is endowed with a unique and mysterious oriental character.

TCM culture has a long history, which is one of the three Chinese treasures, for being extensive and profound.

1. Famous Masters of TCM in Chinese History

Many outstanding medical scientists have shown up during the development of TCM. They heal the wounded, rescue the dying, cure diseases and save people with their excellent medical skills, which makes them widely respected.

(1) Shennong and Chinese Medicine

Yandi grows crops to breed the Chinese people in ancient times and therefore he is honored as Shennong (Farmer God). He tastes hundreds of herbs for his people and opens the age of Chinese medicine. *Shennong's Herbal* (*Shennong Bencao Jing*) is the earliest book on materia medica in the world.

(2) Qi-Huang and the Theory of TCM

Huangdi's Classic on Medicine (*Huangdi Neijing*) is created in the name of Huangdi and Qibo, hence it is known as the "Qi-Huang zhi Shu", which means

Chinese herbal medical science. The book gives a complete and systematic exposition to the following various subjects, the theories of Yin-Yang, Five Elements Theory and the relationship between man and nature, the physiology and pathology of human body, the diagnosis, treatment and prevention of diseases. It lays a preliminary foundation for the theoretical formation of TCM. Moreover, *Huangdi's Classic on Medicine* reflects a "medicine and food homology" idea which is the earliest interpretation of dietetic therapy principle.

(3) Bianque and Four Diagnostic Methods

Through his practice, Bianque, the founder of TCM theories, initiates the four diagnostic methods of TCM, namely inspection, auscultation and olfaction, inquiry, and pulse-taking and palpation. He then builds up a relatively complete scientific system for diagnoses based on those principal techniques. Bianque is respected as the "Medical Forefather" and his *Classic on Medical Problems* (*Nan Jing*) is regarded as one of the four TCM classics in China.

(4) Hua Tuo and TCM Surgery

Hua Tuo, a famous medical scientist in Eastern Han Dynasty, gains his reputation around the world for the reason that he creates anesthesia powder, carries out operation of laparotomy and dispel the poison by scraping the bone. It is Hua Tuo that establishes the basis of TCM surgery.

Hua Tuo, who creates the Five-Animal Exercises, is the first person, who preserves health by the principle of sports in the field of TCM.

(5) Zhang Zhongjing and TDS

Zhang Zhongjing, an outstanding physician in Han Dynasty, who is also considered the Medical Saga in China, writes *Treaties on Febrile and Miscellaneous Diseases* (*Shanghan Zabing Lun*), which is the first conclusive medical work in history to develop from theory to practice. This book establishes the principle of TDS (Treatment of Differentiation Syndromes), which combines the theory,

method, prescription and medicine together.

(6) Lei Xiao and the Processing Method of Materia Medica

Lei Xiao, a famous pharmacologist of Song State in the Nanbeichao Period, is the author of *Leigong Treatise on the Preparation* (*Leigong Paozhi Lun*), which is the earliest Chinese treatise on the preparation of materia medica and the theoretical foundation of its identifying, preparing and cooking. Therefore, there is a saying which goes, "follow Qibo to learn Chinese herbal medical science while Leigong to learn the treatise on the preparation of materia medica".

(7) Sun Simiao and *Valuable Prescriptions*

Sun Simiao, the "King of Herbal Medicine" in Tang Dynasty, writes *Valuable Prescriptions* (*Qianjin Yaofang*), which is the first medical encyclopedia in China.

(8) Meng Shen and *Materia Medica for Dietotherapy*

Meng Shen, a medical scholar in Tang Dynasty, writes *Dietetic Materia Medica* (*Shiliao Bencao*), which is the first work in the world about dietotherapy. The book includes over a hundred kinds of food ingredients which can also be used as medicine. As a frequently quoted book, it is an essential document for studying dietetic therapy and nutriology.

(9) Wang Weiyi and the Science of Acupuncture & Moxibustion

Wang Weiyi, a famous medical scholar in Northern Song Dynasty, writes three volumes of *Map of Acupoints on Copper Man* (*Tongren Shuxue Zhenjiu Tujing*) and records 657 acupoints. He also builds two copper statues for acupuncture practice. The book illustrates Zang-fu organs and twelve meridians in the form of a copper man and notes aside the corresponding acupoints, which epitomizes the science of acupuncture and moxibustion before Song Dynasty.

(10) Li Shizhen and *The Compendium of Materia Medica*

Li Shizhen, a famous physician and pharmacologist in Ming Dynasty, devotes

27 years to finally complete *The Compendium of Materia Medica* (*Bencao Gangmu*) *which consists of* 1,892 medicinal herbs and deals with various subjects like biology, chemistry, astronomy, geography and mineralogy.

(11) Zhu Su and *Prescriptions for Universal Relief*

Zhu Su, the chief of Zhou Prefecture in Ming Dynasty, enlists all his experts in the nation to compile the *Prescriptions for Universal Relief*(*Puji Fang*) , which is the biggest monograph of prescription in Chinese history.

(12) Zhang Jingyue and Homology of TCM and Yi-ology

Zhang Jingyue, a famous physician in Ming Dynasty, advocates the homology of TCM and Yi-ology, who is the first person in Chinese history to comprehensively conclude Yi-ology of medicine.

2. The Theory of Yin-Yang and Five Elements in TCM

The theories of Yin-Yang and Five Elements are Chinese ancient naive materialism and natural dialectics thoughts. According to the theory of Yin-Yang, the world is made of material, developing and changing under the interaction of *Yin* and *Yang*. The theory of Five Elements suggests that wood, fire, earth, metal and water are five basic elements to form the world. These five elements generate and restrict each other, which are always in the state of moving and changing. These theories cast a profound influence to the later ancient materialism philosophies. Such subjects as astronomy, meteorology, chemistry, arithmetic, music and medical science are set up with the help of the theory of Yin-Yang and Five Elements.

The ancient medical scientists have widely applied the theory of Yin-Yang and Five Elements to the medical field, based on their long-term practice. They have used the theories as well to account for the origin of life, physiological phenomena and pathological changes, to guide the clinical diagnoses and the prevention of disease. These two theories are important parts of the TCM theoretical system,

which play an important role in the formation and development of the theoretical system of traditional Chinese medicine.

(1) Theory of Yin-Yang

Yin-Yang, a pair of concepts in Chinese ancient philosophy, is the world view and methodology in ancient China, which has the connotation of the unity and opposites. It summarizes the objects and phenomena in nature which are relevant and opposite at the same time, two opposing objects or two opposing aspects in one object. The theory of Yin-Yang is used to explain the opposite material forces which are mutually consuming. The opposing and consuming are inherent nature of every object, which is also the fundamental law of the Universe. The original meaning of *Yin-Yang* is very simple, the sunshine and shadow, the coldness and warmth, the up and down, the left and right, the inside and outside, and restlessness and stillness. *Yin* and *Yang* can not only represent two opposite objects but also can analyze two opposite aspects within one object.

The theory of Yin-Yang regards the world as a material entirety. All the objects in nature have two sides as *Yin* and *Yang*, they opposing each other and unifying each other. The unity of opposites of *Yin-Yang* is the root cause of the occurrence, development, transformation and extinction of everything.

(2) Four Characteristics of Yin-Yang

Two Conditions There are two conditions inevitable in the theory of Yin-Yang, relativity and regularity.

Relativity Relativity means the opposite objects or phenomena are not irrelevant but belong to one unity. For example, water and fire are two different statuses of natural things, but relating to and opposing each other at the same time. Water is cold and moistens downwards, hence signifying *Yin*, while fire is hot and flares upwards, hence *Yang*. In fact, the theory of Yin-Yang refers to abstract concept of nature rather than specific substances which are irrelevant.

Regularity Regularity means *Yin-Yang* not only can represent two opposite

aspects but also can regulate the nature of these two aspects. Namely, the opposite aspects of relevant objects have in themselves two adverse attributes. *Yang* represents positive, progressing and strong attributes and things with these attributes. On the contrary, *Yin* represents negative, retreating and weak attributes and things with these attributes.

Generally speaking, all those, which are severely moving, extrovert, hot and bright, belong to *Yang*; and all those, which are relatively stable, introvert, cold and dark, belong to *Yin*. As for the Heaven and Earth, the *Qi* of the Heaven, which is pure and light, is *Yang*, but the *Qi* of Earth, which is turbid, is *Yin*. As for water and fire, water which is cold and moistens downwards is *Yin*, while fire which is hot and flares upwards is *Yang*.

Comparativeness *Yin-Yang* is a comparative speaking for the two opposing aspects of things or phenomena, determined by their nature, location, trend, and so on.

(3) Fundamental Contents

The fundamental contents of the theory of Yin-Yang cover four parts, the opposition of *Yin-Yang*, the interdependence of *Yin-Yang*, the mutual consuming of *Yin-Yang* and the inter-transformation of Yin-Yang.

The Opposition of Yin-Yang Everything or every phenomenon in the world is made up of two opposing aspects, *Yin* and *Yang*, such as up and down, the Heaven and Earth, dynamic and static, ascent and descent, in which up, the Heaven, dynamic and ascent are *Yang*, while down, Earth, static and descent are *Yin*.

The Interdependence of Yin-Yang Although Yin and Yang are opposite, they are also interdependent, which means one cannot exist without the other. For instance, up is *Yang* and down is *Yin*, but there will be no up without the existence of down. Similarly, hot is *Yang* and cold is *Yin*, but there will be no hot without the existence of cold. Therefore, *Yang* relies on *Yin* and vice versa. Each side exists only under the existence of its opposite side. This is called interdependence of *Yin-Yang*.

The Mutual Consuming of Yin-Yang *Yin* and *Yang* are in a constant state

of change so that when one increases the other is consumed to preserve the balance. The change is absolute while the balance is comparative. This can be seen in the physiological function of human body throughout the day and night. Human body becomes excited in the day but is suppressed at night. From midnight till noon, the physiological function of human body turns from suppression to excitement, hence *Yin* decreases and *Yang* increases. However, from noon till midnight, the function changes from excitement to suppression, hence *Yang* decreases and Yin increases.

Inter-transformation of Yin-Yang *Yin* and *Yang* can transform one another, which corresponds a Chinese saying that things will develop in the opposite direction when they become extreme. The mutual consuming of *Yin-Yang* is a process of quantitative change, while the transformation is a process of qualitative change. The former is the precondition of the latter, while the latter is the result of the former.

The idea of *Yin-Yang* is reflected everywhere in the theoretical system of TCM. It is applied to demonstrate the organizational structure of human body, the physiological function and the pathological change, and to guide the diagnoses and treatments of diseases.

(4) The Theory of Five Elements

The Chinese version of five elements is *Wuxing*, in which *Wu* means the number five, and *Xing* means the motion. Five Elements then refer to the motion of five materials in nature, wood, fire, earth, metal and water. In the course of their lives and productive labor, the ancient Chinese people realized that wood, fire, earth, metal and water are indispensable for life and then draw a conclusion that everything in the world is resulted from the motion and change of these five basic elements. They generate and restrict each other in order to maintain the balance. This is the fundamental meaning of this theory.

(5) Regularity of the Theory

According to the theory of Five Elements, wood has the nature of growing freely and unfolding. So, anything that is similar to the characteristics is attributed to the

category of wood. Fire has the nature of flaring up. Thereby the things similar to the nature of fire are classified into the attribute of fire. Earth has the nature of giving birth to all things. Thus, those that possess the nature of earth are attributed to earth. Metal has the nature of purifying and descending. Hence, those with the nature of metal can be attributed to metal category. Water has the nature of moistening and flowing downwards. For this reason, the things that have moistening, downward movement and coldness correspond to water.

(6) Generation, Restriction, Subjugation and Counter-restriction

This theory classifies things according to the properties of the Five Elements, relating the characteristics and functions of things and phenomena to it. Among the Five Elements, there exist the relationships of generation, restriction, subjugation and counter-restriction.

Generation implies that one kind of thing can promote, aid or bring forth another. Restriction means bringing under control or restraint. Subjugation means that one of the Five Elements overacts upon another one when the latter is weak. Counter-restriction means that the strong bullies the weak. It is also a morbid condition in which one element fails to restrict the other in the regular order, but in reverse order.

Generation and restriction reflects the inter-relationship among the things, while subjugation and Counter-restriction refer to the interaction among things when the balance is broken.

Generating Sequence In this sequence, fire generates earth, earth generates metal, metal generates water, water generates wood and wood generates fire. Fire generates earth because substances turn into ashes in fire and ashes become earth. Earth generates metal because metal is reserved in earth and stones, so it can be extracted only after smelting. Metal generates water because metal will dissolve into liquid when it is melted in fire, and liquid is water. Water generates wood because after watering, plants can survive and flourish. Wood generates fire because fire uses wood as fuel materials. When wood is burned out, fire will go out.

Restriction Sequence In this sequence, fire restricts metal, metal restricts

wood, wood restricts earth, earth restricts water and water restricts fire. Fire restricts metal because fire can dissolve metal. Metal restricts wood because wood can be sawed down by cutter made of metal. Wood restricts earth because the power of wood will break through the earth above it. Earth restricts water because earth built together is waterproof. Water restricts fire because water can extinguish fire.

(7) Correspondences of Five Elements

Metal dominates west, Autumn, dry, white, nostril, fur, lung and large intestine. Wood dominates east, Spring, wind, cyan and green, tendon, eye, liver and gallbladder. Water dominates north, Winter, cold, black and blue, bone, ear, kidney and bladder. Fire dominates south, Summer, hot, red and purple, arteries and veins, tongue, heart and small intestine. Earth dominates center, long Summer, wet, yellow and brown, flesh, mouth, spleen and stomach.

The theory of Five Elements is applied in TCM to expound the physiological function of human body, to illustrate the pathological change, and to guide the diagnoses and treatments of diseases.

(8) Relationship between Yin-Yang and Five Elements

The theory of Yin-Yang mainly demonstrates the relationship of opposing objects, inter-dependence, mutual consuming and intel-transformation. The theory of Five Elements explains the properties and the relationship among things by attributing everything in nature into one of the Five Elements and the sequences of generation, restriction, subjugation and counter-restriction overact and insult to. In TCM, both of the two theories take Zang-fu organs, meridian-collateral, and Qi, blood and body fluid as their material basis. Both of the two theories are used to analyze, to research and to explain the physiological movements, pathological change and various relations inside and outside human body, and to guide the clinical treatment and differentiation of syndromes relying on the law of changes on natural phenomena and human body by the method of analogy.

3. The Theory of Harmony between Man and Nature in TCM

In TCM, human and nature are considered as a unified entirety, namely the harmony between man and nature. According to this theory, the law of people's life activities and occurrence of diseases are closely connected to all kinds of changes in nature(i. e. season and climate, place and region, day and night, morning and dusk). Different natural environments and different levels of adapting to environments will cause different physical features and diseases' occurrence regularities. Therefore, when physicians try to diagnose and treat the same disease, they should take into consideration the time, place and people.

According to TCM, tissues and organs in human body co-exist in one unity either physiologically or pathologically. They relate to and influence each other, so they should not be treated separately. It is inappropriate to treat head when head aches, or treat foot when foot aches. Rather, disease should be treated and prevented from all the perspectives. This is the holistic view emphasized by the theory of unity of Heaven-Man.

4. The Four Diagnostic Methods

The four diagnostic methods are inspection, auscultation and olfaction, inquiry and pulse-taking and palpation.

Inspection is to observe the patient's vitality, complexion, physical build and state. Vitality refers to the spirit and external conditions. Complexion refers to the outer manifestation of five Zang organs, Qi and blood. Physical build refers to the symptoms of human body. State refers to the dynamic performance of human's reaction. Inspection is therefore to grasp the patient's vitality through observing his face, mouth, nose, teeth, tongue, limbs and skin.

Auscultation means listening to the patient's voice, respiration, coughing, vomiting, hiccup and belching. Olfaction means smelling the patient's odor of the body, fetid breath, nasal discharge and excretion.

Inquiry means asking the patient about the cause and change of disease, chills

and fevers, perspiration, conditions of head and body, defecation and urination, diet and appetite, bosom and abdomen, ear and mouth.

Pulse-taking is to feel the pulse and obtain its condition. And palpation is to touch the patient's body on certain parts and detect his temperature, toughness or softness, for or against pressure, thereby assisting the diagnoses.

5. Differentiation of Syndromes

Differentiation of syndromes in TCM means comprehensive analysis, while syndrome refers to symptoms and signs. So differentiation of syndromes implies that the patient's symptoms and signs collected by the four diagnostic methods are analyzed and summarized by TCM theories (the three pathogenies, four diagnostic methods, six meridians, eight principles, Zang-fu theory, Qi and blood theory) so as to identify the etiology, nature and location of a disease, and the relation between vital Qi and pathogens, thereby determines what syndrome the disease belongs to.

Treatment based on the differentiation of syndromes is carried out according to different syndromes. Thus the differentiation of syndromes is the basis of treatment, while treatment is the purpose of differentiation. Unlike the differentiation of symptoms or diseases, differentiation of syndromes combines the inner relation of human body and the rule of diseases changing together. It is a treatment based on pathogenies.

6. Health Maintenance

Health maintenance is once called as "health conservation" (*Shesheng*) or "Taoism health" (*Daosheng*) in ancient China. It is a traditional health care method, guided by TCM theories, to study principles which can strengthen vitality, prevent disease and lengthen life, and to apply various measures to build the body. Health maintenance requires to keep the balance between *Yin* and *Yang*, to regulate Qi and blood, to consolidate Zang-fu organs, keep genuine Qi, to strengthen vital Qi and to solidify body resistance so that the occurrence of disease can be reduced or prevented, physical and mental health could be maintained and the aging process can

be postponed. Health maintenance includes many factors as environment, emotions, diet, medicine and sport.

7. TCM Allusions

(1) Qi-Huang Zhi Shu

Qi-Huang zhi shu is often known as Chinese herbal medical science, in which "Huang" means Huangdi, and "Qi" was his courtier Qibo. According to the history, Huangdi often discussed with Qibo, Leigong and other courtiers about medical problems and answered questions to pathogenies, diagnoses and treatments of diseases. Many of their discussions were recorded in *Huangdi's Classic on Medicine* (*Huangdi Neijing*). Later generations, out of respect, therefore *Qi-Huang zhi shu* is often used to represent Chinese herbal medical science.

(2) Hang Cucurbit to Practice Medicine

There was a man called Fei Zhangfang in Eastern Han Dynasty. One day, he was drinking in a tavern and saw an old man selling pills, pelvises and pellets with a cucurbit hung beside. He then discovered that the old man secretly drilled into the cucurbit when people scattered away. Figuring out the old man as an unordinary person, Fei bought wine and meat to visit him and respected him as master to learn medical skill. Later Fei practiced medicine like the old man and benefit people there. This story is now quoted to express the essence of medical skill.

(3) Apricot Tree and Virtue of TCM

During the Three Kingdoms Period, Dong Feng was a doctor who treated patients without taking any money. He only asked his patients to plant an apricot tree as a token of gratitude. Gradually the mountain was all covered with apricot trees. And people now refer this story to indicate the virtue of TCM.

第十四章　中国建筑

中国建筑是中国文化中最具独特魅力的部分，是中国文化的标志和象征。中国建筑可分为宫殿建筑、城防建筑、万里长城、礼制建筑、陵墓建筑、宗教建筑、民居建筑等。

一、宫殿建筑

宫殿建筑是中国最宏大、最豪华的建筑，是中国古代建筑艺术的精华，几千年来，历代帝王们都不惜以大量人力、物力，在都城建造规模宏大、巍峨壮丽、金碧辉煌的宫殿，以满足自己穷奢极欲的享受，并在精神上给人们造成一种无比威严的感觉，以巩固他们的政权。以建筑艺术手段烘托出皇权至高无上的威势。宫殿建筑有自己鲜明的特点，可简要概括为中轴对称、左祖右社、前朝后寝、三朝五门等。

（一）中轴对称

为了表现君权受命于天和以皇权为核心的等级观念，宫殿建筑采取严格的中轴对称的布局方式。中轴线上的建筑高大华丽，轴线两侧的建筑低小简单。这种明显的反差，体现了皇权的至高无上，中轴线纵长深远，更显示了帝王宫殿的尊严华贵。

（二）左祖右社

中国的礼制思想有两个重要内容，一是崇敬祖先、提倡孝道；二是要祭祀土地神和粮食神，因为有土地才有粮食，“民以食为天”“有粮则安，无粮

则乱”，风调雨顺、国泰民安是人民共同的最基本的愿望。左祖右社，正是这种观念的体现。所谓“左祖”，是在宫殿左前方设祖庙，祖庙是帝王祭祀祖先的地方，因为是天子的祖庙，故称太庙；所谓“右社”，是在宫殿右前方设社稷坛，社为土地，稷为粮食，社稷坛是帝王祭祀土地神、粮食神的地方。

（三）前朝后寝

前朝，是帝王上朝理政、举行大典的地方，因位于整个建筑群的前部，称“前朝”。后寝是帝王、妃子及其子女生活起居的地方，因位于建筑群的后部，称“后寝”。

（四）三朝五门

宫殿建筑的空间规划及建筑营造是根据帝王的政治活动、日常起居的需要而进行的。宫内的主要政治活动是“朝”，因此宫城营建也围绕“朝”而展开。根据帝王朝事活动内容的不同，分别在不同规模的殿堂内举行。自古就确立了三种朝事活动的殿堂，名为“三朝制”。所谓“三朝”是指外朝、治朝和燕朝。外朝是商议国事、处理狱讼、公布法令、举行大典的场所，位于宫城南门外易于国人进出的地方；治朝用于君王日常朝会治事、处理诸臣奏章、接受万民上书；燕朝是君王接晤臣下、与群臣议事及举行册命、宴饮活动之处。

门，在宫城中不仅起到分隔各朝的作用，还具备交通枢纽、禁卫保安的功能。史料中关于王城门制有多种说法，一般认为是皋、库、雉、应、路五门。皋是远的意思，皋门是王宫最外一重门；应是居此以应治的意思，是治朝之门；库有“藏于此”之意，故库门内多有库房或厩棚；雉门有双观；路者，大也，路门为燕朝之门，门内即路寝，为天子及妃嫔燕居之所。明清紫禁城大体沿袭了上述“三朝”“五门”制度，并根据当时的社会条件和需求有所变通。按位置关系、使用情况和建筑形制分析，明代的“五门”分别对应为大明门、承天门（天安门）、端门、午门和奉天门（太和门），而清代的“五门”则是天安门、端门、午门、太和门和乾清门。

（五）著名的宫殿建筑——北京故宫

故宫也称紫禁城，是明清两朝的皇宫，位于北京市区中心。始建于明永

乐四年（1406 年），永乐十八年（1420 年）基本建成。先后有 24 位皇帝在此登基执政，至今已有 580 余年的历史。故宫占地 72 万多平方米，南北长 961 米，东西宽 753 米，房屋 9 000 余间，建筑面积 15 万平方米，周围还有高 10 多米的城墙和宽 52 米的护城河，是中国现存最大、最完整的建筑群。整个故宫建筑布局严谨，主次有序，青白石底座，红墙、黄琉璃瓦顶，飞檐翘首，既庄严稳重，富丽堂皇，又不乏生动活泼。故宫不仅以其宏大的古代宫殿建筑群闻名于世，而且以丰富的宫廷史迹和灿烂的古代文化艺术享誉海内外。

宫殿分前朝和内廷两部分。前朝是皇帝举行大典、召见群臣、行使权力的场所。主要建筑是坐落在中轴线上的三大殿：太和殿、中和殿、保和殿。

太和殿是最富丽堂皇的建筑，俗称"金銮殿"，是皇帝举行大典的地方，也是中国古建筑中著名的三大殿之一。中和殿是皇帝去太和殿举行大典前稍事休息和演习礼仪的地方。保和殿是举行殿试及除夕皇帝赐宴外藩王公的场所。三大殿都建在汉白玉砌成的 8 米高的三层须弥座台基上，更显得高大、宏伟、庄严。

内廷是皇帝处理日常政务及后妃居住的地方，主要建筑是后三宫：乾清宫、交泰殿、坤宁宫。东西两翼有东六宫和西六宫。内廷富有生活气息，建筑多自成院落，有花园、书斋、馆榭、山石等。在坤宁宫北面是御花园，里面有高耸的松柏、珍贵的花木、山石和亭阁。

二、城防建筑

城防建筑是指旧时在都邑四周用作防御的城垣，一般有两重，里面的称城，外面的称郭。城墙上有城楼、角楼、垛口等防御工事，构成一整套坚固的防御体系。

（一）门　楼

门楼是一个城的重要标志，是权力的象征，所以一般门楼建得比较高大雄伟。门楼在平时作瞭望守卫、储备粮食武器之用，战时则是作战指挥中心和守卫要地。

（二）角　楼

角楼位于城之四角，因为它双向迎敌，所以是城防中的薄弱点，需要努力加强防卫。战时，一般会在角楼中集中较多的兵力和武器。

（三）敌　台

敌台的防御作用是很大的，因城墙正面不便俯射，将士若探身伸头射杀敌人，容易遭到对方的射击，有了突出的城台，进逼城墙脚下的登城者就会遭到左右敌台上的射击，而使登城无法进行。

（四）敌　楼

敌楼一般骑墙而筑，高出城墙之上，有的二层，有的三层，是供储备粮草、军械、火药和士兵居住、躲风避雨以及作战之用。

（五）垛　口

垛口一般筑在城墙迎敌面的顶部，呈上下凹凸状，凸出部分称垛口。垛口中有上下两孔：其上为望眼，用以瞭望来犯之敌；下有射孔，用以射击敌人。垛口作用很大，它既能隐身防敌，又能有力射击敌人，使自己始终处于不败之地。

（六）墙　顶

城墙顶部是军队防御活动的通道，迎敌一面筑有 2 米高的垛口，另一面筑有高 1 米左右用以护身的女墙，墙顶通道一般较宽，可五马并骑，十人排行而走。地势陡峭处，路面筑成阶梯形的梯道。为了排除下雨时的积水，在墙顶还有排水沟等设施。在墙体内侧隔一定距离开有石砌或砖砌的拱形券门，中修磴道，直通墙顶，以便战士们上下。

（七）瓮　城

呈长方形或圆弧形加筑在迎敌的城门之外，以使城门增加一道有力的防线，其迎敌的城台上往往还筑有箭楼。

（八）箭　楼

箭楼往往雄峙在瓮城之迎敌城台上，与门楼遥遥相对，迎敌三面都开有

一排排多层的箭孔，当敌人来犯时，可形成密集的射击点，给敌人以毁灭性的打击。

（九）护城河

护城河即紧接城墙外面深阔的城壕，它一正一负构成了双重的防御体系，在城门处往往还置吊桥。

（十）钟鼓楼

古时，出于“晨钟暮鼓”的报时以及报警之需，凡是重镇城内多建有钟鼓楼。如果四边的城门都开在中央，南、北、东、西四门相对，城内的街道便成十字形，一般钟鼓楼就坐落在这个十字路口附近，西安市内的钟鼓楼便是如此。

（十一）著名的城防建筑

现存的著名的城防建筑有明南京（原称应天府）城墙、明西安城墙、明平遥城墙。

三、万里长城

万里长城是中国特有的建筑形式，其作用虽然主要是防御，但却有自己独特的风格，形成了自己独特的建筑形式。

早在春秋战国时期，各国为了互相防御，均选形势险要的地方修筑长城。战国时齐、魏、燕、赵、秦等国相继兴筑。此后汉、北魏、北齐、北周、隋各代都曾在北边与游牧民族接境地带筑过长城。秦始皇灭六国完成统一后，为了防御北方匈奴贵族的南侵，于公元前214年，将秦、赵、燕长城连接起来，形成西起临洮，北傍阴山，东至辽东，总共6 000多千米的防御工事，俗称“万里长城”。现在看到的长城主要是明长城。

长城是一组有机的防御体系，这一防御体系以城墙为主体，其他还包括敌台、关隘、烽火台等一系列城防建筑。

（一）城　墙

明长城的主体是城墙，城墙多建在蜿蜒曲折的山脉的分水线上。其构造

按地区特点有条石墙、夯土墙和砖墙等。墙高约3至8米，顶宽约在4至6米之间。

（二）敌　台

城墙上每隔30至100米建有敌台。敌台有实心、空心两种。实心敌台只能在顶部瞭望射击，而空心敌台则下层能住人，顶上可瞭望射击。

（三）烽　堠

烽堠是报警的墩台建筑，都建在山岭最高处，相距约1.5千米。一般烽堠用夯土筑成，重要的在外包砖，上建雉堞和瞭望室。雉堞是城上排列如齿状的矮墙，做掩护用。台上贮薪，遇有敌情，日间焚烟，夜间举火，依规定路线，很快传至营堡。

（四）关　隘

凡长城经过的险要地带都设有关隘。关隘是军事要道，所以防御设置极为严密。一般是在关口置营堡，加建墩台，并加建一道城墙以加强纵深防卫。重要关口则纵深配置营堡，多建城墙数重。

（五）长城代表段落

长城代表段落主要有北京延庆县的八达岭、北京怀柔区的慕田峪长城、河北滦平县的金山岭长城、天津蓟县的黄崖关长城、河北秦皇岛市的山海关、甘肃嘉峪关市的嘉峪关等等。

四、陵墓建筑

陵墓建筑是中国古代建筑的重要组成部分，是中国古建筑中最宏伟、最庞大的建筑群之一。中国陵墓建筑与绘画、书法、雕刻等诸艺术门派融为一体，成为反映多种艺术成就的综合体。中国的陵墓建筑，一般都是利用自然地形，靠山而建；也有少数建造在平原上。

中国陵园的布局大都是四周筑墙，四面开门，四角建造角楼。陵前建有甬道，甬道两侧有石人、石兽雕像，陵园内松柏苍翠、树木森森，给人肃穆、

宁静之感。

中国古代的帝王陵寝一般由地下建筑与地面建筑两部分组成。地下建筑部分叫地宫，主要用于埋葬死者的遗体、遗物和随葬品等，多仿死者生前的居住状况。地面建筑部分由封土和陵区建筑组成，主要用于祭祀和护陵之用。

著名陵墓建筑有秦始皇陵、十三陵、清东陵等。

五、礼制建筑

礼制建筑起源于祭祀。伴随着祭祀活动，相应地产生场所、构筑物和建筑，这就是礼制建筑。礼制建筑可分为坛、庙、祠等。

（一）坛

祭坛建筑有着广义、狭义之分。狭义的祭坛仅指祭祀的主体建筑或方形或圆形的祭台，而广义的祭坛则包括了主体建筑和各种附属性建筑。现存著名的祭坛有天坛和社稷坛。

天坛　天坛位于北京崇文区永定门内大街东侧。始建于明成祖永乐十八年（1420 年），原名“天地坛”，是明清两代皇帝祭祀天地之神的地方，明嘉靖九年（1530 年）在北京北郊另建祭祀地神的地坛，此处就专为祭祀上天和祈求丰收的场所，并改名为“天坛”。

天坛是皇帝祭天的场所，皇帝每年冬至要到天坛祭天，新皇帝登基也须祭告天地，以表示他受命于天。

社稷坛　社稷坛原是明清两代皇帝祭祀社（土地神）和稷（五谷神）的地方。该坛坐南朝北，建于明永乐十九年（1421 年），占地 24 万平方米，坛面铺有黄、青、白、红、黑五色土壤，黄土居中，东青、西白、南红、北黑，以道教的阴阳五行学说，象征“天下之地，莫非王土”及国家江山政权之意。1914 年辟为中央公园，1928 年改名中山公园。

（二）庙

庙包括帝王祭祀祖先的太庙、祭祀先师孔子的文庙、祭祀武圣关羽的武庙、祭祀圣哲先贤和神灵的各类庙。

现存著名的庙有太庙、孔庙、关庙、妈祖庙。

太庙 太庙始建于明朝永乐十八年（1420 年），嘉靖二十三年（1544 年）改建。此后于清朝顺治八年、乾隆四年屡次修葺与扩建，太庙面积为 139 650 平方米。位于天安门城楼东侧，原是明清两代皇家的祖庙，现为劳动人民文化宫。

孔庙 孔庙坐落在曲阜城内，其建筑规模宏大、雄伟壮丽、金碧辉煌，为中国最大的祭孔要地。

关庙 解州关帝庙在山西运城市解州镇西关。解州东南 10 千米的常平村是三国蜀将关羽的原籍，故解州关帝庙为武庙之祖。

妈祖庙 湄洲妈祖庙始建于北宋雍熙四年（1998 年），当时规模很小，只有几间平房。后经宋、元、明、清四代扩建，始成今日规模，并升级为天后宫。湄洲妈祖庙是世界所有妈祖庙之祖，世界上所有的妈祖庙都是从湄洲“分灵”出去的。每逢农历三月二十三日妈祖诞辰日和农历九月初九妈祖升天日，四面八方的妈祖信众赶赴湄洲寻根谒祖，举行隆重的祭祀活动。

（三）祠

祠是与帝王宗庙相对的礼制建筑，是上至贵族官僚、下至黎民百姓的祖庙。这些庙被称作家庙、祠堂，简称祠。现存著名的祠有晋祠和武侯祠等。

晋祠 在山西太原市西南 25 千米处的悬瓮山麓，晋水源头，有一片古建园林，统名“晋祠”。晋祠始建于北魏，为纪念周武王次子叔虞而建。

武侯祠 成都武侯祠是中国现存武侯祠中规模最大而又最负盛名的一座，是全国重点文物保护单位。

六、中国宗教建筑

中国宗教建筑包括中国佛寺建筑、中国道教建筑、中国伊斯兰教建筑和中国基督教建筑。

（一）佛教建筑

佛教建筑包括佛寺建筑、石窟和佛塔。中国佛寺建筑，早期与古印度相似，以塔为中心，四周建有殿堂。晋唐以后，殿堂逐渐成为主要建筑，塔被移于寺外。中国佛寺殿堂带有明显的民族特色，由数进四合院组成，具有中

轴线，两偏殿对称，大型的寺院还有廊院。寺院主要殿堂布局比较规范，依次为山门、天王殿、大雄宝殿、法堂、藏经楼、方丈室等。东侧有僧房、香积厨、斋堂、职事房、茶堂、延寿堂等。西侧多为接待云游僧人的禅堂等。

中国著名的中国佛寺建筑有河南洛阳白马寺、浙江杭州灵隐寺、江苏镇江金山寺、湖北武汉归元寺、四川峨眉山伏虎寺、安徽九华山天台古寺、河南嵩山少林寺等。

石窟是一种佛教建筑形式。佛教提倡遁世隐修，因此僧侣们选择崇山峻岭的幽僻之地开凿石窟，以便修行之用。石窟的格局大抵是以一间方厅为核心，周围是一圈柱子，三面凿几间方方的“修行”用的小禅室，窟外为柱廊。中国的石窟起初是仿印度石窟的制度开凿的，多建在中国北方的黄河流域。

中国较早的著名石窟有：山西大同的云冈石窟，甘肃敦煌的莫高窟，河南洛阳的龙门石窟，这就是中国的“三大石窟”。

佛塔是佛教的象征。佛塔最早用来供奉和安置舍利、经文和各种法物。佛塔一般由地宫、基座、塔身、塔刹组成。塔基有四方形、圆形、多角形，塔身以阶梯层层向上垒筑，逐渐收拢，层数多为单数。在中国，佛塔的数量多，形式多样，风格丰富，极富有建筑装饰美感。中国的佛塔按建筑材料可分为木塔、砖石塔、金属塔、琉璃塔等；按类型可分为楼阁式塔、密檐塔、喇嘛塔、金刚宝座塔和墓塔等。

中国著名的佛塔建筑精品山西五台山塔林、河南登封嵩山少林寺塔林、山东济南灵岩寺塔林、宁夏青铜峡塔林、云南景洪市飞龙山白塔林等。

（二）道教建筑

道教建筑叫道观。道观既是供奉、祭祀神灵的殿堂，又是道教徒长期修炼、生活和进行斋醮祈禳等仪式的场所。其建筑的门类很多，有宫、观、殿、堂、府、庙、楼、馆、舍、轩、斋、廊、阁、阙、门、坛、台、亭、塔、榭、坊、桥等，这些建筑按其性质和用途，可分为供奉祭祀的殿堂、斋醮祈禳的坛台、修炼诵经的静室、生活居住的房舍和供人游览憩息的园林建筑五大部分。

中国著名道教建筑有北京白云观、陕西周至楼观台、苏州玄妙观、广东罗浮山冲虚观等。

（三）伊斯兰教建筑

清真寺是伊斯兰教建筑的主要类型，是穆斯林举行礼拜、宗教功课、举办宗教教育和宣教等活动的中心场所。中国传统建筑风格的清真寺多采用中国传统的四合院并往往是一串四合院制度，即沿东西中轴线有次序、有节奏地布置若干进四合院。在建筑设置方面一般都有大殿、水房、讲经堂、邦克楼或望月楼（台），大殿内正向墙正中均设米哈拉布（壁龛），西北角置宣礼楼。

由于伊斯兰教在中国的传播，为人们增添了许多富有特色和魅力的伊斯兰风格的建筑。中国著名伊斯兰教建筑有泉州清净寺、广州怀圣寺、杭州凤凰寺、扬州仙鹤寺、北京牛街清真寺、西安化觉寺、喀什艾提尕尔清真寺、宁夏同心韦州大寺、宁夏石嘴山清真大寺、山东济宁西大寺等。

（四）基督教建筑

基督教三大主流教派在中国俱建有教堂，中国的基督教建筑大多沿袭原有西式建筑，这种具有强烈的西方特征的宗教建筑，打破了中国传统建筑一统天下的格局。

中国著名的基督教特色的建筑有北京南堂和北堂、天津老西开教堂、上海徐家汇天主堂、广州圣心大教堂、哈尔滨圣索菲亚教堂、上海圣母大教堂、上海国际礼拜堂、上海景灵堂等。

七、民　居

中国疆域辽阔，不同的地理条件、气候条件以及不同的生活方式，再加上经济、文化各方面的影响，造成各地居住房屋样式以及风格的不同。按区域分，中国有特色的传统民居建筑包括江南民居、西北民居、北京民居、华南民居以及少数民族民居等。

（一）北京四合院

北京四合院是中国四合院的代表作品。四合院严格按照中轴线布局，主要建筑都分布在中轴线上，左右对称布局。这一布局方式，严格遵循了封建

社会的宗法和礼教制度。在房间的使用上家庭成员按尊卑、长幼等进行分配。

（二）江南民居

江南因为地理原因，水资源丰富，所以大部分的村镇、城市的建筑基本上立于河流两岸，建筑将河流围成一条水街。周庄古镇就是江南水乡的典型代表，这里建筑多临河而建，为了防水防潮，墙壁下部一般使用大块石或用石料贴面。

江南民居的平面布局方式与北方的四合院大致相同，都是封闭式院落，但相对紧凑一些。住宅的大门一般开在中轴线上，中轴线上的第一座房子是用来接待客人和举行典礼的大厅，后面院内多有二层小楼，为了通风采光，院墙上都开有漏窗，房屋也前后开窗。

南方炎热潮湿、多雨的气候特点对江南的建筑产生了极大影响，为了防潮避湿气，江南民居的墙一般较高，开间也大，设前后门，便于通风。同时，为了隔绝地上的湿气，一般为两层建筑，二层作卧室。底层多为砖墙，上层为木结构。

（三）徽州民居

徽州民居最突出的特点是马头墙和青瓦。马头墙有一人多高，能把屋顶都遮挡起来，起到防火的作用。门楼用石雕和砖雕进行装饰，装饰纹样富有生活气息。宅院大多依地而建，分三合院、四合院，合院又有二进、三进之分。徽州民居屋顶的处理以“四水归堂”的天井为特点。四水归堂是指大门在中轴线上，正中为大厅，后面院内有二层楼房，四合房围成的小院称天井，目的是为了采光和排水。四面屋顶的水流入天井，俗称“四水归堂”。

（四）西北窑洞

最具特色的西北民居为因地制宜、利用黄土高原的黄土层建造的独特住宅——窑洞。窑洞依其外形可分为靠崖式窑洞、独立式窑洞、下沉式窑洞。窑洞重视对门窗的装饰，门的洞孔与窗的洞孔一般大小，门窗上装饰有棂格图案。逢年过节时，多在窗上贴各式剪纸。

（五）晋中民居

晋中一带最出名的是晋商们修建的豪宅大院。建筑规模较大，设计精巧，具有独特的建筑造型和空间布局。晋中民居建筑，以四合院居多，一般为砖木结构，砖墙上多为清一色的青砖，墙体厚实，院落中也多用青砖铺地。晋中民居的一大特色是单坡屋顶，而不是人字形坡顶，所以墙体的高度就是屋脊的高度。另外，院落纵深较长，即南北长，东西窄。

晋中大规模的民居建筑有乔家大院、王家大院等。院中有院，明楼院、统楼院、栏杆院错落有致，卷棚顶、硬山顶形式各异。

（六）客家土楼

客家最具代表性的民居建筑为土楼。客家人修建的土楼中数量最多的是方形土楼，方形土楼规模庞大，土墙单面墙的长度一般在 20 ~ 50 米之间，楼层一般为三到四层，最高可达五层半。方形土楼的瓦顶屋檐通常一样高，屋顶为悬山顶式，木穿斗结构，也有的屋顶为九脊歇山顶。方形土楼一般底层作厨房，二层作谷仓，一、二层均不开窗，三层以上是卧室，对外开小窗。祖堂一般设在院内的底层，正对着大门，位于中轴线的尽头。整座方楼的采光通风都是依靠内院的天井。

（七）少数民族民居

中国少数民族众多，建筑风格各异，最具典型的少数民族民居有竹楼、吊脚楼、蒙古包和云南的“一颗印”建筑。

竹楼 竹楼主要指两层或两层以上的竹结构楼房，属于南方干栏式建筑的一种。根据用途及造型差异，可分为宾馆楼、餐酒茶楼、观景楼及景致楼等等，非常适合于旅游景区的观赏、住宿、餐饮等用途，绿色环保，贴近自然。竹楼主要分布在中国云南的西双版纳傣族自治州和德宏傣族景颇族自治州的傣族、基诺族等民族地区。由于傣族竹楼比较有代表性，现在说到竹楼一般都指的是傣族竹楼，又称傣家竹楼。

吊脚楼 吊脚楼属于干栏式建筑，但与干栏式建筑又有所不同。干栏式建筑为全悬空，吊脚楼可称半干栏式建筑。

吊脚楼多依山就势而建，整体风水布局讲究“左青龙，右白虎，前朱雀，后玄武”。形式包括单吊式、双吊式、四合水式、二屋吊式、平屋起吊式等。吊脚楼一般底层用来堆放物品；二楼住人，同时还设有客厅，用来接待客人；三楼除设起居室外，还有隔出来用于储存粮食或物品的小间。

蒙古包　蒙古包的外形为圆形，由架木、毡、绳带组成，原料以木和皮毛为主，大小不等，但基本构造相同。

蒙古包一般门朝东南方向，内部正面和西侧供长辈起居，东面供晚辈起居。

云南“一颗印”建筑　滇中高原地区，四季如春，无严寒，多风，故住房墙厚重。最常见的形式是毗连式“三间四耳”，即正房三间，耳房东西各两间，有些还在正房对面，即进门处建有倒座。房屋通常为楼房，为节省用地，改善房间的气候，促成阴凉，采用了小天井。外墙一般无窗、高墙，主要是为了挡风沙和保证安全，住宅地盘、外观方整，被称为“一颗印”。

Chapter 14 Chinese Architecture

Chinese architecture is a symbol of Chinese culture for its unparalleled charm. It includes palatial architecture, defensive architecture, the Great Wall, ritual architecture, mausoleum architecture, religious architecture, and residential constructions.

1. Palatial Architecture

Palace buildings, the most grand and the most luxurious buildings in China, are the essence of ancient Chinese architectural art. Over thousands of years, in capital cities, emperors are all at the expense of a large amount of manpower and material resources in the construction of large-scale, majestic, and magnificent palaces to meet their own extravagant enjoyment. Meanwhile, the splendid palaces also create a tremendous sense of dignity in spirit, which can consolidate their power. Architectural art is also a means of foiling the supreme imperial power. Palaces have their own striking features, which can be briefly summarized as axial symmetry, the ancestral temple in the left and the altar of Land and Grain in the right, the court in front and resting palaces in back, and three courts and five gates.

(1) Axial Symmetry

To show monarchical power given from the Heaven and sense of hierarchy centering in the imperial power, palatial architecture takes strictly the layout axial symmetry. The buildings on the central axis are tall and gorgeous. Those on the two

sides are low and simple. This apparent contrast reflects the imperial supremacy. The far-reaching longitudinal axis also embodies the dignity and luxury of the imperial palace.

(2) Ancestral Temples in the Left, Altar of Land and Grain in the Right

For the norm of Chinese etiquette, there is a key idea that it is important to revere ancestor, advocate filial piety, and worship the Land God and the Grain God. Where there is land, there is food. Some old sayings, which go like, "food is the first necessity of the people", "hunger breeds discontentment", "favorable weather leads to peaceful country and happy people", are well known and regarded as unalterable principles. The ideas mentioned above are well embodied in the principle of ancestral temples in the left and altar of Land and Grain in the right. "Ancestral temples in the left" means the ancestral temples are in the left front of palaces. Ancestral temple is the place where the emperors offer sacrifices to ancestors. It is called the Imperial Ancestral Temple for the reason that it is the emperors' ancestral temple. "Altar of land and grain in the right" means the altars of Land and Grain are in the right front of palaces. The altar of Land and Grain is also called Shejitan Altar, in which "She" means land, and "Ji" means grain. So Shejitan Altar is the place where the Emperor worshiped the God of Land as well as the God of Grain.

(3) Front Court and Back Palace

Front court is located in the front of the entire buildings, and is used for day-to-day affairs of state and ceremonial purposes. The back palace, which is also called the resting palace of the emperors, is located at the back, and is the residence of the emperor and his family.

(4) Three Courts and Five Gates

Space planning and construction of the palace buildings are carried on according to the needs of the emperor's political activities and daily living. The

main political activities in the palace are around the court. Therefore, the building groups are also around the court. Different imperial events are held in different courts with different sizes, which are named as "Three Courts System" since ancient times. Three Courts refer to the outer court, governance court, and living court. The outer court is the place where the emperors discuss state affairs, deal with lawsuits, issue decrees, and hold ceremonies, so it is located outside the south gate which is accessible for people. Governance court is the place where the emperors treat daily affairs, memorials from the ministers and report from common people. Living court is the place where the emperors meet and discuss affairs with his ministers, confer titles, and hold banquets.

The gate in palace not only plays the role of separating each court, but also has the transportation hub and guard security functions. There are many versions about the gates in imperial palace in historical documents. It is generally considered that there are 5 gates for a palace, namely, *Gaomen*, *Kumen*, *Zhimen*, *Yingmen*, and *Lumen*. *Gao* means far in Chinese, so *Gaomen* is the gate which is the outmost one of the palace gates and is the gate of governance court. *Ku* means storage in Chinese, so in *Kumen* is the gate, which is for storerooms and stables or sheds. *Zhimen* has two gate towers. *Lu* means huge. *Lumen* is the gate of living court. Inside the gate is the home of the emperors and their households. The Forbidden City of Ming and Qing Dynasties generally follow "Three Courts and Five Gates System" with flexibility according to the prevailing social conditions and needs. Based on the position, usage and architectural form, Five Gates in Ming Dynasty are corresponding to Damingmen Gate (Great Ming Gate), Chengtianmen Gate (Gate for Receiving the Mandate of Heaven, Tian'anmen Gate), Duanmen Gate (Upright Gate), Wumen Gate (Meridian Gate) and Fengtianmen Gate (Gate for Paying Tribute to Heaven Gate, Gate of Supreme Harmony); in Qing Dynasty, Tian'anmen Gate, Duanmen Gate (Upright Gate), Wumen Gate (Meridian Gate), Taihemen Gate (Gate of Supreme Harmony), and Qianqingmen Gate (Gate of Heavenly Purity).

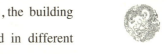

(5) Famous Palatial Architecture, Beijing Palace Museum

The Palace Museum is also called the Forbidden City which is the Chinese imperial palace from Ming Dynasty to the end of Qing Dynasty. It is located in the center of Beijing, and now it is called the Palace Museum. The construction and completion of the emperor's palace are under the request of Emperor Yongle, an emperor in Ming Dynasty, in 1406 A. D. and in 1420 A. D. respectively. During over five centuries, the Forbidden City has been home to 24 emperors. The Forbidden City covers an area of more than 720,000 square meters, 961 meters from north to south and 753 meters from east to west. It consists of over 9,000 bays of rooms with building area of 150,000 square meters. The Forbidden City is surrounded by a 10 meters high city wall and a 52 meters wide moat. It is the largest and best-kept palace buildings in China. The palace buildings are featured with rigor, order, greenish white porcelain as the base, red walls, yellow glazed tile roof, cornices wing angle, which create a sense of solemnity, magnificence and liveliness. Together with its awe-inspiring architecture, the Forbidden City is world-renowned for the impressive historical and cultural richness hiding behind the walls.

The Forbidden City Palace grounds are divided into two main sections, the Front Court and the Inner Palace. The Front Court is the place where the emperors exercise his power over the nation by attending ceremonies and conducting state affairs. It is composed of three main buildings in the central axis, Taihedian Hall (the Hall of Supreme Harmony), Zhonghedian Hall (the Hall of Central Harmony), and Baohedian Hall (the Hall of Preserving Harmony).

Taihedian Hall is the most magnificent building, commonly known as the *Jinluandian* (throne room), where the emperors hold the ceremony, and it is one of the most famous three Chinese ancient halls. Zhonghedian Hall located behind is the usual resting and rehearsing place of emperors prior to presiding over grand events. Finally, Baohedian Hall is the building used for holding banquets and imperial examinations. The three halls all stand on eight-meter-high terraces which

are made up of three layers of white marble bounded by a low balustrade. All these make them tall, grand and solemn.

The Inner Palace is the place where the emperor and his royal family and concubines lived. It is also the place where the emperors handle daily affairs. That section is composed of three main structures, Qianqinggong Palace (the Palace of Heavenly Purity), Zhonghedian Palace (the Palace of Union and Peace), and Kunninggong Palace (the Palace of Earthly Tranquility). Beside them, twelve more palaces stand, six on the eastern side, six on the western side. This inner court contains rich flavor of life, in which most buildings are independent with the garden, study, pavilions, rocks, and so on. In the north of the Kunninggong Place stands the Imperial Garden, where there are towering pines and cypress, precious flowers and trees, rocks and pavilions.

2. Defensive Architecture

Defensive architecture refers to the walls around the city in ancient times for military defense. Generally, there are inner and outer city walls. Towers, turrets, crenels and other fortifications on the walls constitute a complete set of solid defense system.

(1) Gate Houses

The gate house is an important symbol of the city and a symbol of power, so it is generally quite tall and majestic. Usually it is used for guarding, reserving food and weapons, but in war time, it is the command center and guard point.

(2) Turrets

The turret is located in the four corners of the city. It is the weak point in the city defense, for the reason that it is a two-way point against the enemy. During the war, more troops and weapons concentrate in the turret.

(3) Garrison Towers

The defensive role of garrison towers is great. Soldiers are vulnerable to be

attacked by the enemy if they stretch out the heads here for the reason that the front of the walls is inconvenient to shot. However, with the highlight of enemy terrace, the enemy is too easy to be shot and they are unable to board the city.

(4) Watch Towers

Generally built on the walls, watch towers are higher than the walls with two or three stories. They are used to reserve army provisions, ordnance, gunpowder, shelters for the soldiers from the wind and rain and war purposes.

(5) Crenel

Generally built on the top of walls facing enemy, the crenel is the convex part of this concave-convex construction. There are two holes in the crenel. The upper one is named watching hole, which is used for monitoring the invading enemy. The lower one is arrow hole for shooting at the enemy. With crenel, the defensive part can not only be invisible from the enemy, and shoot the enemy effectively, so it can remain an invincible position.

(6) Top of a Wall

The top of the wall is the channel for military defense activities, on which 2-meter-high crenels are built on the enemy side and 1-meter-high parapet is built on the other side. The channel is so wide that 5 horses or 10 persons can walk side by side. On steep occasion, the road is built into the stepped stairway. In order to get rid of the rain water, drains and other facilities are constructed on the top of the wall. Stone or brick arches open in the inner part of the wall at some distance, together with stone path to the top of the wall, so the soldiers can walk up and down.

(7) Barbican

Rectangular or circular in shape, the barbican, which is built outside the gates facing the enemy, aims to reinforce the defense, accompanying with the

construction of the arrow tower on the platform facing the enemy.

(8) Arrow Towers

Arrow towers, facing the gate house, stand on the platforms of the barbican. Their three faces are provided with a row of arrows holes, so when the enemy launches an attack, they can form dense firing points, which give the enemy a devastating blow.

(9) Moat

Moat is a deep and wide gap closely outside the city walls. It constitutes a double defense system. At the gate, the drawbridge is often set.

(10) Bell and Drum Tower

In ancient times, morning bell and evening drum are time reminders or signs of warning, so bell and drum towers are built in key cities. If the gates of four directions are open in the center, four gates face each other, which lead to the streets in the city a cross. Generally the bell and drum tower is located near the crossroad. Bell and Drum Tower in Xi'an City is the case.

(11) Famous Defensive Architecture

The existing famous defensive architecture includes the City Wall in Nanjing City (Ming Dynasty), the City Wall in Xi'an City (Ming Dynasty), and the City Wall in Pingyao County (Ming Dynasty).

3. The Great Wall

The Great Wall is a unique type of architecture, and beside the defensive function, it forms a style, which is exclusively-owned by China.

It is said that the history of the Great Wall starts from the Spring and Autumn Periods when seven powerful states co-exist at the same time. In order to defend themselves, they all build walls and station troops on the borders. In 221 B. C., the

Emperor Qin conquers the other six states and sets up the first unified kingdom in Chinese history. In order to defend Xiongnu, an ancient nationality in China, in the north, in 214 B. C., he orders connecting the walls once built by such states as Qin, Zhao, and Yan. Thus the Great Wall comes into being. The Great Wall starts from the east of today's Liaodong and ends at Lintao County in the north, stretches to Yinshan Mountain in the north. At that time, the total length of the wall has already reached more than 6,000 meters, which is known to the Chinese as the "Wanli Changcheng". Han Dynasty, Northern Wei, Northern Qi, Northern Zhou of Nanbeichao Period and Sui Dynasty all built their own sections in order to consolidate the frontier. However, the Great Wall, which we can see today, is the Great Wall, which is mostly built during Ming Dynasty (1368 – 1644 A. D.).

The Great Wall is not merely a wall but instead a complete and rigorous defensive project, which is composed of countless garrison towns, passes, and beacon towers, and so on.

(1) Wall

During Ming Dynasty, the Great Wall is mainly built on the ridge of meandering mountains. And in accordance with the terrain, bricks are heavily used in many areas of the wall, as are materials such as rammed earth and stone. The average height of it measures about 3 to 8 meters, and the top width is about 4 to 6 meters.

(2) Garrison Towers

On the wall, garrison towers, solid or hollow, are built each 30 to 100 meters. Solid garrisons are only used for observation and shooting, while the hollow ones are used for living in the underlayer, and on the upper layer, soldiers can watch and fire at the enemies.

(3) Beacon Towers

Beacon towers are built continually to pass military messages. Therefore, the

Great Wall contains countless beacon towers every 1.5 kilometers on the top of mountains, and they are of rammed-loam construction. They are composed of battlements and observation room. The city battlements are arranged like the dentate parapet, so soldiers can hide behind it. In ancient times, if intruders approached, soldiers on the wall will create smoke in the daytime and light a fire at night to warn their troops.

(4) Passes

Being the stronghold where the troops station, passes are often located in the key position of the Great Wall with an extremely tight defense. Generally speaking, the pass is composed of a city wall, city gate, gate tower, even many city walls for important passes.

(5) Famous Sections

The famous sections of the Great Wall include Badaling Great Wall in Yanqing County, Beijing City; Mutianyu Great Wall in Huairou District, Beijing City; Jingshanling Great Wall in Luanping County, Hebei Province; Huangyaguan Pass in Ji County, Tianjin City; Shanhaiguan Pass in Qinhuangdao City, Hebei Province; Jiayuguan Pass in Jiayuguan City, Gansu Province.

4. Mausoleums

Mausoleums architecture is another important component of Chinese ancient architecture, revealing the imposing majestic manner of royalty. It is also a combination of various artistic achievements like painting, calligraphy, sculpture, and so on. Many are set against mountains to take advantage of the natural terrain, but a few mausoleums are built in the plain.

Chinese mausoleums are mostly surrounded by walls and gates as well as corner towers in four directions. Leading into the mausoleum, there is a paved path leading to a main hall or a tomb. On the both sides of the paved path there are stone statues, and green and dense pines and cypresses in it, which creates a sense of

quietness and solemnity.

Chinese ancient imperial mausoleum generally consists of two parts, underground buildings and buildings on the ground. Underground part is called underground palace, which is mainly used for the burial of the dead body, remains and funerary objects. In the underground palace, a copy of living conditions of the dead is also presented. The buildings on the ground are composed of a sealing soil and buildings, which are mainly used for the sacrifices and protections.

Famous mausoleums in China are Qinshihuang Mausoleum, Ming Tombs, and Eastern Qing Mausoleums.

5. Ritual Architecture

Ritual architecture is originated in the worship activities. Along with the sacrifice, the corresponding places, structures and buildings are formed, which are called the ritual buildings. Ritual architecture can be divided into the altar, temple, shrine, etc.

(1) Altar

The altar building can be divided into altars in a broad sense and in a narrow sense. The altar in a narrow sense refers only to the main building for sacrifice with square or circular shape, while in a broad sense, it includes the various affiliated buildings, too. The existing famous altars are Altar of Heaven and Altar of Earth and Grain.

Altar of Heaven The Altar of Heaven is the building groups situated in the east side in Yongding Gate, Chongwen District of central Beijing. The Altar of Heaven is the place, where the emperors of Ming and Qing Dynasties worship the God of Heaven and Earth. The Altar of Heaven is first built in 18th gear of Emperor Yongle in Ming Dynasty (1420 A. D.). It is firstly called the Altar of Heaven and Earth at that time. However, in 9th year of Emperor Jiajing in Ming Dynasty (1530 A. D.), it is renamed as the Altar of Heaven because the Altar of Earth is also built in the north of Beijing. It is used to hold a memorial ceremony for the God in Winter Solstice

Festival and to pray for harvest in the first month of the lunar year by the emperors. When the new emperor ascends the throne, he must offer sacrifices to the Heaven, to show his mandate from the Heaven.

Altar of Earth and Harvests The Altar of Land and Grain or the Altar of Earth and Harvests, which is built in 1421 A. D. by Emperor Yongle, is the place where the emperors of Ming and Qing Dynasties worship the gods of land and grain. The altar covers an area of 240, 000 square meters. The alter surface are covered with five colored earth, which are yellow, green, red, white and black. The five colored earth are placed in five directions respectively, yellow in the middle, green in the East, white in the West, red in the South, and black in the North, which accords with the theory of Yin-Yang and the Five Elements of Taoist. Besides, it also indicates that all the earth in the country belongs to the emperor. In the center of the platform stands a square column, signifying that the emperor's reign will be everlasting just as the mountains and rivers. By 1914, the altar grounds become a public park known as the Central Park. That park is then further renamed in 1928 after Sun Yat-Sen (Zhongshan Park).

(2) Temples

The temple includes Imperial Ancestral Temple that the emperors worship their ancestors, Temples of Literature (Confucius Temples) built to commemorate great sage Confucius, Martial Temple (Guan Yu Temple) enshrining of Guan Yu, and different temples for worshiping sages, saints and gods.

The existing famous temples are Imperial Ancestral Temple, Confucius Temple, Guan Yu Temple, Mazu Temple.

Imperial Ancestral Temple The Imperial Ancestral Temple, which is built in 1420 A. D. by Emperor Yongle and rebuilt in 1544 A. D. by Emperor Jiajing, is where the emperors of Ming and Qing Dynasties hold sacrificial ceremonies in honor of the imperial family's ancestors. The temple is repaired and expanded by Emperor Shunzhi and Emperor Qianlong many times in Qing Dynasty. The Imperial Ancestral Temple is now the Cultural Palace of the Laboring People.

Confucius Temple Confucian Temple is located in Qufu City in Shandong Province, with large-scale, magnificence, and beautiful decoration is China's largest place worshiping Confucius.

Guan Yu Temple The Guan Yu Temple is situated at the west pass in Xiezhou Town, Yuncheng City of Shanxi Province. Changping village, 10 kilometers southeast away from Xiezhou Town, is the hometown of Guan Yu, who is a general of Shu State in the Three Kingdoms Period.

Mazu Temple Mazu Temple in Meizhou City is first built in Northern Song Dynasty, 4th year of Yongxi period (984 A. D.) with only a few bungalows. After expansion in Song, Yuan, Ming, and Qing Dynasties, it has upgraded to Tianhou Temple. Meizhou Mazu Temple is the ancestor of all the Mazu temples in world, and all Mazu temples get their "spirits" from it. Every March 23th in Chinese lunar calendar is Mazu's birthday and September 9th is Mazu's Ascension Day, so on these two days, numerous followers of Mazu will come to Meizhou City to find their roots and hold grand sacrifice activities.

(3) Shrine

The shrine, a ritual architecture different from imperial temples, is a kind of temple, which is dedicated to a specific deity, ancestor, hero, martyr, saint, daemon or similar figure of awe and respect for noblemen or common people.

Jin Shrine Jin Shrine is located at the origin of Jinshui River, as well as the foothill of Xuanwengshan Moutain, 25 kilometers away from Taiyuan City, Shanxi Province. It is also the location of several ancient gardens. Jin Shrine is first founded in the Northern Wei State of the Nanbeichao Period to commemorate Shuyu, the second son of Emperor Wu in Zhou Dynasty.

Wuhou Shrine (Memorial Temple of Marquis Wu) Wuhou Shrine in Chengdu City is the largest and most prestigious one among the existing Wuhou Shrines in China. It is a national key cultural heritage unit.

6. Religious Architecture

Chinese religious architecture includes Chinese Buddhist architecture, Chinese

Taoist architecture, Chinese Islamic architecture and Chinese Christian architecture.

(1) Buddhist Architecture

The main Buddhist architectural items include temples, pagodas, and grottos. Initially, the Chinese Buddhist temples follow Indian style, which sets the stupa as its center. The Buddhist temple is adapted to Chinese tastes after Jin and Tang Dynasties. Its general layout follows Chinese traditional type, courtyard with halls as its principal parts. Generally speaking, the mountain gate (front gate) is the entrance part. The Hall of Heavenly King is the first main hall. Next follows the Grand Hall. Bodhisattva Hall is located behind. Next is the lecture hall. Refectories, monks' rooms and other attached architecture are distributed in the east and west along the central axis.

Famous Chinese Buddhist temples are Baimasi Temple in Luoyang City, He'nan Province, Lingyinsi Temple in Hangzhou City, Zhejiang Province, Jinshansi Temple in Zhenjiang City, Jiangsu Province, Guiyuansi Buddhist Temple in Wuhan City, Hubei Province, Fuhusi Temple in Emeishan Mountain, Sichuan Province, Tiantaisi Temple in Jiuhuashan Mountain, Anhui Province, Shaolinsi Temple in Songshan Mountain, He'nan Province.

Grotto, another type of Buddhist architecture, is often chiseled into cliffs. Buddhism advocates the reclusion as hermits, for which the monks choose high mountains and lofty hills to dig caves. The layout of grottoes is probably to set a square hall as the core, the surrounding is a circle of pillars, three facets are chiseled several square meditation halls for practice and outside the cave stands the colonnade. Chinese grottoes originally followed the Indian caves system, and many are built in the Huanghe River basin of northern China.

The three famous grottoes in China are Yungang Grottoes in Datong City, Shanxi Province, Mogao Caves in Dunhuang City, Gansu Province, and Longmen Grottoes in Luoyang City, He'nan Province.

Pagoda, which is a symbol of Buddhism, where monks worship and place relics, scriptures and various dharma-vessels, is often composed of underground palace,

base, tower, and *Tasha*. Pagodas have an odd number of layers, and their bodies gradually step upward and gradually gathered. The shape of cross-section is rectangular, eight-sided or even multi-sided. Pagodas in China are featured with large numbers, different forms, various styles, and rich architectural decorative beauty. Pagodas can be made of stone, wood, brick, colored glaze or metal. According to the types, they can be divided into the pavilion style pagoda, multi-eaves pagoda, Lamaist pagoda, pagoda with Vajra-base, and relics pagoda, etc.

China's famous pagodas are Pagoda Forest of Wutaishan Mountain in Shanxi Province, Pagoda Forest of Shaolinsi Temple of Songshan Mountain, in Dengfeng City, He'nan Province, Pagoda Forest of Lingyansi Temple in Ji'nan City, Shandong Province, Pagoda Forest of Qingtongxia City in Ningxia, White Pagoda Forest of Feilongshan Mountain in Jinghong County, Yunnan Province, etc.

(2) Taoist Architecture

Taoist architecture is called Taoist temple, or generally called *Daoguan* in Chinese, Taoist temple is not only the place to worship the gods but also the place for Taoists to live in and to perform their religious ceremonies. It includes, palaces, temples, halls, nunneries, altars, huts, rooms, houses, pavilions, platforms, storied buildings, colonnades, pavilions on terrace, waterside pavilions, pagodas, bridges, and so on. It can be divided into holy halls for sacrifice, altars to pray at, houses to live in, rooms to chant scriptures gardens for guests and visitors in according to their use.

Famous Chinese Taoist temples are Baiyunguan Temple in Beijing City, Zhouzhilou Taoist Temple in Shaanxi Province, Xuanmiaoguan Taoist Temple in Suzhou City, and Chongxuguan Taoist Temple of Luofushan Mountain in Guangdong Province, and so on.

(3) Islamic Architecture

Islam mosque is not only the holy place where Muslims fulfill their divine services, but also the miniature of Islamic architecture. The whole layout is composed of a series of courtyards distributed orderly along the central axis. The construction

contains generally hall, water room, a lecture hall, minaret or Mochizuki, and in the hall right facing the wall are equipped with mihrab(niche) , in the northwest corner are the minaret tower.

The famous Chinese Islamic architectures include Qingjingsi Mosque in Quanzhou City, Huaishengsi Mosque in Guangzhou City, Fenghuangsi Mosque in Hangzhou City and Xianhesi Mosque in Yangzhou City, Niujie Mosque in Beijing City, Huajuesi Mosque in Xi'an City, Yidigaer Mosque in Kashi Prefecture, Tongxing Weizhou Mosque and Shizuishan Mosque in Ningxia Hui Autonomous Region, and West Mosque in Ji'ning City.

(4) Christian Architecture

Three main sects of Christianity all have built churches in China, and Chinese Christian Architecture mostly follows the original western architecture, which breaks the dominant status of traditional Chinese architecture.

The famous buildings with Christian characteristics include the South Church and North Church in Beijing, the Laoxikai Church(St Joseph's Cathedral Church) in Tianjin, Xujiahui Catholic Church in Shanghai, Shi Sacred Heart Cathedral in Guangzhou, San Sofia Cathedral in Harbin, Shanghai Notre Dame Cathedral, Shanghai Community Church and Shanghai King Hall.

7. Residential Architecture

The patterns and styles of residential architecture in China differ in regions because of the vast territory, different geographical conditions, climatic conditions and different ways of life, coupled with the impact of economy and culture. According to the regions, the traditional residential architecture of China has five major styles, dwelling in the regions south of the Yangtze River, Northwestern cave dwelling, Beijing courtyard, dwellings in south China, and minority residential houses.

(1) Beijing Courtyard

Beijing courtyard(*Siheyuan* in Chinese) is the representative work of Chinese

courtyard. The layout of courtyard is in strict accordance with the axis, so the main buildings are distributed in the central axis, the left and the right ones are symmetrical. This arrangement reflects the patriarchal and ethical system in feudal society. The rooms also assigned based on the age and status in the family.

(2) Dwelling in the Regions South of the Yangtze River

The region in south of the Yangtze River are rich in water resources because of geography. Most of the villages and towns, cities constructions basically remain on the banks of the river. The buildings around the river make it a water street. Zhouzhuang Town is the typical representative of Water Village in this region. Buildings here are built along the rivers. Moreover, in order to achieve the waterproof effect damp proof effect, massive stones or stones are used for the surface for sticking the lower part of the walls.

The plane layout of the dwelling, roughly the same as the northern courtyard, is an enclosed courtyard, but relatively more compact. The gates of houses generally open in the central axis, and the first house on the axis is used to receive guests and hold ceremony. Behind it is two-storied building, and for better ventilation and lighting, the walls in it are provided with leaking windows, and windows are both on front and back walls.

The hot, humid, and rainy climate exerts a great influence on the dwellings in this region. In order to avoid humidity, the residential walls are generally higher and wider with front and back doors which are convenient for ventilation. At the same time, to isolate the ground moisture, two-storied building is commonly found and the bedroom is in the second floor. The base is made of brick wall, while the upper part is in wooden structure.

(3) Huizhou Dwelling

The most prominent feature of Huizhou dwelling lies in Matouqiang walls and black tiles. The Matouqiang walls are as high as a man, so they can protect the roofs to prevent from fire. The gatehouse is decorated with stone and brick cravings which

are full of life flavor. Houses are built under the natural conditions. Three-section or four-section compounds both can be seen here, and the compound consists of two or three main buildings. The roof of Huizhou dwelling is characterized by "four water gathering in the court" in the courtyard. It refers to that the door in the central axis, the back hall, and the two-storied building form a yard which is also called patio for lighting and drainage. Water from four sides of the roofs flow into the courtyard is what commonly known as "four water gathering in the court".

(4) Northwestern Cave Dwelling

The most characteristic house in the Northwest is cave dwelling building which suits the local conditions, using the loess layer of the Loess Plateau. According to the shape, the cave can be divided into cliff cave, independent cave and sunken cave. The decoration of cave doors and windows is emphasized here and the doors and windows are in the similar size to holes. They are generally decorated with the lattice patterns. And kinds of paper-cut are posted on the windows in festivals.

(5) Dwelling in Middle Shanxi

Middle Shanxi is famous for the fancy dwellings built by the local merchants. The dwellings are built in large scale, together with exquisite design, special style and unique spatial distribution, and they mainly use brick wood structure to form a courtyard. Thick black bricks are paved for the walls as well as for the ground in the yard. One of the characteristics of middle Shanxi dwelling is single slope roof instead of herringbone slope roof, so the height of the walls is identical to that of the house. Another one is deep courtyard, which is long from north to south, narrow from east to west.

Grand residential buildings here are, Qiao Clan Courtyard, Wang Clan Courtyard, and so on. In the courtyard, different buildings can be seen.

(6) Earthen Houses of Fujian

Earthen houses, *Tulou* in Chinese, are the most representative residential

buildings for the Hakkas. They are mostly square with large amount. The length of single side wall generally reaches between 20 – 50 meters, and there are three to four even five floors. The tile of the square earthen house is usually as high as the roof eaves, and the roof belongs to the hanging top type, wooden structure, but Xieshan top with nine ridges type is also the case. The bottom of square house is for kitchen, the second floor is used as the barn, and they both have no windows. And above them are the bedrooms with small windows. The ancestral hall is generally located in the bottom floor inside the courtyard, facing the door, and in the end of the central axis. Ventilation and lighting of the entire building both depend on the patio of the courtyard.

(7) Ethnic Minority Residential Dwellings

China has many ethnic minorities with different architectural styles, and the most typical ethnic minority dwellings are bamboo houses, upland dwellings, Mongolian yurt and seal-like compound in Yunnan Province.

Bamboo Houses Bamboo houses, a kind of Ganlan type dwelling in south China, mainly refer to bamboo buildings with two or more floors. According to the purpose and shape, they can be divided into the hotel building, restaurant building, and sightseeing building, and so on. Bamboo houses are very suitable for tourism, accommodation, catering and other purposes for they are environmentally friendly and natural. They are mainly distributed in Dehong and Xishuangbanna Prefectures of Yunnan Province and are used by Dai, Ji'nuo and other ethnic groups. Now the bamboo houses generally mean the Dai bamboo houses for their representation.

Upland Dwellings Upland dwellings belong to half-Ganlan style architecture for they are half-suspended.

Upland dwellings are mostly built against the mountains, with special attention to the geomancy like *Qinglong* (Green dragon) on the left, *Baihu* (White tiger) on the right, *Zhuque* (Rose finch) in front, and *Xuanwu* (Black turtle) at behind. The forms include single hanging type, double hanging type, courtyard type, two houses hanging type, and flat roof lifting type, etc. The bottom is used to store goods. The second floor

is for living and has a hall for receiving guests. The upland dwelling with three floors provides a separate small room for storage in the third floor besides the living function.

Mongolian Yurt Mongolia yurt is round in shape and composed of wood frame, felt, rope, and the raw materials are wood and fur. Mongolia yurts are different in size, but the basic structure is the same.

The door of Mongolia yurt is generally toward the southeast, and the west side in it is for elders, the east for the juniors.

Seal-Like Compound in Yunnan(Yikeyin) It is warm and windy in central Yunnan plateau. Therefore, the house walls are thick. The most common dwelling form is a building with three adjacent rooms and four wing rooms. That means there are three main rooms, and on the left and right stand two rooms respectively, and in some cases, there is a room opposite to the main rooms. Sometimes, a small courtyard is used instead of a room in order to save the land and improve the climate of the house. The exterior walls are high and without windows so as to prevent the wind and the sand. Here the compound is called *Yikeyin* in Chinese, which means seal because the layout and whole building both resemble the shape of the square seal.

第十五章　中国园林艺术文化

园林是中国传统建筑文化的集大成者，也是中国文化的精华之一。中国古典园林是以自然山水为基础，以植被作为装点，以山水、花木、石、建筑为表现手段，在有限的空间里创造出一个精练的、概括的、典型化的自然。达到所谓的“虽为人做，宛自天开”的意境。

中国园林的精髓在于通过造园者的构思创作，表现出园林景观上的形象化、典型化的自然环境以及它显露出来的诗情画意，这是造园艺术所追求的最高境界。中国园林通常还与一些诗文、书画、楹联相结合，更增添了园林的诗情画意。

中国园林建筑类型丰富，有殿、堂、厅、馆、轩、榭、亭、台、楼、阁、廊、桥等，以及它们的各种组合形式，不论其性质与功能如何，都能与山水、树木有机结合，协调一致，互相映衬、互相渗透、互为借取。有的建筑能成为园林景观的主体，成为构图中心，有的建筑对自然风景起画龙点睛的作用。

一、中国园林分类

按占有者身份分，中国园林可以分为皇家园林和私家园林。

皇家园林是专供帝王休息享乐的园林。其特点是规模宏大，真山真水较多，园中建筑色彩富丽堂皇，建筑体型高大。现存最为著名的皇家园林有北京的故宫、圆明园、香山公园、北海公园、颐和园和河北承德的避暑山庄等。

私家园林是供皇家的宗室外戚、王公官吏、富商大贾等休闲的园林。其特点是规模较小，所以常用假山假水，建筑小巧玲珑，表现出淡雅素净的色彩。现存的私家园林较多，如北京的恭王府，苏州的拙政园、留园、沧浪亭、

网狮园，上海的豫园等。

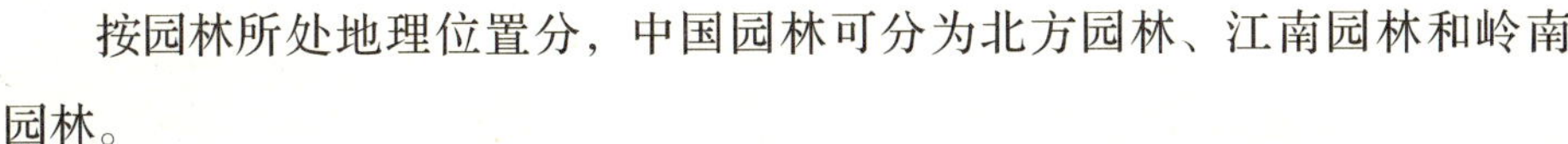

按园林所处地理位置分，中国园林可分为北方园林、江南园林和岭南园林。

北方园林，因地域宽广，所以范围较大，建筑富丽堂皇；因自然气象条件所局限，河川湖泊、园石和常绿树木都较少。由于风格粗犷，所以秀丽媚美则显得不足。北方园林的代表大多集中于北京、西安、洛阳和开封，其中尤以北京最具代表性。

江南因人口较密集，所以园林地域范围小；又因河湖、园石、常绿树较多，所以园林景致较细腻精美。因上述条件，其特点为明媚秀丽、淡雅朴素、曲折幽深，但毕竟面积小，略感局促。江南园林的代表大多集中于南京、上海、无锡、苏州、杭州、扬州等地，其中尤以苏州为代表。

岭南因为其地处亚热带，终年常绿，又多河川，所以造园条件比北方、南方都好。其明显的特点是具有热带风光，建筑物都较高而宽敞。现存岭南类型园林，有著名的广东顺德的清晖园、东莞的可园、番禺的余荫山房等。

二、中国古典园林的组成要素

（一）筑　山

筑山是造园的重要组成要素之一。筑山是为了表达造园者对仙境的向往。造园时常造一池三山，一池象征东海，三山象征东海中的蓬莱、方丈、瀛洲三座传说中的神山。秦汉的上林苑，用太液池所挖土堆成岛，象征东海神山，开创了人为造山的先例。

筑山有时是为了模仿自然山水。在园中垒土构石为山是对自然山水的模仿，体现了造园艺术以现实生活作为创作起点的思想。宋徽宗时的艮岳是历史上规模最大、结构最奇巧、以石为主的假山。

筑山有时是为写意山水。造园者采用概括、提炼手法，将所造之山的真实尺度大大缩小，但力求体现自然山峦的形态和神韵。这种写意式的筑山，比自然主义模仿大大前进一步。苏州拙政园、常熟的燕园和上海的豫园，其筑山便是此意。

（二）理　水

理水也是造园最主要的组成要素之一。古代园林理水之法一般有三种：掩、隔和破。

所谓掩就是用建筑和绿化将曲折的池岸加以掩映。比如，临水建筑，不论亭、廊、阁、榭，皆前部架空挑出水上，以形成水好像从其下面流出的错觉，这样可以打破岸边的视线局限。也可以在池水的岸边种上芦苇和杂木，造成池水无边的视觉印象。

所谓隔就是在水面上筑堤把水面隔断，也可在水面上架上曲折的小桥，来增加景深和空间层次，使水面有幽深之感。

所谓破就是当水面很小时，如曲溪绝涧、清泉小池，可用乱石为岸，怪石纵横、犬牙交齿，并植配以细竹、野藤、朱鱼、翠藻，那么虽是一洼水池，也令人似有深邃山野风致的审美感觉。

（三）花　木

花木是造山理水不可缺少的要素。花木犹如山峦之毛发，所筑之山，如果缺了花木的衬托，就没有美感可言，水景如果离开花木的掩映，也失去了美感。造园时，要选择姿美、色美、味香、有意境的花木。

（四）建　筑

园林中建筑有十分重要的作用，它可满足人们生活享受和观赏风景的愿望。中国园林，其建筑一方面要可行、可观、可居、可游，一方面要起到点景、隔景的作用，产生移步换景、渐入佳境，以小见大的效果，使园林显得自然、淡泊、恬静、含蓄。中国自然式园林中的建筑形式多样，有宫、殿、堂、厅、楼、阁、馆、轩、斋、塔、榭、舫、亭、廊、桥、墙等。

宫、殿具有高大严肃、堂皇富丽的审美性格，一般处于中轴线上，占据中心位置，是整个园林的主体。宫、殿是专供皇帝居所或供奉神佛之用的建筑。

厅、堂具有庄严的气度，在私园中通常作为主体建筑，是全园的中心。厅、堂是专供园主团聚家人、接待客人、进行宴会等重要活动的建筑，空间大。该类建筑不仅要满足不同的功能要求，也要体现主人的身份、修养和志趣。

楼是在宽敞的地方，构筑高耸的建筑，可供人更上一层楼，以观远处的风景。

阁是古典园林中的常见建筑类型，一般为重檐，并且四面都开窗，造型通透轻盈。层数一般在两层以上，用于观景和藏书。

馆既可指园林中供起居、燕乐、观览、眺望的建筑，也可以指园主专门招待宾客，供客人居住的建筑。

轩是置于高敞或临水之处，用作观景的小型单体建筑。

斋是园林中的一座小院，是用于修身养性的场所，处于僻静之处，常以叠石、植物进行遮掩，环境素雅、幽静，适合学习。

塔是多层建筑，常建于曲水转折处或山峰之巅，以控制局势，也暗含镇守一方平安的吉祥寓意。

榭是依水架起的观景平台，平台一部分架在岸上，一部分伸入水中。榭四面敞开，平面形式比较自由，常与廊、台组合在一起。

舫多建于水池边，且三面临水，或四面临水，是专供游览赏景的船形建筑。

亭通常四面临空，常筑于山顶或山腰，是供人休息的地方。

廊是古典园林中最具特色的建筑之一，通常是指有顶的过道，可避风雨、遮太阳，具有轻灵美好的风格特征，是联系建筑物的脉络，又常是赏景的导游线。

桥有拱桥、平桥、廊桥、曲桥等类型，有石制的、竹制的、木制的。桥不但有增添景色的作用，而且用以隔景可在视觉上产生扩大空间的作用。

三、中国古典园林构景手段

构景手段是在造园构景中运用多种手段来表现自然，以求得渐入佳境、小中见大、步移景异的理想境界，以取得自然、淡泊、恬静、含蓄的艺术效果。常见的构景手段有布局、对景、框景、漏景和借景。

（一）布　局

布局是指以天然景观为主，人工景观为辅的园林构景手段。布局应用于大

多数的皇家园林和寺庙园林，如颐和园、避暑山庄、乐山大佛寺，普陀山观音寺等。这些园林本来就是建筑在景色优美的地方，观赏能直接欣赏到大自然的本来面目，其中建筑只是作为风景的点缀。这种园林的特点是以山水作为风景主体，人工艺术的建筑庭院只是作为大自然的烘托和陪衬，二者相得益彰，天然美和自然美融为一体。

（二）对　景

对景是指在园林中，登上亭、台、楼、阁、榭可观赏堂、山、桥、树木，反之在堂桥廊等处可观赏亭、台、楼、阁等。

（三）框　景

框景是指园林中的建筑的门、窗、洞或乔木树枝抱合成的景框，往往把远处的山水美景或人文景观包含其中。

（四）漏　景

在园林的围墙上，或走廊（单廊或复廊）一侧或两侧的墙上，常常设以漏窗，或雕以带有民族特色的各种几何图形，或雕以民间喜闻乐见的葡萄、石榴、老梅、修竹等植物，或雕以鹿、鹤、兔等动物，透过漏窗的窗隙，可见园外或院外的美景，这叫做漏景。

（五）借　景

借景是指在造园时有意识地把园外的景物“借”到园内视景范围中来，目的是在有限的空间里，在横向或纵向上，让游人扩展视觉和联想，从而达到以小见大的艺术效果。借景有远借、邻借、仰借、俯借、应时而借之分。借远方的山，叫远借；借邻近的大树，叫邻借；借空中的飞鸟，叫仰借；借池塘中的鱼，叫俯借；借四季的花或其他自然景象，叫应时而借。

Chapter 15　Chinese Garden Art and Culture

Chinese classical gardens are one of the greatest achievements of Chinese traditional architectural culture and also one of the Chinese cultural quintessence. Taking natural landscape as their basis, ground vegetation covers as their decorations, mountains, waters, flowers, trees, stones and architectures as their means of expression, Chinese classical gardens use the limited space to create a refined, summarized and typified nature, which creates an artistic effect of being natural without any artificial decoration.

The essence of Chinese gardens is that it can express the visualized and typical natural environment of garden landscape and the poetic prospect, which they expose, through the design and creation of garden creators, which is the highest realm pursued by garden creators. People usually combine Chinese gardens with poetry, calligraphy, traditional Chinese paintings and Chinese couplets, which greatly increases the poetic and pictorial splendor of the gardens.

Chinese gardens contains different architectural types, including palace, hall, lounge, lodge, pavilion with windows, pavilion on terrace, pavilion, platform, storied building, loft, corridor, bridge and various integrated forms. No matter what their properties and functions are, they all form an organic combination with mountains, waters and trees, which are in harmony with each other, set each other off beautifully, integrate into each other harmoniously and bring out the best in each other naturally. Some constructions become the subject of Chinese gardens and the center of layout, and some buildings add the finishing touch to the natural scenery.

1. The Classifications of Chinese Gardens

According to the identity of their possessors, Chinese gardens can be divided into royal gardens and private gardens.

Royal gardens are gardens which are specially built for emperors' relaxation and entertainments. Royal gardens are characterized by their large scale, abundant natural mountains and waters, majestic colors and magnificent constructions. The existing famous royal gardens include the Palace Museum, the Winter Palace, Xiangshan Park, Beihai Park and Summer Palace in Beijing and the Mountain Resort in Chengde in Hebei Province, and so on.

Private gardens are those which are built for imperial princes, court ministers, rich merchants and tycoons to relax themselves. Therefore, they are characterized by their small scale, artificial mountains and waters, small and exquisite constructions to create a light, elegant, plain and neat tone. The existing private gardens include the Prince Gong's Palace (Gongwangfu Garden) in Beijing, the Humble Administrator's Garden (Zhuozhengyuan Garden), the Lingering Garden (Liuyuan Garden), Canglang Pavilion, the Garden of Master of the Net (Wangshiyuan Garden) in Suzhou, Yu Garden in Shanghai, and so on.

According to the geographical locations, Chinese gardens can be divided into northern gardens (gardens in northern China), Jiangnan gardens (gardens in regions south of Yangtze River) and Lingnan Gardens (gardens in regions south of the Five Ridges).

Northern gardens are characterized by their large scope and magnificent constructions for the spacious lands. However, being limited by climate conditions, there are less rivers, lakes, stones or evergreen woods in northern gardens. Northern gardens are lacking of obsequious beauty in aesthetics due to their rough and straightforward architecture styles. The representatives of northern gardens mostly gather in Beijing, Xi'an, Luoyang and Kaifeng, especially in Beijing.

Jiangnan gardens are usually small because of the intensive populations in South China. However, Jiangnan gardens are characterized by their exquisite and

elegant landscapes for the reason that there are plenty of rivers, lakes, stones and evergreen woods in the South. On one hand, for the conditions mentioned above, Jiangnan gardens are bright, beautiful, plain, elegant, tortuous and deep. On the other hand, due to their small size, Jiangnan gardens take on somewhat a sense of constrain. The representatives of Jiangnan gardens mostly gather in Nanjing, Shanghai, Wuxi, Suzhou, Hangzhou, Yangzhou, and so on, especially in Suzhou.

Located in the subtropical areas with many evergreen woods and rivers, when creating gardens, Lingnan has better advantages richly endowed by nature than that of in north and south. Lingnan gardens are characterized by their tropical scenery, tall and spacious constructions. The existing Lingnan gardens are the famous Qinghui Garden in Shunde, Keyuan Garden in Dongguan, and Yuqian Mountain House in Fanyu of Guangdong Province.

2. The Important Elements of Chinese Classical Gardens

(1) Hill Making

Hill making is one of the most important components for Garden making. The purpose of hill making is to express the creators' pursuits for fairyland. When making gardens, it is usual to build a pool and three hills. The pool symbolizes the East China Sea and three mountains represent three legendary holy mountains, namely Penglai Mountain, Fangzhang Mountain, Yingzhou Mountain in the East China Sea. For example, Shanglinyuan in Qin and Han Dynasties is made of the soil dug out from Taiye Pool to symbolize the holy mountain in the East China Sea, which set a precedent of hill making in Chinese history.

Sometimes, hill making is to imitate the natural mountains and waters. Turning from building hills in the garden by heaping up earth and stones to imitating natural scenes marks that the art of garden creation begin to take the real life as the starting point of creation. For example, Genyue, which is built by Emperor Songhuizong in Northern Song Dynasty, is an artificial hill mainly heaping up by stones with the largest scale and most elaborate structure in Chinese history.

Sometimes, hill making is just to imitate the shape and charm of the natural mountains and waters. The garden creators minimize the real size of the created mountains by largely generalizing and extracting just keeping the shapes and charms of natural mountains. The method of hill making, which just imitate the shape and charm of natural mountains has made a big step forward. The examples are the Humble Administrator's Garden in Suzhou, Yan Garden in Changshu and Yu Garden in Shanghai.

(2) Water Layout

Water layout is also one of the most important components for Garden making. There are generally three means for water layout in ancient gardens, namely hiding, separation and breakage.

Hiding is to use architectures and greening to shade the winding pool bank. For example, waterside constructions, whether pavilion, corridor, cabinet or shed, are all built on the water surface to form the optical illusion that water is flowing under them, which breaks the visual limits of the banks. We can also plant reeds and trees near the pool banks to make the pool boundless.

Separation means that the water surface is separated by dams or we can construct winding bridge on it to increase the scenery's depth and spatial levels, making people feel the water surface deep and quiet.

Breakage is that when water surface is small, for example, crooked creeks and streams or small pools, we can use some stones to form banks with fantastic stones spreading vertically and horizontally and plant thin bamboos, wild vines and put golden fish and green algae around or in it. Hence, although visiting a small pool, we can have aesthetic feeling as being in deep and wild mountains.

(3) Flowers and Trees

Flowers and trees are the indispensable elements for hill making and water layout. Flowers and woods are like mountains' hairs. Hill making without the foils of flowers and woods has no aesthetic feelings. Water landscape without the foils of flowers and woods also loses its aesthetic feelings. When making gardens, we should choose beautiful, flagrant, colorful and meaningful flowers and woods.

(4) Architecture

Architecture plays a very important role in gardens. It can satisfy people's desire to enjoy life and sightseeing. Architecture in Chinese gardens, on one hand, should have such functions as walking, looking, living and traveling, on the other hand, it can decorate and separate the landscape, making the scenery in the garden changeable, beautiful and mystic and also making the garden natural, plain, quiet and implicit. The architecture forms in Chinese gardens are various and have such forms as palace, hall, mansion, lounge, storied building, loft, lodge, pavilion with windows, monastic room, tower, pavilion on terrace, boat house, pavilion, corridor, bridge, wall, and so on.

The aesthetic characteristics of palace are large, serious, spatial and beautiful and it is usually located on the central axis and occupies the central position. It is the main body of the whole garden and used specially as the place for emperors to live or for people to worship gods.

Hall has serious atmosphere. Usually regarded as main buildings in private garden, hall is the center for the whole garden and used as the place for host to hold such important activities as family union, guest reception and banquet. It not only has various functions to satisfy different needs, but also embodies the host's status, morality and interests.

Storied building is built as a tall architecture in a spacious place. It can make people view the scenery in distance easily.

Loft is a common architecture type, which has double eaves with windows on its four sides and which is transparent and graceful structure. It has more than two stories for sightseeing and collecting books.

Mansion both refers to the architecture used for living, Yan music, sightseeing and overlooking and to the building host uses to receive and accommodate guests.

Pavilion with windows is usually built on waterside or high place and used as

a small single architecture for sightseeing.

Zhai(studio) is a small yard in a garden. It is used for self-cultivation and usually located in a quiet place shaded by stones and plants. Its environment is elegant and silent and it is suitable for learning.

Tower is a multi-story building which is usually built in the winding water or the top of mountains to control the situation. Tower also connotes that it can guard the safety and peace of the place where it locates.

Shed is a sightseeing platform set up by water. The one part of shed is on the bank and the other stretches into water. The shed's four sides are open and its plat form is very free, usually combined with corridor and stand.

Boat house is mostly built beside pools with its three or four sides facing water and it is a boat-like architecture specially provided for viewing.

The four sides of pavilion are usually above the ground and it is mostly built at hillside or hilltop for people to have rests.

Corridor is one of the most unique architectures in the classical gardens. It usually refers to the passage with roof to shelter people from wind, rain and sunshine. It is characteristic of beautiful and lively and it is used as the vein to connect buildings and also used as the tour guideline.

Bridge's types include vaulted bridge, flat bridge, corridor bridge, curved bridge, and so on. It can be made of stone, bamboo or wood, which not only beautify the scenery but also separate views to enlarge the space visually.

3. The Means of Landscape Design in Chinese Classical Gardens

In garden landscaping, many means of landscape design are employed to express nature in order to make people appreciate the scenery gradually, get the big picture from small details, and see changeable scenes in different places to achieve the natural, plain, quiet and implicit art effects. The common means of landscape design are layout, view in opposite place, enframed view, leaking through view and view borrowing.

(1) Layout

Some Layouts regard artificial view as subject and natural view as supplement. These gardens, for example, the Wangshiyuan Garden, the Lingering Garden and the Humble Administrator's Garden in Suzhou and so on, are not the places for sightseeing directly but highly generalize and extract natural views. With such natural elements as hills, stones, pools, woods, flowers and grass, these gardens form symbolic landscapes to give people aesthetic feeling.

Some Layouts regard natural view as subject and artificial view as supplement. Most royal gardens and temples, for example, the Summer Palace, the Mountain Resort in Chengde, Leshan Giant Buddha Temple, Putuoshan Guanyin Temple, and so on, are actually built in the beautiful places for people to enjoy nature's true features. Meanwhile, architectures are only embellishments for scenery . The characteristic of those gardens is that they regard water and mountain as subject but regard artificial architectures and yards as foils for nature. Both complement each other so that natural beauty and artificial beauty could integrate harmoniously.

(2) Opposite View

Opposite view refers to the scenery that when we stand at pavilion, stand, house, and cabinet or shed, we can view hall, hill, bridge and woods. And when we are in hall, bridge or corridor, we can see pavilion, stand, house, cabinet, and so on.

(3) Enframed View

Enframed view refers to the confined picture formed by tree branches or architects' doors, windows and holes, usually enframing natural beauty or artificial landscape in distance into it.

(4) Leaked View

Leaked view refers to the designing means that on walls or on one or both

sides of corridor (single or double) in gardens, we make ornamental windows, or carve geometric shapes with ethnic features, or carve such common folk plants as grape, pomegranate, plum and fixed bamboo, or carve such animals as deer, crane and rabbit. Through ornamental windows, people can see beautiful scenery outside gardens or yards. That is called leaked view.

(5) Borrowed View

Borrowed view means that when making garden, we consciously borrow scenery outside the garden into it, in order to make tourists expand their sight and imagination horizontally or vertically in a limited space. Thus, the artistic effect in which people could predict the whole scenery from a small angle can be achieved. Borrowed views include far borrow, neighboring borrow, upward borrow, overlook borrow and seasonal borrow. Borrowing mountains in distance is called far borrow; borrowing trees nearby is called neighboring borrow; borrowing birds in air is called upward borrow; borrowing fish in pools is called overlook borrow; borrowing seasonal flowers or other natural phenomena is called seasonal borrow.

第十六章　中国的风物特产

中国风物特产是中华文化的重要组成部分，也是人类的物质文明与精神文明的完美体现。

一、陶瓷器

陶瓷器是陶器制品和瓷器制品的总称。陶瓷生产在中国有悠久的历史。远在六七千年以前，中国人就开始使用陶器了。中国瓷器的使用，大约也有3 000年的历史了。

（一）陶　器

陶器是指以黏土为胎，经过手捏、轮制、模塑等方法加工成型后，在800℃~1 000℃高温下焙烧而成的物品。坯体不透明，有微孔，具有吸水性，叩之声音不清。陶器可区分为细陶和粗陶，白色或有色，无釉或有釉。品种有灰陶、红陶、白陶、彩陶和黑陶等。陶器具有浓厚的生活气息和独特的艺术风格。

宜兴紫砂器　宜兴紫砂器产于中国江西省宜兴市。宜兴制陶业历史久远，素有“陶都”之称。宜兴陶器以日用陶器为主要产品。紫砂陶是无釉细陶器，有天下“神品”之称。它采用质地细腻、含铁量高的特殊陶土烧制而成。其造型古朴，色泽素雅，胎壁多孔，用作茶具泡茶，存放数天仍能保持茶香，同时，还具有保温性好、传热慢、不烫手等特点。

佛山石湾陶器　佛山石湾陶器产于中国广东省佛山市，是用当地陶土和岗砂为原料生产的陶器。主要产品有日用陶、艺术陶塑、琉璃陶和建筑陶。

佛山石湾陶器以实用为原则，秀美与实用相结合，胎壁厚，釉层厚，技法多姿多彩。艺术陶塑是别具特色的民间民俗工艺品。造型朴实粗犷，有浓郁的乡土气息。陶塑人物脸部和裸露的肌肉选用有色陶土制成，不施釉彩（称为露胎）。

钦州泥兴陶器　钦州泥兴陶器产于中国广西壮族自治区钦州市，是采用当地钦江两岸的红土为原料制作而成的陶器。钦州泥兴陶器主要有花瓶、茶具、咖啡具、花盆、文具、食具、熏鼎及仿古等八大类，花色品种400多个。其中以各式茶具、花瓶、笔筒、盆景盆和食具最负盛名。钦州泥兴陶器质地细腻，音质铿锵，坚硬结实，古朴幽雅。无毒、耐酸、耐碱、吸水性强、透气性能好。

洛阳唐三彩　唐三彩是唐代洛阳一带生产的彩陶工艺品，因其主要以黄、白、绿为基本釉色，因称“唐三彩”。它吸取了中国国画、雕塑等工艺美术的特点，采用堆贴、刻画等形式的装饰图案，线条粗犷有力。唐三彩是一种低温釉陶器，在色釉中加入不同的金属氧化物，经过焙烧，便形成浅黄、赭黄、浅绿、深绿、天蓝、褐红、茄紫等多种色彩，但多以黄、褐、绿三色为主。它主要是陶坯上涂上的彩釉，在烘制过程中发生化学变化，色釉浓淡变化、互相浸润、斑驳淋漓、色彩自然协调，花纹流畅，是一种具有中国独特风格的传统工艺品。

（二）瓷　器

瓷器是从陶器发展来的，但它和陶器有着本质的区别。制造瓷器要用比较纯净的瓷土做原料；要经过1 100℃以上高温的焙烧；还要在器物的表面涂上釉料，只有同时具备这三个条件，才能生产出瓷器。瓷器有胎质致密、经久耐用、便于清洗、外观华美等特点。中国瓷器的使用，大约有3 000年的历史了。

景德镇瓷器　景德镇是中国著名“瓷都”，制瓷的历史已有约2 000年。景德镇瓷器瓷质细腻，造型精巧，滋润清雅。以“白如玉、薄如纸、明如镜、声如磬”的独特风格闻名于世。青花瓷、玲珑瓷、粉彩瓷和高温颜色釉瓷被称为“景德镇四大名瓷”。

淄博美术陶瓷　淄博美术陶瓷沉静典雅、凝重高贵、造型新颖、工艺精

湛。雨点釉和茶叶末釉为其突出代表。雨点釉是漆黑的釉面上均匀地布满银色小圆点，被视为茶道精品。茶叶末釉是釉面色如橄榄，上面均匀地散布茶叶末状的细微晶粒，深受中外茶客的珍爱。

绍兴越瓷 越瓷的故乡浙江省绍兴市，被认为是中国青瓷的著名发源地。越瓷是中国陶瓷艺术园地中的一朵奇葩。早在商朝中期，古越人民就率先制造彩叠压的“龙瓷”，这是一种印纹硬陶，釉色绿中泛黄，具有一定的光泽度，这就是历史上的原始青瓷。目前仍保持传统制作工艺“变色釉瓷器”。

唐山骨瓷器 唐山是中国北方瓷都，该地生产的骨瓷属中国首创，填补了中国高档瓷生产的空白。骨质瓷简称骨瓷，是世界公认的最高档的瓷种。质地轻巧，细密坚硬，不易磨损及破裂，在灯光的照射下晶莹、白皙、透亮，色泽成天然骨粉独有的自然奶白色。骨瓷的特色是白度高、透明度好、光泽柔和、装饰效果极佳、声音特别悦耳。

醴陵釉下彩瓷 釉下彩是先作画于瓷坯，然后在其上覆盖透明的釉料，经过高温焙烧而成。瓷质洁白如玉，釉下五彩晶莹，画面在薄釉的掩映下，极富流动感。耐高温、抗腐蚀、花纹不易褪色。

德化白瓷 福建省德化县是中国白瓷的著名产地。它所生产的瓷器质地洁白，细腻如玉，釉面光润如镜，胎质坚实致密，敲声如磬。

龙泉青瓷 浙江省龙泉市的青瓷，釉色多呈青色，美如玉，明如镜，声如磬。

二、织　锦

织锦是用染好颜色的彩色经纬线，经提花、织造工艺，织出图案的织物，当代三大名锦是指云锦、蜀锦、宋锦。

（一）云　锦

云锦产于江苏南京，因锦纹如云，故名云锦。云锦始于南朝，盛于明清。它纹路多样，古朴浑厚，配色灿烂，匀称和谐，极富地方特色。主要品种有雨花锦、凹凸锦和双面锦等。既可用于家具装饰，也可作为艺术挂屏。

（二）蜀　锦

蜀锦产于四川成都，是以地名命名的著名织锦，其质地坚韧，五彩缤纷，

构图独特，富有浓郁的地方风格。

（三）宋　锦

宋锦产于江苏苏州，相传始织于宋代，故而得名。其色彩文雅，平整挺实。它非常适合装裱书画之用，深受文人墨客的青睐。

三、刺　绣

（一）苏　绣

苏绣是江苏苏州一带刺绣产品的总称。苏绣具有绣工精细、针法活泼、图案秀丽、色彩雅致等特点。现代苏绣以绸、缎、绢、纱为底，经过若干工序，使用针法40余种，配用色线上千余种。

（二）湘　绣

湘绣是湖南长沙一带刺绣工艺品的总称。湘绣融传统绘画、书法和刺绣等艺术手法为一体，构图优美，章法严谨，色彩鲜明，风格写实，生动自然，被称为“超级绣品”。

（三）粤　绣

粤绣是流传于广东地区的一种民间刺绣。粤绣构图丰满，形象逼真，色彩鲜艳。金银线垫绣是粤绣的特技，它使所绣景物形象丰满，富有立体感。

（四）蜀　绣

蜀绣是四川成都一带刺绣工艺品的总称。蜀绣一般以软缎和彩线为主要原料，构图明丽美观，针法严谨，色泽光亮，浓淡适宜，疏密得体，有水墨写意画的艺术效果。

四、文房四宝

在笔、墨、纸、砚“文房四宝”中，湖笔、徽墨、端砚、宣纸为上品。

(一) 湖　笔

湖笔因产于中国浙江省湖州市善琏镇而得名。湖笔一般都是用上等山羊毛经过浸、拔、梳、连、合等近百道工序精制而成。

(二) 徽　墨

徽墨因产于中国安徽省徽州地区而得名。徽墨是以松烟、桐油烟、漆烟、胶为主要原料制作而成的一种主要供传统书法、绘画使用的特种颜料。徽墨有色泽黑润、坚而有光、入纸不晕、舔笔不胶、经久不褪、馨香浓郁、防蛀等特点。其正面镌绘名家的书画图案，美观典雅，是书画艺术的珍品。

(三) 端　砚

端砚产于广东肇庆市，因古代肇庆称为端州，因此称为端砚。端砚自古深受文人墨客的喜爱，并受到达官贵人和帝王将相的赏识。端砚制作要经过探测、开凿、运输、选料、整璞、设计、雕刻、打磨、洗涤、配装等十多道艰辛而精细的工序。端砚石质幼嫩、纯净、细腻、滋润、坚实、严密。传说端砚具有呵气可研墨、发墨不损毫、冬天不结冰的特色。

(四) 宣　纸

宣纸因原产于宣州府（今安徽宣城市）而得名，现主要产于安徽泾县。宣纸起于唐代，历代相沿。宣纸具有良好的润墨性、耐久性、变形性和抗虫性，是中国古代用于书写和绘画的纸。由于宣纸有易于保存、经久不脆、不会褪色等特点，故有“纸寿千年”之誉。

五、中国五大名玉

中国的五大名玉是指新疆和田玉、陕西蓝田玉、河南独山玉、甘肃祁连玉、辽宁岫岩玉。

(一) 和田玉

和田玉因产于新疆和田地区而得名，又称“软玉”或“真玉”，硬度为

6～6.5，按照产出地的不同，可分为子料、山流水、山料三种类型，和田玉以质地致密、细腻、温润、坚韧、光洁而著称。

（二）蓝田玉

蓝田玉因产于陕西蓝田县而得名，俗称“菜玉”，玉质从外观上看，有黄色、浅绿色等不均匀的色调，并伴随浅白色的大理岩，玉质硬度为 4 左右，容易加工。

（三）独山玉

独山玉因产于河南南阳市的独山而得名，也称“南阳玉”或“河南玉”，独山玉以色泽鲜艳、透明度好而著称。

（四）祁连玉

祁连玉因产于甘肃祁连山而得名。祁连玉以玉色暗绿，有较多的黑色斑点而著称。

（五）岫岩玉

岫岩玉因产于辽宁省岫岩满族自治县而得名。岫岩玉是一种软玉，属蛇纹石，以其质地温润、晶莹、细腻、性坚、透明度好、颜色多样而著称。

六、中国三大佳石

中国三大佳石是指浙江昌化鸡血石、青田冻石和福建寿山石。

（一）昌化鸡血石

昌化鸡血石产于浙江省昌化镇西北的玉岩山，因其色如鸡血而得名，是中国特有的珍贵宝石，它具有鸡血般的鲜红色彩和美玉般的质地，历来与珠宝翡翠同样受人珍视，以“国宝”之誉驰名中外。

（二）青田冻石

青田冻石因产于浙江青田县而得名，其主要成分为叶蜡石，又称为图章

石，以灯光冻石最为名贵。灯光冻石因其色微黄，纯净细腻，温润柔和，色泽鲜明，半透明，光照下灿若灯辉而得名。灯光冻石质雅易刻，明初已用于刻印，名扬四海，为青田石之极品，价胜黄金。

（三）福州寿山石

福州寿山石因产于福州北郊寿山而得名，是中国传统“四大印章石”之一。其石料以叶蜡石为主要成分，其中“田黄石”最为名贵。1 克品相普通的田黄石材要价已达 300 元人民币。

七、金属工艺

金属工艺是中国工艺艺术的一个特殊门类，主要包括景泰蓝、烧瓷、花丝镶嵌、斑铜工艺、锡制工艺、铁画、金银饰品等。

（一）北京景泰蓝

景泰蓝是北京著名的传统手工艺品，又称“铜胎掐丝珐琅”，俗名“珐蓝”，又称“嵌珐琅”，是一种在铜质的胎型上，用柔软的扁铜丝，掐成各种花纹焊上，然后把珐琅质的色釉填充在花纹内烧制而成的器物。因其在明朝景泰年间盛行，制作技艺比较成熟，使用的珐琅釉多以蓝色为主，故而得名“景泰蓝”。

（二）北京烧瓷

北京烧瓷，又名“铜胎画珐琅”，与景泰蓝同为金属工艺中的姐妹艺术。它与景泰蓝的区别在于不用掐丝，而是在以铜制胎之后，在胎体上敷上一层白釉，烧结后用釉色进行彩绘，经两三次填彩，修正后再烧结、镀金、磨光而成。北京烧瓷种类繁多，有瓶、盘、碗、罐、碟、盏、酒具、烟具，以及炉、鼎、爵、熏、挂瓶、插瓶等。

（三）北京和成都的花丝镶嵌

花丝镶嵌，又叫“细金工艺”，是“花丝”和“镶嵌”两种制作技艺的结合。它是用金、银等材料，镶嵌各种宝石、珍珠或用编织技艺制造而成。

花丝镶嵌分为两类：花丝，是把金、银抽成细丝，用堆垒、编织技法制成工艺品；镶嵌则是把金、银薄片捶打成器皿，然后錾出图案，镶以宝石而成。花丝镶嵌工艺以北京、成都最负盛名。花丝镶嵌的代表作品有明代的万历皇帝金冠、清代的金瓯永固杯、银六方盆金桃树盆景、金嵌珠宝朝冠顶、现代的珠宝天坛祈年殿、中华世纪龙等。

（四）芜湖铁画

芜湖铁画，也称铁花，因产于安徽省芜湖市而得名，是中国独具风格的工艺品之一。铁画是以低碳钢为原料，将铁片和铁线锻打焊接成的各种装饰画。它将民间剪纸、雕刻、镶嵌等各种艺术的技法融为一体，采用中国画章法，黑白对比，虚实结合，别有一番情趣。铁画的制作起源于宋代，盛行于北宋。清代康熙年间，安徽芜湖铁画才自成一体，并逐渐享誉四海。

（五）龙泉宝剑

龙泉宝剑是中国著名的传统工艺品之一，因产于浙江龙泉市而得名。相传，龙泉宝剑创始于2 000 多年前的春秋战国时代。唐朝时，龙泉剑名声大震。龙泉宝剑具有坚韧锋利、刚柔相济、寒光逼人、纹饰巧致四大传统特色。龙泉宝剑名扬海内外，东南亚国家的华侨、华人，喜爱把它挂在室内或床头，既为避邪，又是装饰。

八、年　画

年画是中国画的一种，始于古代的“门神画”。清光绪年间，正式称为年画，是中国特有的一种绘画体裁，也是中国农村老百姓喜闻乐见的艺术形式。因其大都用于过年时张贴，不仅可以装饰环境，而且含有祝福新年吉祥喜庆之意，因此称作年画。河南开封的朱仙镇、山东潍坊的杨家埠、江苏桃花坞、天津杨柳青在历史上久负盛名，被誉为中国“年画四大家”。

（一）朱仙镇年画

朱仙镇年画因产生于河南开封市的朱仙镇而得名，属于木版印绘制品，历史悠久，源远流长，距今已有800 多年的历史，诞生于唐，兴于宋，鼎盛

于明，被誉为中国木版年画之鼻祖。传说唐朝时候，唐太宗命画工绘大将秦琼、尉迟敬德画像悬挂宫门，以避邪，成为门神之始。由于它的使用量大，单一手绘的年画很难满足需求，于是民间艺人用木版刻印来大量生产，从而得到发展，进而形成年俗。

（二）杨家埠年画

杨家埠年画因产生于山东省潍坊市杨家埠村而得名，属于木版印绘制品，始于明代，兴于清朝。杨家埠年画构图完整匀称，造型粗壮朴实，线条简练流畅，多反映理想、风俗和日常生活，具有浓厚的民间风味、乡土气息和节日氛围。

（三）天津杨柳青年画

天津杨柳青年画因产于天津市杨柳青镇而得名，属于木版印绘制品，是中国著名民间木版年画。与苏州桃花坞年画合称“南桃北柳”。约产生于明代崇祯年间。清雍乾至光绪初期为鼎盛期。天津杨柳青年画具有笔法细腻、人物秀丽、色彩明艳、内容丰富、形式多样、气氛祥和、情节幽默、题词有趣等特色。

（四）江苏桃花坞年画

江苏桃花坞年画因产生于江苏苏州市以北的桃花坞而得名。桃花坞年画源于宋代的雕版印刷工艺，到明代发展成为民间艺术流派，清代雍正、乾隆年间为鼎盛时期，每年出产的桃花坞木版年画达百万张以上。桃花坞年画构图对称、丰满，色彩绚丽，常以紫红色为主调表现欢乐气氛，具有精细秀雅的江南民间艺术风格，主要表现吉祥喜庆、民俗生活、戏文故事、花鸟蔬果和驱鬼避邪等民间传统审美内容。

九、编织工艺

编织工艺是指利用韧性较好的植物纤维（如细枝、柳条、竹、灯心草）以手工方法编织成的一种工艺品（篮子或其他物品）。编织工艺品既有实用性，又有装饰性艺术。根据所用材料不同可以分为竹编和草编。竹编比较有

名的是东阳竹编、嵊州竹编和傣家竹编。草编比较有名的是山东草编和宁波草编。

（一）东阳竹编

东阳竹编因产生于浙江省东阳市而得名，兴起于宋代，以制作龙灯、花灯、走马灯为主。现在东阳竹编主要以实用产品和工艺品为主。东阳竹编实用产品有篮、盘、包、箱、瓶、罐、家具等20多种。工艺品以动物竹编产品最为传神，有鸡、鸭、鹅、兔、狗等，其形象夸张生动，表情细腻。

（二）嵊州竹编

嵊州竹编因产生于浙江东部的嵊州市而得名，始于战国，成熟于汉晋，兴于明清。嵊州竹编以编织精巧、工艺繁杂、花色丰富著称。嵊州竹编有篮、盘、罐、盒、瓶、屏风、动物、人物、建筑物、家具、灯具、器具等12个大类，6 000多个花色品种。

（三）云南傣家竹编

云南傣家竹编因云南傣族人擅长竹编而得名。自古以来，傣族就和竹子结下了不解之缘，傣寨大多竹林环绕，傣家人在饮食上喜欢吃鲜竹笋和用竹笋腌制的酸笋，各种生活用具也多用竹制作而成。一踏上那别致的竹楼，仿佛进入了一个竹子编织的世界：墙壁用竹子编成，地毯是竹编席垫，室内陈设的家具什物，大到衣柜，小到饭盒、小凳，以及凉帽、雨帽，随身携带的小背篓，无一不是竹编的，最具有代表性的竹编漆器主要有贡桌、提箩、腊条盒、饭盒、滴水葫芦（傣语称“棚腊”“撒毫”“嘎顶”“喘毫”和“南噪哇”），这些漆器上镶嵌五彩图案，富丽堂皇，专供佛寺祭扫之用。是傣族群众从事佛教活动时的必需用品，家家户户都备有一套。每到泼水节或开门节、关门节时，傣家老人用“嘎顶”装腊条，“喘毫”装糯米饭，“南噪哇”装水，“撒毫”装各种礼佛用品，子女们则用“棚腊”和“撒毫”给父母、佛爷送斋饭，老人们则用“拿佛”给佛爷送斋饭。这些竹编漆器平时则置于高处，不能乱放东西。由于傣族人民笃信佛教，竹器漆制品较多装饰荷花、蝴蝶、龙、五角星等图案，寓意祈求佛祖赐福予人，保佑来年风调雨顺、吉庆

有余。

（四）山东草编

山东是草编大省，山东草编起源于莱州，至少有6 000多年的历史，草编工艺品是山东的特色产品，山东草编采用天然蒲草、茅草、玉米皮、玉米秸、麦草等编织而成。山东草编产品主要分两类：一是具有使用功能的工艺品，如提篮、提袋、茶垫、地席、草帽、门帘、果盒、纸篓、婴儿篮、储物箱等；二是具有形式美感的装饰品，如草屏风、草地毯、灯伞、墙壁装饰纸、草墙纸草编等。

（五）宁波草编

浙江宁波自古以来就有传统的编织技艺，宁波草编已有2 000多年的历史，宁波的草编资源丰富，有席草、麦秆、咸草、蒲草、龙须草、玉米壳等多种。宁波草编除草帽外，还编织草篮、提袋、草扇、草拖鞋、草茶垫等，以及各种花纹图案的物品。

十、漆　器

中国人民从新石器时代起就认识了漆的性能并用以制器。历经商周直至明清，中国的漆器工艺不断发展，达到了相当高的水平。

（一）北京漆器

北京漆器主要有两种，一是雕漆，这种工艺成熟于公元14世纪，历史相当悠久。雕漆也以铜为胎并烧衬珐琅里，口边还要镀金，胎上需用红、绿、黄等色漆敷涂，有的要涂数百层，等漆阴干后才能进行雕刻，雕刻的方式有浮雕和镂雕等；另一种是金漆镶嵌，分为彩漆勾金、螺钿镶嵌、金银平脱以及刻灰和磨漆画等。两种漆器都有珠光宝气、古朴沉稳的特色。

（二）福州脱胎漆器

福州脱胎漆器，质地固轻巧，装饰精细，色泽鲜艳，结实耐用，具有独特的民族风格和浓厚的地方特色，与北京的景泰蓝、江西景德镇的瓷器并称

为中国传统工艺的“三宝”，享誉国内外。福州脱胎漆器产品大致分为实用和欣赏两大类，包括大花瓶、大屏风、各种磨漆画以及茶具、咖啡具、文具、餐具等300多个规格的3 000多个品种。

（三）扬州镶嵌漆器

扬州漆器起源于战国，兴旺于汉唐，鼎盛于明清。其工艺齐全，技艺精湛，风格独特，驰名中外，是中国传统的工艺品种。

（四）天水漆器

甘肃天水名产有雕填、镶填、镶银、描金等品种，其中以雕填最为著名。天水漆器已有近百年历史，在清代主要有木胎、皮胎，髹饰技法仅雕填一种，生产木碗、手杖等日用品。新中国成立以来，天水雕填漆器技艺有很大提高，在设计、雕刻、填彩、研磨等方面都超过历史水平。主要产品有花瓶、盘、套盒、烟具、茶具以及各种柜、围屏、沙发桌等近百个花色品种，特别是满堂嵌螺钿围屏、折叠沙发桌等产品，造型优美，制作精工，纹饰典丽，富有独特的地方风貌。

十一、民间艺术

中国民间艺术历史悠久，内容丰富多彩，形式多样。皮影、泥塑、剪纸、狮子舞等等都是很著名的民间艺术，不仅是极具地方特色的风物特产，也是中华文化的瑰宝。

（一）西北的皮影

皮影戏是中国的一种民间艺术形式，它是工艺美术与戏曲巧妙结合而形成的独特的艺术品种，起源于明清时期，是甘肃、陕西、宁夏农村的一种民间艺术。皮影戏中的平面偶人以及场面道具景物，是中国民间艺人用手工进行刀雕、彩绘而成的皮制品。制作时，先用水把牛皮洗净，晒干，然后进行画图雕刻，然后进行彩绘，熨烫而成。演出时，由表演者在幕后控制、操作皮影人物身体的每一个部分，观众在幕布前面看光源照射下的人物剪影，表演时配合振奋人心的歌曲或独白来演绎故事情节。

（二）汉族的剪纸

剪纸艺术是中国汉族最古老的民间艺术之一，是中国民间艺术中的瑰宝，它的历史可追溯到公元 6 世纪。剪纸在中国农村是一种流传很广的汉族民间艺术形式。剪纸是用剪刀把纸张、金银箔、树皮、树叶、布、皮、革等片状材料剪成各种各样的图案，如窗花、门笺、墙花、顶棚花、灯花等。这种民俗艺术的产生和流传与中国农村的节日风俗有着密切关系，逢年过节抑或新婚喜庆，人们把美丽鲜艳的剪纸贴在雪白的窗纸或明亮的玻璃窗上、墙上、门上、灯笼上，节日的气氛便被渲染得非常浓郁。

（三）陕西凤翔彩绘泥塑

陕西凤翔县彩绘泥塑，始于西周时期，在民间流传已有 3 000 年之久，是至今中国保留最古老、最具民族特色的泥塑类手工制品。凤翔彩绘泥塑造型优美，生动逼真，具有浓厚的乡土生活气息。泥塑内容有人物、动物，也有植物，大都是空心的圆塑作，也有浮雕式的挂片。其制作方法简便易行，将黏土和纸浆搅拌成塑泥，先制好模子，翻成胎坯晾干，上白色底粉，随后涂彩、绘画和上光。凤翔泥塑的色彩别具一格，以大红、大绿和黄色为主，用色不多，却鲜艳明快，对比强烈的感觉。以黑墨勾线和简练的笔法涂染，给人以明快醒目的感觉。凤翔彩塑取材立意极为广泛，戏剧脸谱、吉祥图案、民间传说、历史故事、乡俗生活等无所不有。

Chapter 16 Chinese Local Specialties

China's local specialty is one of important parts of Chinese culture and a perfect embodiment of material civilization and spiritual civilization of human beings as well.

1. Ceramics

Ceramic is the general name of pottery and porcelain products. Ceramic production has a long history in China. It has been 6,000 or 7,000 years since Chinese people invented the pottery. As for Chinese porcelain, it also has been about 3,000 years since being invented.

(1) Pottery

Pottery refers to an article that uses the clay as its body, which is molded by hand pinching, wheel braking, molding and then fired in 800℃ - 1 000℃. The pottery has opaque body with water-absorptive microporous without a clear and melodious sound when being knocked upon. Pottery can be divided into fine pottery and crude pottery, white or colored as well as unglazed or glazed. As for the varieties, pottery can be divided into gray pottery, red pottery, white pottery, painted pottery and black pottery, etc. It is with a strong flavor of life and a unique artistic style.

Yixing Zisha Pottery Yixing Zisha pottery is produced in Yixing City in Jiangxi Province of China. The Yixing pottery industry has a long history, hence it is

known as"City of Pottery". The main products of Yixing pottery are potteries for daily use. Yixing Zisha pottery, which is called as "Holy Masterpiece", is unglazed fine pottery. It is made of special pottery clay with fine texture and high iron content. It has an antique shape, a simple but elegant color and porous side walls. When being used as a tea set to make a tea, it can keep a tea's aroma for several days. Besides, it has good heat insulating properties, conducting heat slowly, not scalding, etc.

Foshan Shiwan Pottery Shiwan Pottery, which is produced in Foshan City in Guangdong Province of China, uses local clay and mound sand as raw materials. The main products are household pottery, art pottery, glazed pottery and architectural pottery. Shiwan pottery sticks to the principle of utility in combination with elegance. It has thick walls, thick enamel and varied techniques. Art pottery is distinctive folk crafts. The modeling is plain and rugged with a strong local flavor. The pottery figure's face and exposed muscle are made from colored clay, and are not glazed(called as"exposed pottery tube").

Qinzhou Nixing Pottery Qinzhou Nixing pottery is made in Qinzhou City in Guangxi Zhuang Autonomous Region of China. The pottery is made of local red clay from both sides of the Qinjiang River. Qinzhou Nixing pottery includes eight categories, the vase, tea set, coffee service, flowerpot, stationery, tableware, smoked tripod and antique earthenware, and has more than four hundred types. Among them, the most prestigious are tea set, the vase pen container, bonsai pots and tableware. Qinzhou Nixing pottery has the characteristics of delicate texture, sonorous sound, solid and sturdy, simple and elegant. It is non-poisonous, acid proof, alkali proof, strong water absorption and strong air permeability.

Luoyang Tang Tri-colored Glazed Pottery Tang tri-colored glazed pottery is a painted pottery handicraft, which is made in the area of Luoyang City in Tang Dynasty. It mainly uses the yellow, white and green as its basic glaze, therefore it is called "tri-colored glazed pottery". It absorbs such traits of arts and crafts as traditional Chinese painting, sculpture, and uses the decorative patterns in the form of the sticking pile, carving, etc., and has the bold powerful lines. Tang tri-colored glazed pottery is a low-temperature glazed pottery. When added in different metal

oxides, the glaze, after being fired, then it forms a variety of colors including light yellow, deep yellow, light green, deep green, blue, red and purple, etc. But the main colors are yellow, brown and green. It is mainly the colored glaze on the pottery cup that has a chemical reaction during the process of being fired. Tang tri-colored glazed pottery has the characteristics of glaze shade change, mutual infiltration, mottled dripping, natural color coordination, and smooth pattern, and it is a kind of traditional Chinese arts and crafts with unique style.

(2) Porcelain

Porcelain is developed from pottery. There are essential differences between porcelain and pottery. The porcelain is made by using relatively pure porcelain clay as the raw material, being fired in above 1,100℃; and the surface of the utensils is coated with glaze. It is only provided with these three conditions that the porcelain can be produced. Porcelain has the traits of dense compaction base, durability, easily cleanable quality, gorgeous appearance, etc. The invention of Chinese porcelain has been about 3,000 years.

Jingdezhen Porcelain Jingdezhen City, which is called "ceramics capital" of China, is famous for its porcelain, and has about 2,000 years' porcelain producing history. Jingdezhen porcelain is exquisite with delicate design and elegant moisturizing. Jingdezhen porcelain has been well-known in the world for its own four special features, "white like jade, thin as paper, bright as a mirror, and sound like a chime". The blue and white porcelain, exquisitely wrought blue and white ware, the faille rose porcelain and the high-temperature colored glaze porcelain are called "Four Great Famous Excellent Jingdezhen Porcelain Wares".

Zibo Art Ceramics Zibo art ceramics are characterized by their quiet, elegant, dignified, and innovative design and exquisite techniques. Raindrop glaze ceramics and tea-dust glaze ceramics are its prominent representatives. Raindrop glaze ceramics are silver dots evenly covered with the black glaze. The raindrop glaze is regarded as the boutique of teaism. Tea-dust glaze ceramics has olive-color glaze over which tea powder-like are evenly scattered, favored by Chinese and foreign patrons.

Shaoxing Yue Porcelain Yue porcelain's hometown, Shaoxing City in Zhejiang Province, is considered to be the famous birthplace of Chinese celadon porcelain. The Yue porcelain is an outstanding craft in China's ceramic art garden. During Shang Dynasty, ancient Yue people firstly product color pressure-superposed"Dragon Porcelain", Which is stamped hard pottery with yellow in green glazing color and certain luster. This is the original celadon in history. Nowadays, the traditionally processed"allochroic glazed porcelain"still exists.

Tangshan Bone Porcelain Tangshan City is the northern porcelain capital in China. The production of bone porcelain is a Chinese initiative, filling the gaps in porcelain production in China. Bone porcelain is a short form of Tangshan bone porcelain in China, recognized worldwide as the highest grade. The bone porcelain is characterized by light weight and hard fine texture, and not easy to wear or break. Under the light exposure, it is white translucent crystal, a natural milk white color the natural bone dust has in peculiar. Bone porcelain is featured as high brightness, nice transparency, soft luster, special decorative effect, and peculiarly pleasant sound.

Liling Underglaze Colour Porcelain Underglaze colour porcelain is formed by being painted on its body first, and covered with the transparent glaze, and then fired in high temperature. Porcelain is white as jade with crystal underglaze color. Hidden under the thin glazes, the painting is full of a sense of movement. The porcelain is high temperature resistant, corrosion resistant, and not easy to fade.

Dehua Porcelain Dehua County of Fujian Province is famous for producing white porcelain in China. Its production has white texture, fine as jade, and its glazed surface is smooth like mirror, the body is dense and solid, and the sound is like a chime.

Longquan Celadon Ceramics Longquan celadon ceramics is produced in Longquan City in Zhejiang Province of China. The glaze color is mainly cyan, beautiful as jade, and its bright is like a mirror, and sound like a chime.

2. Brocade

Brocade is weaving pattern fabrics made by the dyed color latitude and longitude lines through jacquard and weaving techniques. Three famous contemporary brocades are Yun brocade, Sichuan brocade, and Song brocade.

(1) Yun Brocade

Yun brocade is produced in Nanjing City of Jiangsu Province. Brocade pattern seems like the cloud (in Chinese, cloudis pronounced *yun*), thus the name of Yun brocade comes into being. Brocade begins from the period of Nanbeichao, develops in Ming and Qing Dynasties. Its texture is diverse, ancient and vigorous, color-bright, well proportioned and harmonious, full of local characteristics. Main varieties are Yuhua brocade (raindrops brocade), concavo-convex brocade and double-sided brocade. It can be used for furnishing decoration, or as art picture.

(2) Shu Brocade

Shu brocade (Sichuan brocade), which is made in Chengdu of Sichuan Province, is named after the place. It has tough texture, colorful and unique composition, and rich local style.

(3) Song Brocade

Song brocade is produced in Suzhou City of Jiangsu Province. It is said that it originates from Song Dynasty, hence the name Song brocade comes into being. Being elegant, smooth and firm, it is suitable for calligraphy and painting, thus favored by men of letters very much.

3. Embroidery

(1) Su Embroidery

Su embroidery refers to the embroidery products made in Suzhou City of Jiangsu

Province. Embroidery is characterized by its fine needlework, lively stitch, beautiful pattern, and elegant colors. Modern embroidery uses silk, satin and yarn as the bottom, adopts various processes, uses over 40 kinds of needle techniques, and applies more than a thousand species of colored threads.

(2) Xiang Embroidery

Xiang embroidery (Hu'nan embroidery) is the general name of the embroidery handicraft in the area around Changsha of Hu'nan Province. Xiang embroidery synthesizes traditional painting, calligraphy and embroidery art gimmick. It has a beautiful design, rigorous composition, bright color, style of realism, and vivid and natural form, also known as "super embroidery".

(3) Yue Embroidery

Yue embroidery (Guangdong embroidery) is a kind of folk embroidery popular in the region of Guangdong Province. Yue embroidery has plump composition, vivid and lifelike image and bright color. Gold and silver cushion embroidery is the unique skill of Yue embroidery. It can make the image of embroidery scenery rich and produce a three-dimensional effect.

(4) Shu Embroidery

Shu embroidery (Sichuan embroidery) is the foundation of the embroidery handicraft in the area around Chengdu of Sichuan Province. Shu embroidery generally uses satin and threads as the main raw materials, and its composition is bright and beautiful, stitch is rigorous, color and luster are light, shade is appropriate, and density is adequate. It has the artistic effect of abbreviated ink painting

4. The Four Treasures of the Study

Among the four treasures of the study "writing brush, ink stick, ink slab and paper", Huzhou writing brush, Hui ink stick, Duan ink slab, and Xuan paper are the four treasures of top grade.

(1) **Huzhou Writing Brush**

Huzhou writing brush gets the name for being produced in Shanlian Town of Huzhou City in Zhejiang Province. Huzhou writing brush is commonly made of super goat hair after nearly hundreds of refining processes, such as soaking, epilating, combing, etc.

(2) **Hui Ink Stick**

Hui ink stick is produced in Huizhou area of Anhui Province. Hui ink stick uses turpentine soot, China wood oil soot, lacquer soot and glue as its main raw materials, and is a major special paint for the use of traditional calligraphy and painting. Hui ink stick has the characteristics of black and moister color, tough and bright luster, no gluing brush, no fainting into the paper, rich ink fragrance and moth proofing, etc. Hui ink stick makes the names of calligraphy masters and the painting patterns engraved beautiful and elegant, and thus is valued greatly by calligraphy and painting art.

(3) **Duan Ink Slab**

Duan ink slab is produced in Zhaoqing City of Guangdong Province. For the reason that Zhaoqing City is called Duanzhou Prefecture in ancient time, hence the ink slab produced there is called Duan ink slab. Duan ink slab has been the scholars' favorites long before, and appreciated by the emperors and dignitaries. The production of Duan ink slab needs more than ten kinds of difficult and delicate processes of exploration, excavation, transportation, material selection, program, design, engraving, polishing, washing and equipment. The calcarea of Duan ink slab is slender, pure, delicate, moist, firm and tight. There is a legend that ink will not lose or freeze in winter once rubbed on Duan ink slab.

(4) **Xuan Paper**

Xuan paper is named after being originated in Xuanzhou Prefecture (today

Xuancheng City of Anhui Province). It is now mainly produced in Jingxian County of Anhui Province. Xuan paper, also called "rice paper", comes from Tang Dynasty and is inherited generation by generation. Rice paper has good moistening deformation of ink, durability, and resistance to insects and is appropriate for writing and drawing. Because the rice paper has the characteristics such as being easy to save, enduring the crisp, not fading, and so on, it wins the reputation of "paper longevity of the millennium".

5. Chinese Five Types of Famous Jade

Chinese five types of famous jade refer to Xinjiang Hetian jade and Shaanxi Lantian jade, He'nan Dushan jade, Gansu Qilian jade, Liaoning Xiuyan jade.

(1) Hetian Jade

Hetian jade is also known as nephrite which gets the name because it is produced in Hetian Prefecture of Xinjiang. Hetian jade is also called "soft jade" or "real jade" and its hardness is 6 – 6.5. According to different places of outputs, Hetian jade can be divided into three types, pebble, water and mountain. Nephrite is famous for its dense texture, and delicate, soft, smooth and resilient characteristics.

(2) Lantian Jade

Lantian jade is named after its birth place Lantian County of Shaanxi Province, and is commonly known as "dish jade". From the appearance of its texture, it has uneven colors such as yellow, light green, etc., along with light white marble. Its jade hardness is around 4 and is easy to be processed.

(3) Dushan Jade

Dushan jade is named because it is produced in Dushan of Nanyang City, and is also known as Nanyang jade or He'nan jade. Dushan jade is known for its bright color and good transparency.

(4) Qilian Jade

Qilian jade is produced in Qilianshan Mountain. It is renowned for dark green color and black spots.

(5) Xiuyan Jade

Xiuyan jade is produced in Xiuyan Man Autonomous County of Liaoning Province. It belongs to serpentine and is renowned for its moist, crystal, subtle, tough, transparent texture and diverse colors.

6. Chinese Three Types of Wonderful Stone

Three types of wonderful stone of China refer to Changhua Bloodstone of Zhejiang Province, Qingtian bacon stone and Fujian Shoushan stone of Fujian Province.

(1) Changhua Bloodstone

Changhua bloodstone is produced from Yugan Mountain in northwest of Changhua Town in Zhejiang Province, named after its color of blood. Changhua bloodstone is a precious gemstone peculiarly produced in China, with chicken blood-like red color and beautiful jade-like texture. It is cherished as jade all the time and considered as treasure both at home and abroad.

(2) Qingtian Bacon Stone

Qingtian bacon stone is named because it is produced in Qingtian County of Zhejiang Province. Its main components are pyrophyllite, also known as stone of stamp. Lamplighter bacon stone is the most expensive of this kind. Lamplighter bacon stone is named after its characteristics of being light yellow, pure and delicate, moist and soft, bright and lustrous, translucent, and fantastic under the lights. It has elegant quality and is easy to be carved, once used to stamp in early Ming Dynasty. Lamplighter bacon stone is the masterwork of Qingtian stone and well-known everywhere with a very high price.

(3) Shoushan Stone

Shoushan stone is produced in the northern suburbs of Shoushan Village of Fuzhou City. It is one of the traditional Chinese "four seal-stone". The main ingredients are pyrophyllite, among which larderite is the most expensive. The price of 1 gram of larderite with the ordinary quality has reached 300 yuan.

7. Metal Craft

Metal craft is a special category of Chinese art and craft, including cloisonné, enamel ware, filigree inlaying, variegated copper-ware, tin craft, iron painting, gold and silver jewelry, and so on.

(1) Beijing Cloisonné

Cloisonné is Beijing's famous traditional handicraft, known as the copper wiry enamel or enamel ware, and it is also known as "embedded wiry enamel". It is a ware fired by the pattern which is filled with enamel glaze after pinching into a variety of pattern welded on with a soft flat copper wire. It was prevalent in the period of Jingtai of Ming Dynasty with mature skills and blue-dominated glaze enamel, hence the name cloisonné.

(2) Beijing Enamel

Beijing enamel, also known as copper tires painted enamel, is called the sister art of cloisonne. Its difference from cloisonné lies in that it needs no pinching, but applies a layer of white glaze on the carcass in copper after a tire tread and is painting after sintering glaze, filled with color and amended twice or three times, and then sintered, gold-plated, and polished up. Beijing enamel has a wide range of varieties, such as bottles, plates, bowls, pots, dishes, and the wine facilities, smoking accessories, as well as furnaces, tripod, *Jue* (an ancient wine vessel with three legs and a loop handle), sandalwood burner and plug hanging bottles, bottles and other

decorations.

(3) Filigree Inlaying in Beijing and Chengdu

Filigree inlaying, also fine gold, is the combination of two production skills filigree and inlaying. It is made of materials like gold, silver, inlaid precious stones, and pearls, and made in woven art. Filigree inlaying falls into two categories, filament and inlaying. Filament is an art ware made with heaps, in weaving techniques through a thin gold, silver silk. Inlaying is hammering gold, silver slices into containers caved with pattern and inlayed with gems. Filigree technology is well-known in Beijing and Chengdu. The representative works of filigree are the crown of Ming Dynasty Emperor Wanli, Qing Dynasty Jin'ou yonggu cup, gold peach bonsai in silver square basin, gold inlaid jewelry crown, hall of prayer for Good Harvests of modern jewelry and China century dragon.

(4) Wuhu Iron Picture

Wuhu iron picture, also known as iron flower, gets the name because it is produced in Wuhu City of Anhui Province and is one of the unique arts and crafts of China. Iron picture is using low carbon steel as raw materials, forging and welding metal palter and steel wire into variety of decorative painting. It integrates folk paper-cutting, sculpture, mosaics, and a variety of art techniques as a whole using Chinese painting art, black and white contrast, combination of excess and deficiency, and having some fun. Iron picture originates from Song Dynasty, being rampant in Northern Song Dynasty. During the period of Kangxi in Qing Dynasty, Wuhu iron picture has its own style and is renowned throughout the world gradually.

(5) Longquan Sword

Longquan sword, which is one of the famous Chinese traditional handicrafts, gets the name because it is produced in Longquan City of Zhejiang Province. Legend has it that Longquan sword is originated from more than 2,000 years ago, the Spring and Autumn Period and the Warring States Period. Longquan sword is very famous in

Tang Dynasty. Longquan sword has the four traditional features, tough and sharp, the pressing cool-radiance, tamper force with mercy, skillful and delicate emblazonry. Longquan sword is popular both at home and abroad. Overseas Chinese and ethnic Chinese in Southeast Asian countries like to hang it in the room or bedside, to ward off evil spirits and take them as decorations.

8. New Year Picture

New Year picture is a form of Chinese painting, dating from ancient Gate-god picture. It is officially called New Year picture during the period of Emperor Guangxu in Qing Dynasty. It is a unique painting genre in China, and a popular art form for China's rural people. Because most of them are posted when New Year comes, which are not only used to decorate environment but also as an indication of good luck and blessing for the new year, so it is called New Year's pictures. Zhuxianzhen Town in Kaifeng City of He'nan Province, Yangjiabu Village in Weifang City of Shandong Province, Taohuawu of Jiangsu Province, and Yangliuqing Town, have enjoyed a good reputation for a long time and are known as China's "four masters of New Year picture".

(1) New Year Picture of Zhuxianzhen Town

New Year picture of Zhuxianzhen Town gets the name because it comes from Zhuxianzhen Town in Kaifeng City of He'nan Province. It belongs to woodblock prints painting products, has a long history and is a long standing of history of more than 800 years. It was born in Tang Dynasty, prevailing in Song Dynasty and reaching its peak in Ming Dynasty which was honored as the founder of Chinese woodblock New Year pictures. Legend has it that, in Tang Dynasty when Emperor Tangtaizong ordered painters to hang senior general Qin Qiong and Yuchi Jingde portraits in the palace gate to ward off evil spirits, hence it becomes the beginning of the Door God. Because of the short supply, hand-painted prints are difficult to keep up with demand, so folk artists used woodblock carving to have mass production, resulting in development, which formed annual custom.

(2) Yangjiabu New Year Picture

Yangjiabu New Year picture gets the name because it is produced in Yangjiabu Village of Weifang City in Shandong Province. It belongs to the woodblock prints painting products, originated in Ming Dynasty and was prosperous in Qing Dynasty. The composition of Yangjiabu New Year picture is proportional and full. The model is sturdy and simple, and the line is concise and smooth, reflecting the ideals, customs and daily life with a strong folk flavor, local color and holiday atmosphere.

(3) Yangliuqing New Year Picture

Yangliuqing New Year picture gets the name because it is produced in Yangliuqing Town of Tianjin City, belonging to the woodblock prints painting products. As famous Chinese folk New Year wood-block print, it is called "South peach and North willow" with Taohuawu New Year pictures arising from the Chongzhen Era in Ming Dynasty. Yangliuqing New Year picture has characteristics of fine and smooth drawing, pretty characters, brightly beautiful color, rich content, diverse forms, harmonious atmosphere, humorous plot, interesting inscription, and so on.

(4) Taohuawu New Year Picture

Taohuawu New Year picture gets the name because it is produced in the area of Taohuawu in the north of Suzhou City of Jiangsu Province. Taohuawu New Year picture originates from Song Dynasty woodblock printing technology, develops into a folk art genre in Ming Dynasty, and is prosperous in Yongzheng and Qianlong eras of Qing Dynasty. The amount of production of Taohuawu woodblock New Year picture reaches millions or more per year. The composition of Taohuawu New Year picture is proportional, full, magnificent, which is often dominated by amaranth to show joyful atmosphere, with beautiful and refined Southern folk art style, mainly showing traditional folk aesthetic content of being auspicious folk life, local opera story, flowers, birds, fruits, vegetables, but avoidance of ghosts andevils.

9. Knitting Technology

Knitting technology is a kind of art ware (baskets or other goods) waved by manual method with better toughness fiber (such as twigs, wicker, bamboo, juncus effuses). Knitting technology is both practical and decorative arts. Depending on the materials used, it can be divided into bamboo plaiting and straw plaiting. Bamboo plaiting is famous for Dongyang bamboo plaiting, Shengzhou bamboo plaiting and Dai bamboo plaiting. Straw plaiting is famous for Shandong straw plaiting and Ningbo straw plaiting.

(1) Dongyang Bamboo Plaiting

Dongyang bamboo plaiting gets the name because it is produced in Dongyang City of Zhejiang Province. It rises in Song Dynasty, making mainly dragon lantern, festive lantern, and trotting horse lamp. Dongyang bamboo plaiting is mainly practical products and crafts now. Dongyang practical products include more than 20 varieties of bamboo baskets, dishes, bottles, cans, packs, boxes, furniture, and so on. Among crafts, animal bamboo plaiting is the most expressive, such as chickens, ducks, geese, rabbits, and dogs with vivid and exaggerated image, fine and sooth looking.

(2) Shengzhou Bamboo Plaiting

Shengzhou bamboo plaiting gets the name because it is produced in Shengzhou City in the East of Zhejiang Province. It begins in the Warring States Period, matures in Han and Jin Dynasties and is prosperous in Ming and Qing Dynasties. Shengzhou bamboo painting is known for its exquisite weaving, various craft and rich color. Shengzhou bamboo plaiting has twelve categories of baskets, dishes, pots, boxes, vases, screens, animals, people, buildings, furniture, lamps, appliances, etc. with more than 6,000 varieties of color and design.

(3) The Bamboo Weaving of Dai People in Yunnan Province

The bamboo weaving of Dai people in Yunnan Province gets the name for Dai

people in Yunnan Province so skilled in bamboo weaving. Dai people establish tight connection with bamboo since ancient times. Their stockade villages are often located in bamboo forests, and thus the various kinds of utensils in their life are made of bamboo naturally. When it comes to diet, Dai people enjoy fresh bamboo shoots as well as some kind of sour pickled bamboo shoots. It just seems like turning into a world of bamboo weaving when you step on the chic bamboo house. You can see bamboo weavings everywhere, the bamboo weaving wall, the bamboo weaving mat, the interior furnishings woven of bamboo from wardrobe to dinner bucket, besides the little stool, summer hat, rain cap, little portable pack basket, and so on. There are mainly tribute table, lift basket, bacon box, lunch box and drip gourd as the most representative bamboo weaving lacquer, and they are called *Pengla*, *Sahao*, *Gading*, *Yanhao* and *Nanduowa* respectively in Dai language. Bamboo weaving equipments with colorful gorgeous patterns are the necessities when Dai people engaged in Buddhist activities for the temple martyrs, and nearly every family gets one set of the equipment. When the Water-splashing Day or the Door Opening/Closing Festival comes, old Dai people put the bacon in *Gading*, glutinous rice in *Yanhao*, water in *Nanduowa* and various kinds of Buddha tributes in *Sahao*. The children deliver their parents and the Buddha vegetarian food with Pengla and Sahao, as for the olds, they use *Nafo*. Bamboo weaving lacquers are often placed high up, staying away from other things. Patterns like lotus, butterflies, dragon and pentagon are used so popular in bamboo weaving lacquer decorating, and they implied wishes for the Buddha's blessing, blessing people good and happy.

(4) Shandong Straw Weaving

Straw weaving is very popular in Shandong Province. Shandong Straw weaving originates from Laizhou City with at least 6, 000 years history. Straw weaving handicraft is a local specialty in Shandong Province. Its straw weaving uses the raw materials, such as rushes, grass, corn husk, corn stalk, wheat straw, and so on. Shandong straw weaving products are mainly divided into two categories. One is the arts and crafts with the function of use, such as lift basket, bags, mat of tea,

ground mat, straw hat, door curtain, fruit box, wastepaper basket, baby basket, straw storage bins, etc. The other is the decorations with the beauty in form, such as grass screen, grass carpet, lamp cover, wallpaper, wallpaper of straw weaving, etc.

(5) Ningbo Straw Weaving

The traditional weaving techniques of Ningbo City of Zhejiang Province has existed since ancient times with the history of more than 2,000 years. Ningbo City has abundant resources of straw, such as mat grass, culm, salty grass, rush, Chinese alpine rush and corn husks, etc. Ningbo straw weaving is famous for its straw hat, in addition with grass basket, bags, grass fan, straw sandals, straw tea mat, etc. , as well as a variety of wonderful decorative pattern designs.

10. Lacquerware

Chinese people began to make lacquerware with their knowledge about the strength of lacquer, as early as the New Stone Age. From then on, thanks to the technique evolution from Shang Dynasty (1600 – 1100 B. C.), and Zhou Dynasty (1100 – 256 B. C.) all the way to Ming Dynasty (1368 – 1644 A. D.) and Qing Dynasty (1644 – 1911 A. D.), the lacquerware craft has reached quite a advanced level.

(1) Beijing Lacquerware

There are two major types of lacquerwares, carved lacquerwares and inlayed metal (gold, silver, etc.) pattern lacquers. Possessing a long history, the former's craft grows to be mature in 14th century. Its manufacture begins with a copper mold being prime coated with melted lacquer together with enamel, then the coating materials in red, green and yellow, etc. are applied to it one layer after another layer with hundreds of times of repetition. The edges of the ware are galvanized with gold. When the coats completely dry in shade, they can be carved to be either reliefs or cutting-out. The latter is known as "Jinqi xiangqian", lacquer with inlayed metal patterns, which can be broken down into, color lacquer with metal patterns, lacquer engraved

with tiny shinning shells, golden/silver foil patterns flushed with lacquer coating, intaglio lacquer, and lacquer with polished painting. Both of the two major lacquerware show their classic style with luxury and stable features.

(2) Fuzhou Bodiless Lacquerware

With strong Fujian local ethnic characteristics, Fuzhou bodiless lacquerware lives up to its fame as one of the "Top Three Crafts" in China (cloisonné ware and Jingdezhen porcelain), thanks to its sophisticated decoration in vivid colors as well as its strong durability but light in weight. Nowadays, there are over 3,000 types of products in 300 styles of each type, which are mainly wares for daily-use and art wares. The former includes giant vase, screen, various polished paintings, etc., the latter can be used as stationary and serve tea, coffee and dinner.

(3) Yangzhou Engraved Lacquer

Originated in the Warring States Period, Yangzhou engraved lacquerwares evolution from Han Dynasty to Tang Dynasty and finally blooms in Ming and Qing Dynasties. Today, this Chinese traditional craft has won its world-class reputation, due to its sophisticated tech making a complete list of products with strong characteristics.

(4) Tianshui Lacquerware

The techniques include carving and filling up, engraving and filling up, engraving silver patterns, golden edging, etc., among which the craft of carved and filled-up is the most popular one. With a history of over 100 years, the products are made out of a wooden or leather mold in Qing Dynasty. The "Xiu" (a traditional coating technique) can only be applied to the process of carving and filling up for manufacturing a wood bowl, a hand stick, etc. Since the P. R. C. founded in 1949, Tianshui lacquerware makes unprecedented progress in the fields of its design, carving, pigment filling up, polish, etc. There are almost a hundred types of major products, vase, plate, box set, cigarette holder, tea set screens, sofa-table, various

kinds of cabinets, etc. Particularly the screen of engraved spiral shell and foldable sofa-table, etc. display their great regional ethnic features with elegant shape and sound decorative patterns made out of outstanding crafts.

11. The Folk Art

The traditional Chinese folk art has a long history with richness and colorfulness. For example, shadow play, the clay sculpture, paper cut and lion dance etc. are famous folk art. They are not only the specialties with local characteristics, but also treasures of Chinese culture.

(1) The Shadow Play in the Northwest of China

The shadow play is a form of folk art in China which originates in Ming and Qing Dynasties. It is a unique art which combines art and drama, and it is a kind of folk art in the rural area of Gansu Province, Shaanxi Province and Ningxia Hui Autonomous Region. The shadow puppets and the pros of the scene are leather products which are carved and painted manually by Chinese folk artist. They are made by procedures of washing the cowhide, drying, drawing, carving, painting and ironing. During the performance, each part of the puppet characters is controlled by the performer who is behind the scenes, and it casts many lifelike actions on the screen in front of the audience. The plot of the story is interpreted by adding some inspiring songs or monologue.

(2) Paper-cut of Han Nationality

The art of paper-cut is one of the most ancient folk arts of Han nationality. Its history can be traced back to the sixth century A. D. . It is a treasure of Chinese folk art, and it is a form of long-history and wide-spread folk art in Chinese rural areas. Paper-cut is to cut paper, gold foil, bark, leaves, cloth, leather, leather sheet material into a variety of patterns with scissors, such as window paper-cut, wall paper-cut, ceiling paper and snuff paper-cut, etc. The origin and the popularization of the folk art are closely related to the customs of celebrating the festivals in Chinese rural

areas. People put beautiful paper-cut on the window paper or on the bright windows, walls, doors, the lanterns on holidays or on wedding celebration. It can greatly enrich the atmosphere of the festival.

(3) Shaanxi Fengxiang Painted Clay

Fengxiang painted clay of Shaanxi Province originates in the Pre-Qin Dynasty. It has been handed down for three thousand years, and is still the oldest and well-preserved clay sculpture among the handmade products in China with its full national characteristics. Fengxiang painted clay is elegant and vivid with the strong flavor of rural life. The characters of the clay include human, animals and plants. Most of the works are hollow plastic circular or the hanging pieces of relief style. Its production method is simple. Firstly, the clay and paper pulp are mixed together and is put into a mould. Then the white powder is brushed on it after the mould is dried. The following procedures are coloring, painting and varnishing. Fengxiang painted clay has its own style of bright colors which is presenting strong contrast. The coloring is simple, mainly in bright red, bright green and yellow. It gives people striking and eye-catching feeling by sketching the outline with black ink lines and brushing and dyeing the pictures with simple drawing. The derived conceptions of Fengxiang painted clay are colorful. The theatrical makeup, auspicious patterns, folk legends, historical stories, rural folk life etc. are all contents of the conceptions.

参考文献

References

[1] 中国56个民族简介［J］. 当代贵州，2011（04）.

[2] 中国56个民族简介［J］. 当代贵州，2011（05）.

[3] 中国56个民族简介［J］. 当代贵州，2011（06）.

[4] 中国56个民族简介［J］. 当代贵州，2011（07）.

[5] 中国56个民族简介［J］. 当代贵州，2011（08）.

[6] 中国56个民族简介［J］. 当代贵州，2011（09）.

[7] 中国56个民族简介［J］. 当代贵州，2011（10）.

[8] 中国56个民族简介［J］. 当代贵州，2011（11）.

[9] 中国56个民族简介［J］. 当代贵州，2011（12）.

[10] 中国56个民族简介［J］. 当代贵州，2011（13）.

[11] 中国56个民族简介［J］. 当代贵州，2011（14）.

[12] 中国56个民族简介［J］. 当代贵州，2011（15）.

[13] 中国56个民族简介［J］. 当代贵州，2011（16）.

[14] 中国56个民族简介［J］. 当代贵州，2011（17）.

[15] 中国56个民族简介（一）［J］. 地理教育，2004（02）.

[16] 56个民族简介（二）［J］. 地理教育，2004（04）.

[17] 慰南. 龙崇拜与望子成龙的文化观念［J］. 江西社会科学，1999（01）.

[18] 刘蔚华. 龙文化根源的考古探索［J］. 中州学刊，2000（02）.

[19] 杨海鹏. 金代铜坐龙的发现与研究［J］. 北方文物，2009（01）.

[20] 蔡贝贝. 中国的龙文化［J］. 西部大开发，2012（Z1）.

[21] 高黎，崔哲．用英语介绍中国［M］．北京：中国水利水电出版社，2011.

[22] 庞进．龙的基本神性与民族文化心理［J］．人文杂志，2000（01）.

[23] 李运航，琚文英．中国龙文化［J］．中州统战，1997（06）.

[24] 黄能馥．龙袍探源［J］．故宫博物院院刊，1998（04）.

[25] 龙芃穆．试论中国龙文化的起源［J］．大众文艺，2010（19）.

[26] 孙小美．中国古代四大发明——纸［J］．中国科技月报，1999（01）.

[27] 孙小美．中国古代四大发明——印刷术［J］．中国科技月报，1999（02）.

[28] 孙小美．中国古代四大发明——火药［J］．中国科技月报，1999（03）.

[29] 孙小美．中国古代四大发明——指南针［J］．中国科技月报，1999（04）.

[30] 于希贤．中国古代四大发明及其西传［J］．文史知识，1994（05）.

[31] 赵文润．我国人民在科技史上的杰出贡献——指南针、造纸法、印刷术和火药四大发明简介［J］．陕西师师范大学报：哲学社会科学版，1977（03）.

[32] 贺彦凤，张德才．中国宗教文化的特征及其生成原因［J］．长春理工大学学报：社会科学版，2009（02）.

[33] 洪修平．中国宗教与传统文化［J］．南京社会科学，1992（01）.

[34] 贺彦凤．当代中国宗教问题的文化研究［D］．东北师范大学，2007.

[35] 王彧．中国宗教文化之原始图腾崇拜再认识［J］．林区教学，2014（06）.

[36] 吾敬东．古代中国宗教的基本精神［J］．上海师范大学学报：哲学社会科学版，2008（03）.

[37] 赵嚣，蔡新芝．英语畅谈中国文化风俗［M］．北京：科学出版社，2011.

[38] 周济．中国人的文化［M］．上海：上海文化出版社，2009.

[39] 孙金玲．从礼仪文化的发展看中国的文明进程［J］．科技资讯，2006（23）.

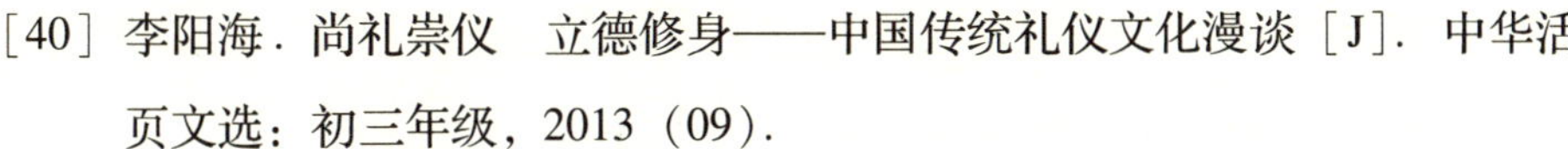

[40] 李阳海．尚礼崇仪　立德修身——中国传统礼仪文化漫谈［J］．中华活页文选：初三年级，2013（09）．

[41] 金品卓．中西方礼仪文化差异［J］．中国科技信息，2007（02）．

[42] 吉恩煦．中国明代士民揖礼习俗小考［J］，首都师范大学学报：社会科学版，2011（S1）．

[43] 刘洋．拱手以礼［J］．中学生百科，2008（18）．

[44] 曹乃玲．“拜见”礼节的变迁［J］．苏州教育学院学报，1995（04）．

[45] 季鸿崑．《三礼》与中国饮食文化［J］．中国烹饪研究，1996（03）．

[46] 小白．初次见面的礼仪［J］．职业，2003（1）．

[47] 朱健．传统礼仪文化与现代化［J］．殷都学刊，2000（01）．

[48] 舒安娜．交际礼仪的产生及其历史演变［J］．郑州大学学报：哲学社会科学版，1996（03）．

[49] 管丽莉．中国传统礼仪的蕴意及现代价值［J］．合作经济与科技，2012（06）．

[50] 盛邦和．《礼记》与中国礼文化［J］．江苏社会科学，2009（01）．

[51] 吴央．中国传统礼节［J］．中学生，2005（05）．

[52] 梅桑榆．闲话握手［J］．现代交际，1998（05）．

[53] 曹砚农．中国古代坐法与礼仪文化［J］．湖南师范大学社会科学学报，1997（04）．

[54] 苏振兴．先秦饮食与礼仪文化初探［J］．华夏文化，2003（02）．

[55] 关小燕．礼仪文化中的“位”、“序”研究［J］．江西社会科学，2003（03）．

[56] 冬青．古代待客之礼［J］．语文之友，2005（04）．

[57] 晓月．敬酒礼仪［J］．应用写作，2005（08）．

[58] 余琳．从婚礼习俗看中西文化差异［J］．山西青年管理干部学院学报，2012（02）．

[59] 马芳琴．从传统婚俗看中西方文化差异［J］．旅游纵览：下半月，2012（09）．

[60] 王伊韩．中国传统婚俗文化中“六礼”的传承与应用研究［D］．内蒙古师范大学，2014．

[61] 徐惠婷，粟丹. 浅析西周婚姻制度对中国传统婚俗的影响 [J]. 浙江社会科学，2012（10）.

[62] 王茜，魏铭清. 维吾尔族婚俗历史演变研究 [J]. 新疆大学学报：哲学社会科学版，2002（01）.

[63] 佤族婚俗 [J]. 云南农业，2005（02）.

[64] 黄光兴. 苗族婚俗 [J]. 西南民兵，1995（03）.

[65] 陆友昌. 侗族婚俗 [J]. 影像材料，2004（04）.

[66] 夏洋. 土家族婚俗探析 [J]. 才智，2013（08）.

[67] 刘容. 小议土家族婚俗的民族特色 [J]. 重庆教育学院学报，2008（04）.

[68] 罗中玺. 土家婚俗中的哭嫁与伴嫁——以黔东北土家族为例 [J]. 时代文学：下半月，2010（01）.

[69] 廖从刚. 土家族婚俗中的哭嫁习俗 [J]. 寻根，2005（02）.

[70] 姚文华. 浅析数字禁忌的文化隐义 [J]. 文教资料，2005（02）.

[71] 陶芸. 数字禁忌的文化内涵 [J]. 江西社会科学，2013（07）.

[72] 数字禁忌 [J]. 现代语文：文学研究，2007（06）.

[73] 韩学山. 中国早期的节日禁忌形态 [J]. 农业考古，2010（04）.

[74] 节日禁忌（二）[J]. 新农业，2004（06）.

[75] 节日禁忌（三）[J]. 新农业，2004（07）.

[76] 詹秦川，王悦. 浅析中国节日民俗中的禁忌民俗 [J]. 美与时代：下半月，2009（02）.

[77] 钟巧玲. 浅谈传统节日中的禁忌民俗 [J]. 广西师范学院学报，2006（S1）.

[78] 冯小丽. 浅论传统节日——春节里的禁忌 [J]. 沧桑，2013（06）.

[79] 龙武生. 招待客人的礼节 [J]. 家庭科技，1997（01）.

[80] 王智勇. 浅谈生活中的语言禁忌 [J]. 科技信息，2009（16）.

[81] 朱华斌. 浅谈我国民俗文化中的禁忌 [J]. 新余高专学报，2005（03）.

[82] 李红. 中国人用筷子的忌讳 [J]. 农村百事通，2010（17）.

[83] 祁建. 中国古代服饰颜色禁忌 [J]. 中国纤检，2008（03）.

[84] 有趣的生肖婚配禁忌歌谣 [J]. 创业者，2006 (06).
[85] 刘琳. 民间礼仪禁忌 [J]. 农村·农业·农民，2003 (11).
[86] 周汛. 中国服饰的演变历程 [J]. 上海艺术家，1996 (03).
[87] 匡义. 中国服饰的演变 [J]. 神州学人，1996 (05).
[88] 高春明. 垂衣裳而天下治——中国古代服饰的演变 [J]. 文明，2013 (09).
[89] 李珊珊. 中国历代服饰的演变 [J]. 山东行政学院山东省经济管理干部学院学报，2003 (03).
[90] 邝金凤. 浅谈原始服饰文化 [J]. 大众文艺，2012 (2).
[91] 冀艳波，徐军，张华君. 商周服饰初探 [J]. 西安工程科技学院学报，2002 (01).
[92] 宋镇豪. 春秋战国时期的服饰 [J]. 中原文物，1996 (02).
[93] 薛芳芳. 秦汉服饰制度研究 [D]. 江西师范大学，2010.
[94] 辜国娟. 魏晋南北朝服饰美学研究 [D]. 四川师范大学，2013.
[95] 武天合，张艳喜. 隋唐服饰述略 [J]. 乾陵文化研究，2010 (01).
[96] 谷莉. 浅谈隋唐服饰艺术 [J]. 兰台世界，2008 (17).
[97] 王雪莉. 宋代服饰制度研究 [D]. 浙江大学，2006.
[98] 乔婷. 宋代服饰特点的研究与探析 [J]. 2010 (10).
[99] 闫晶，仇华美，尹利琴. 中国明朝服饰文化探析 [J]. 东华大学学报：社会科学版，2007 (01).
[100] 李一萱. 明朝服饰体现的等级差别 [J]. 职业时空，2013 (06).
[101] 王耘. 清代服饰变化与满汉文化交融 [J]. 纺织科技进展，2008 (06).
[102] 陈娟娟. 清代服饰艺术 [J]. 故宫博物院院刊，1994，(02).
[103] 陈娟娟. 清代服饰艺术（续）[J]. 故宫博物院院刊，1994，(03).
[104] 陈娟娟. 清代服饰艺术（续）[J]. 故宫博物院院刊，1994，(04).
[105] 中国“八大菜系“ [J]. 现代班组，2007 (03).
[106] 我国的八大菜系 [J]. 致富之友，2000 (10).
[107] 我国的八大菜系 [J]. 林产化工通讯，1996 (04).
[108] 小周. 八大菜系名菜 [J]. 食品健康，2001 (01).

［109］沈军霞．八大菜系的渊源［J］．今日南国，2007（12）．

［110］王主玉．揭示中国茶文化精蕴［J］．中国社会科学，1994（01）．

［111］姜天喜．论中国茶文化的形成与发展［J］．西北大学学报：哲学社会科学版，2006（06）．

［112］梁晓宇．中国茶文化的特征［J］．乌蒙论坛，2014（02）．

［113］谭振．中国茶文化的历史溯源与海外传播［D］．青岛理工大学，2014．

［114］苏叶．中国茶文化中的雅与俗［J］．杨州教育学院学报，2011（01）．

［115］程启坤．中国茶文化的历史与未来［J］．中国茶叶，2008（07）．

［116］苏雪．中国茶文化［J］．学理论，2013（24）．

［117］张进华．也议中国茶文化［J］．中国茶叶，2009（03）．

［118］曲焕云．中国茶文化研究［J］．吉林农业，2012（06）．

［119］吴慧，张秀军，张晓．对中国酒文化的内涵、形态与特点的探讨［J］．学理论，2010（05）．

［120］丁季华．中国酒文化的结构与功能［J］．历史教学问题，1991（02）．

［121］陆平．论中国酒文化及其发展特点［J］．赤峰学院学报：汉文哲学社会科学版，2009（11）．

［122］黄亦锡．酒、酒器与传统文化——中国古代酒文化研究［D］．夏门大学，2008．

［123］高枫．中国酒文化的精神内涵［J］．山西师大学报：社会科学版，2011（S3）．

［124］木鱼．中国酒文化［J］．地图，2006（06）．

［125］卞怡菁，范希嘉．中国酒文化与酒包装容器［J］．上海包装，2004（04）．

［126］王玲，张克复．春节文化的传承与创新［J］．甘肃社会科学，2012（04）．

［127］李翠华．先秦至唐宋时期春节习俗研究［D］．中山大学，2010．

［128］王杰．谈春节习俗及其现代化演变的文化内涵［J］．长春教育学院学报，2013（11）．

［129］韩梅．元宵节起源新论［J］．浙江大学学报：人文社会科学版，预印

本，2010（06）.
［130］王志振．元宵节史话［J］．科学新闻，2000（06）.
［131］元宵节的来历及习俗［J］．现代农村科技，2013（02）.
［132］付秋婷．清明节的演变及其文化内涵探析［J］．德宏师范高等专科学校学报，2008（01）.
［133］江玉祥．清明节的来历及文化意义［J］．西华大学学报：哲学社会科学版，2010（03）.
［134］不二．中国最主要的八节之一清明节［J］．中华魂，2013（08）.
［135］秦立．端午节溯源［J］．山东文学，2010（06）.
［136］梅边．论端午节及其文化［D］．华中科技大学，2012.
［137］费伟健．我国传统节日“端午节“的演变发展与传承［J］．产业科技论坛，2011（12）.
［138］张柏林．中秋节［J］．中学课程辅导：初二版，2004（09）.
［139］中秋节［J］．吉林农业，2014（17）.
［140］杨择．中秋节起源［J］．江淮，2004（09）.
［141］中国传统节日——中秋节［J］．神州学人，2008（09）.
［142］张训浩．浅议中医文化与中医发展［J］．中国民间疗法，2013（11）.
［143］谭舯．中医文化［J］．统一论坛，2013（06）.
［144］刘子志．中医阴阳学说探微［J］．新中医，2011（04）
［145］郝万山．中医药学讲座（二）第二讲中医阴阳学说的基本内容［J］．中国自然医学杂志，2000（01）.
［146］罗元恺．阴阳学说是中医理论体系的核心［J］．新中医，1991（04）.
［147］陈吉全．中医五行学说属性与本质探析［J］．中医研究，2014（02）.
［148］申文．中医五行学说［J］．天津中医，1987（05）.
［149］杜青雄．五行学说是中医理论的核心架构［J］．世界中医药，2009（04）.
［150］徐云生．论中医学基本观［D］．广州中医药大学，2001.
［151］焉石，樊长征，等．中医四诊信息与形神一体观［J］．中华中医学刊，2007（12）.
［152］中医四诊基本知识（上）［J］．陕西新医药，1976（03）.

[153] 王瑞华，董国力．论中医的辨证施治与遣方用药［J］．中国当代医药，2010（14）．

[154] 徐正德．中医养生理论与实践［D］．南京中医药大学，2010.

[155] 程强．中国古建筑的形式与施工程序［J］．建筑工人，1992（04）．

[156] 石增礼．中国古代建筑类型与分类［D］．浙江大学，2004.

[157] 李纯．中国宫殿建筑美学三维论［D］．武汉大学，2011.

[158] 陈莉．清代宫殿建筑的文化社会学解析［D］．哈尔滨工业大学，2006.

[159] 张伟．北京故宫的建筑伦理思想研究［D］．湖南工业大学，2010.

[160] 王雪芹．浅析中国古塔建筑艺术［J］．大众文艺，2010（24）．

[161] 王福和．中国古典宫殿建筑琐谈［J］．黑龙江农垦师专学报，1994（04）．

[162] 李洋．中国宫殿艺术的认识和思考［J］．科技风，2012（01）．

[163] 朱黎明．开封城墙防御体系研究［D］．河南大学，2011.

[164] 闫梦婕．潼关故城城防体系研究［D］．西安建筑科技大学，2009.

[165] 宁倩．荆州城墙古代城防设施研究及实例分析［D］．西安建筑科技大学，2005.

[166] 吴健骅．万里长城：世界伟大的建筑工程奇迹［J］．中国房地产信息，1998（08）．

[167] 晓东．中国人工程技术的结晶——万里长城［J］．飞碟探索，2011（12）．

[168] 居阅时．帝王陵墓建筑的文化解释［J］．同济大学学报：社会科学版，2004（05）．

[169] 李金娜，底素卫．唐代帝王陵墓的建筑特点［J］．兰台世界，2013（10）．

[170] 朱士光．初论我国古代都城礼制建筑的演变及其与儒学的关系［J］．大同高等专科学院学报，1998（03）．

[171] 李栋．先秦礼制建筑考古学研究［D］．山东大学，2010.

[172] 姜波．汉唐都城礼制建筑研究［D］．中国社科院研究生院，2001.

[173] 吴维伟．中国宗教建筑的文化解析［J］．科教文汇：下旬刊，2008

（02）.
[174] 续昕．浅论中国道教建筑的美学思想［J］．社会科学研究，2012（02）.
[175] 孙宗文．中国道教建筑艺术的形成、发展与成就［J］．华中建筑，2005（s1）.
[176] 谢科．中国道教建筑的起源发展及分布［J］．现代装饰：理论，2013（05）.
[177] 樊天华．中国佛寺建筑的空间表达［J］．上海工艺美术，2009（02）.
[178] 马若琼．中国伊斯兰教建筑艺术研究［D］．兰州大学，2011.
[179] 王绍周．北京民居——四合院的形成与发展特点［J］．时代建筑，1989（01）.
[180] 洪烛．四合院：中国的盒子［J］．家具与环境，2003（06）.
[181] 于杨．解读江南民居［J］．农家之友，2010（05）.
[182] 吕国伟．浅析江南民居的建筑设计风格［J］．无锡南洋学院学报，2007（04）.
[183] 王光明．浅谈徽州民居［J］．建筑学报，1996（01）.
[184] 刘俊．气候与徽州民居［D］．合肥工业大学，2007.
[185] 王军．《西北民居》［J］．中国西部，2011（05）.
[186] 李宁．浅析西北民居及民居文化［J］．青海师范大学学报：哲学社会科学版，2006（12）.
[187] 沈纲，沈昌乙．晋中民居初探［J］．建筑知识，2005（04）.
[188] 何佳，赵暄．晋商文化和晋中民居［J］．建筑与文化，2005（03）.
[189] 廖文．客家民居建筑文化初探［J］．韶关学院学报：社会科学版，2002（01）.
[190] 黄红生．客家民居建筑——浅谈龙南围屋［J］．商品与质量，2009（S7）.
[191] 高立士．西双版纳傣族竹楼文化［J］．德宏师范高等专科学校学报，2007（01）.
[192] 张爱武．土家族吊脚楼营造技艺及其传承与保护研究——以兴安村为例［D］．中南民族大学，2012.
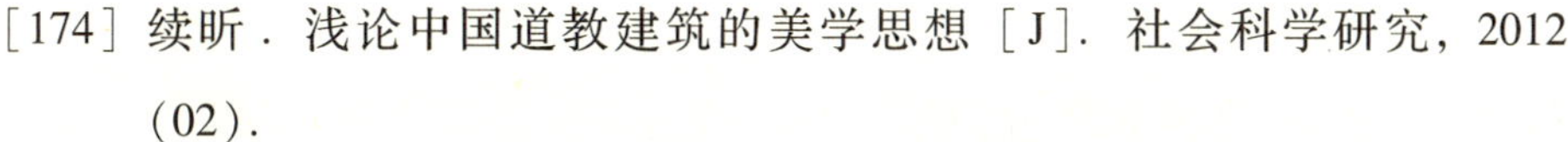

［193］许丽．中西园林艺术比较——中西园林艺术观念与手法比较分析［D］．山东师范大学，2009.
［194］王建英．试论园林艺术的诗情与画境［D］．东南大学，2005.
［195］邓文．对园林艺术的解读［J］．城市地理，2014（14）.
［196］李松强．浅谈中外园林艺术及中国现代园林的发展方向［J］．科技风，2012（12）.
［197］姚琳．中国传统园林天人合一之人与自然和谐交融［D］．东北林业大学，2011.
［198］刘希娟．传统园林天人合一之思诗交融的艺术境界［D］．东北林业大学，2012.
［199］易宁．中国传统园林艺术特质初探［J］．人民论坛，2011（17）.
［200］由国林．中国传统园林造型艺术初探——以西安曲江池遗址公园为例［D］．西安建筑科技大学，2010.
［201］张晓春．“有若自然”——苏州传统园林的设计精髓［D］．苏州大学，2004.
［202］罗正浩．点题——中国传统园林“意境”理解的探索［J］．福州建筑2013（10）.
［203］李黄山．中国古典园林理水艺术及其应用研究［D］．河南大学，2013.
［204］卓拉．蒙古包建筑构造方法研究［D］．北京建筑大学，2013.
［205］蒋昕萌，王冬．云南“一颗印”民居建筑空间原型解析［J］．铁道勘探与设计，2014（03）.
［206］惠飞．炊烟犬吠人家——云南一颗印［J］．中华民居，2010（10）.
［207］孙天健．中国陶瓷起源的探索［J］．景德镇陶瓷，1998（01）.
［208］朱乃诚．中国陶器的起源［J］．考古，2004（06）.
［209］徐建亚．中西交流史上的宜兴紫砂艺术［J］．文化月刊，1998（03）.
［210］程勉中．论宜兴紫砂陶艺术［J］．陶瓷工程，1997（02）.
［211］黄静．灵动质朴的石湾陶器［J］．收藏，2011（07）.
［212］郭有权．钦州泥兴［J］．中国工商，1989（02）.
［213］范万武．洛阳唐三彩艺术研究——对洛阳唐三彩镇墓神物的艺术探索

[D]. 陕西师范大学，2007.
[214] 张变玲. 景德镇瓷器艺术的历史变迁 [J]. 兰台世界，2012 (19).
[215] 周燕儿. 绍兴越窑初探 [J]. 南方文物，2004 (01).
[216] 赵鸿声. 唐山骨瓷之路 [J]. 山东陶瓷，2014 (01).
[217] 夏金凤. 浅析醴陵釉下五彩瓷的创新工艺 [J]. 美术界，2012 (07).
[218] 陈万利. 浅谈德化白瓷雕烧制技艺 [J]. 艺术科技，2014 (01).
[219] 彭勃. 龙泉青瓷技术的研究 [D]. 浙江大学，2010.
[220] 周海燕. 论南京云锦艺术的传承与发展 [D]. 东南大学，2006.
[221] 胡光俊，谭丹. 浅谈蜀锦及其传统织造技艺 [J]. 现代丝绸科学与技术，2013 (02).
[222] 茅惠伟. 从两块现代宋锦面料话说宋锦 [J]. 四川丝绸，2006 (02).
[223] 王欣. 当代苏绣艺术研究 [D]. 苏州大学，2013.
[224] 谢洋慧. 湘绣文化与工艺传承研究 [D]. 湖南师范大学，2013.
[225] 张蕾. 粤绣传承和发展研究 [J]. 大众文艺，2013 (16).
[226] 吴文轩. 绘画和刺绣的交融——蜀绣的文化特色与价值研究 [J]. 中华文化论坛，2013 (04).
[227] 肖. “文房四宝”之宝——湖笔、徽墨、宣纸、端砚简介 [J]. 赣江经济，1985 (03).
[228] 黄正彪. 中国的四大名玉 [J]. 地球，2000 (03).
[229] 黄正宏. 陕西蓝田玉初考 [J]. 西北地质，1984 (04).
[230] 毛麒瑞. 中国工艺雕刻三大佳石 [J]. 珠宝科技，2000 (02).
[231] 于宏艳. 谈金属工艺的发展 [J]. 消费导刊，2008 (11).
[232] 北京景泰蓝制作技艺 [J]. 时代经贸，2008 (06).
[233] 贾关法. 北京景泰蓝 [J]. 集邮博览，2008 (07).
[234] 朱家溍. 铜掐丝珐琅和铜胎画珐琅 [J]. 文物，1960 (01).
[235] 司晨卉. 浅谈花丝镶嵌工艺的传承与发展 [J]. 科技致富向导，2011 (35).
[236] 司晨卉. 北京、四川、广东三地花丝镶嵌工艺之比较 [J]. 科技致富向导，2012 (15).
[237] 褚力. 论芜湖铁画的艺术传承与延伸 [J]. 中国包装，2011 (09).

[238] 史启新. 设计、手工艺及芜湖铁画 [J]. 创意与设计，2010（05）.

[239] 雷云飞，项红梅. 名扬天下的龙泉宝剑 [J]. 今日浙江，2003（11）.

[240] 关明新. 龙泉宝剑——中国宝剑文化的承载者 [J]. 文艺争鸣，2010（06）.

[241] 化金莲. 年画艺术展望 [J]. 集宁师专学报，2002（03）.

[242] 李青青. 年画艺术中的情感意味 [D]. 江西科技师范学院，2010。

[243] 于鹏飞. 浅析我国的年画艺术及特征 [J]. 现代交际，2011（06）.

[244] 郑海涛. 开封朱仙镇年画与天津杨柳青年画比较研究 [J]. 美术教育研究，2013（19）.

[245] 曹晓飞. 杨家埠木版年画考 [D]. 福建师范大学，2005.

[246] 中国民间艺术赏析——苏州桃花坞年画 [J]. 思维与智慧，2005（05）.

[247] 冬竹. 东阳竹编 [J]. 风景名胜，1998（12）.

[248] 止裕. “东方珍宝”嵊州竹编 [J]. 百姓生活，2012（11）.

[249] 燚林. 草编 [J]. 秘书，2003（11）.

[250] 张金庚. 山东民间编织考略 [J]. 民俗研究，1991（04）.

[251] 郝云华. 云南德宏傣族竹器艺术简析 [J]. 楚雄师范学院学报，2012（07）.

[252] 田静. 西双版纳傣族竹文化研究 [J]. 重庆工商大学学报：自然科学版，2009（02）.

[253] 薛步青. 淳朴、健美的工艺美术之花——浙江草编纹样简介 [J]. 新美术，19890（2）.

[254] 张燕. 二十世纪中国漆器艺术 [J]. 文艺研究，1997（03）.

[255] 王敏. 华盛于实之北京漆器 [J]. 东方养生，2009（03）.

[256] 孟祥玲，孙薇，等. 民族科技的瑰宝——福州脱胎漆器 [J]. 民营科技，2010（05）.

[257] 李志倩. 扬州镶嵌漆器 [J]. 中国生漆，1992（02）.

[258] 李志倩. 扬州镶嵌漆器 [J]. 中国生漆，1992（03）.

[259] 李志倩. 扬州镶嵌漆器（续二）[J]. 中国生漆，1992（04）.

[260] 赵娟. 甘肃天水漆器的艺术特征 [J]. 牡丹江大学学报，2009（02）.

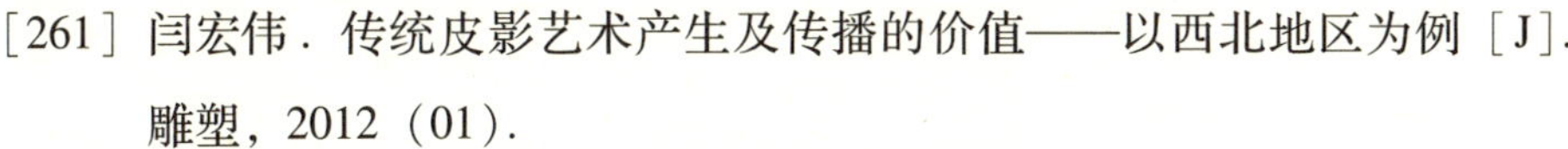

[261] 闫宏伟. 传统皮影艺术产生及传播的价值——以西北地区为例 [J]. 雕塑，2012 (01).

[262] 李倩倩. 中国南方与北方民间剪纸的图形特征比较研究 [D]. 四川大学，2007.

[263] 别淑花. 剪纸艺术的形式特征及象征意蕴 [D]. 山东师范大学，2010.

[264] 刘爱丽. 浅谈凤翔彩绘泥塑 [J]. 艺术设计研究，2012 (02).

[265] 鲁凤华. 浅谈凤翔彩绘泥塑的艺术特色 [J]. 数位时尚：新视觉艺术，2013 (03).